DYNO RUN 383SBCVY.DYN

HORSEPOWER ——
TORQUE ——

RPM	HP	TQ
2000	131	344
2500	187	393
3000	233	407
3500	291	437
4000	362	475
4500	436	509
5000	507	532
5500	560	535
6000	599	524
6500	621	502
7000	631	473
7500	635	445
8000	622	408

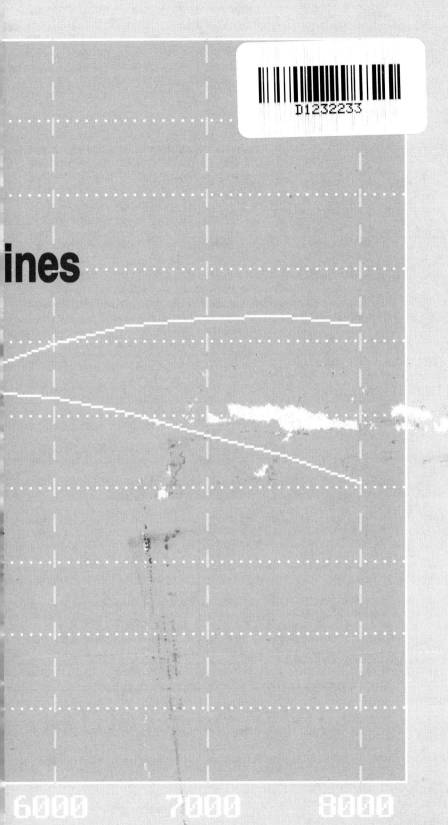

ines

CALC PROGRESS

MOTION SOFTWARE
2.5.7 (C) 1996

6000 7000 8000

[R]eturn [P]rint

By
Larry Atherton

DeskTop DYNOS

Using Computers To Build And Test Engines

WRITTEN AND PRODUCED BY:
LARRY ATHERTON

TECHNICAL CONSULTANT:
CURTIS LEAVERTON

OVERSEAS DISTRIBUTION BY:

Brooklands Books Ltd.
P.O. Box 146, Cobham, Surrey, KT11 1LG, England
Telephone 01932 865051 FAX 01932 868803

Brooklands Books Ltd.
1/81 Darley Street, P.O. Box 199, Mona Vale, NSW 2103, Australia
Telephone 2 999 78428 FAX 2 997 95799

TECHNICAL DRAWINGS BY:
JIM DENNEWILL

ISBN 1-884089-23-2
PART No. 51

CARTECH, INC., 11481 KOST DAM ROAD, NORTH BRANCH, MN 55056

CONTENTS

1—INTRODUCTION 4
  ACKNOWLEDGMENTS 5
2—ENGINE & DYNO BASICS 6
  THE OTTO-CYCLE ENGINE 6
  AN OVERVIEW OF THE OTTO-CYCLE PROCESS 7
  MODERN ENGINE DEVELOPMENT AND TESTING 8
  THE DYNAMOMETER AND WHAT IT MEASURES 9
  TORQUE 9
  POWER 10
  HORSEPOWER 10
  HORSEPOWER BY ANY OTHER NAME 11
  HORSEPOWER & TORQUE IN THE REAL WORLD ... 12
  OTHER TYPES OF DYNOS 13
  THE HYDRAULIC DYNAMOMETER 14
  THE ELECTRIC DYNAMOMETER 15
  SCHIZOPHRENIC COURSE OF DEVELOPMENT 16
  THE DYNO: ULTIMATE TRIAL-AND-ERROR TOOL .. 17
3—SIMULATING ENGINE PRESSURES 18
  ENGINE PRESSURES 18
  INDICATED CYLINDER PRESSURES 19
  THE PRESSURE CRANK-ANGLE DIAGRAM 20
  THE PRESSURE VOLUME DIAGRAM 20
  CALCULATING HORSEPOWER: THE BASICS 22
  CALCULATING CYLINDER PRESSURES 22
  INTAKE CYCLE PRESSURES 23
  POWER CYCLE PRESSURES 24
  EXHAUST CYCLE PRESSURES 24
  INDICATED HORSEPOWER AND MEP 26
  SIMULATING FRICTIONAL LOSSES 28
4—THE GROWTH OF SIMULATIONS 30
  EARLY MODELING EFFORTS 30
  ZERO- AND QUASI-DIMENSIONAL MODELS 31
  MULTIDIMENSIONAL MODELS 32
  FILLING-AND-EMPTYING MODELS 32
  GAS-DYNAMIC MODELS 33
  MODERN ENGINE MODELING MEETS THE PC 36
  DYNOMATION: GLEAM IN A YOUNG MAN'S EYE 37
  THE FUTURE OF IC MODELING 39
5—INSIDE FILLING-AND-EMPTYING 42
  FILLING-AND-EMPTYING BY ANY OTHER NAME 42
  MOTION ENGINE SIMULATION BASICS 43
  THE ON-SCREEN MENU CHOICES 44
  THE BORE/STROKE MENU 44
  WHAT'S A SHORTBLOCK 44
  BORE, STROKE, & COMPRESSION RATIO 45
  BORE AND STROKE VS. FRICTION 45
  FALLACY ONE: STROKE VS. PUMPING WORK 47
  FALLACY TWO: LONG VS. SHORT STROKE 49

  CYLINDERHEAD AND VALVE DIAMETER MENUS 50
  CYLINDERHEADS AND DISCHARGE COEF. 51
  RAM TUNING AND PRESSURE WAVES 53
  SORTING OUT CYLINDERHEAD MENU CHOICES ... 55
  WHEN TO CHOOSE SMALL/BIG-BLOCK HEADS ... 57
  VALVE DIAMETERS AND AUTO CALCULATE 58
  THE COMPRESSION RATIO MENU 59
  COMPRESSION RATIO BASICS 59
  CHANGING COMPRESSION RATIO 60
  WHY HIGHER C/R PRODUCES MORE POWER 61
  OTHER EFFECTS OF INCREASING C/R 61
  COMPRESSION RATIO ASSUMPTIONS 62
  THE INDUCTION MENU 62
  AIRFLOW SELECTION 62
  AIRFLOW MENU ASSUMPTIONS 64
  INDUCTION MANIFOLD BASICS 64
  MANIFOLD SELECTION ADVICE 66
  THE EXHAUST MENU 70
  WAVE DYNAMICS IN THE EXHAUST SYSTEM 71
  EXHAUST MENU SELECTIONS 73
  THE CAMSHAFT MENU 77
  CAM BASICS 77
  VISUALIZING & CALCULATING VALVE EVENTS 78
  HOW VALVE EVENTS AFFECT POWER 81
  CAMSHAFT MENU—LIFTER CHOICES 85
  CAMSHAFT MENU—SPECIFIC CAMSHAFTS 87
  ENTERING 0.050-INCH & SEAT-TO-SEAT TIMING 90
  CAMSHAFT ADVANCE AND RETARD 91
  CALCULATING VALVE EVENTS 92
6—GAS DYNAMICS AND DYNOMATION 94
  THE IC ENGINE: AN UNSTEADY FLOW MACHINE ... 94
  ACOUSTIC VS. FINITE-AMPLITUDE WAVES 95
  COMPRESSION AND EXPANSION WAVES 95
  PRESSURE WAVES AND ENGINE TUNING 97
  PRESSURE-TIME HISTORIES 97
  GAS FLOW VS. ENGINE PRESSURES 99
  INTAKE TUNING 99
  INDUCTION RUNNER TAPER ANGLES 100
  PORT FLOW VELOCITIES 101
  EXHAUST TUNING 102
  EXHAUST FLOW VELOCITIES 103
  VALVE EVENTS AND STRATEGIES 105
  OPTIMIZE VALVE EVENTS WITH DYNOMATION 106
APPENDIX—A: SOFTWARE INSTALLATION 108
APPENDIX—B: GLOSSARY 120
APPENDIX—C: BIBLIOGRAPHY 126
SOFTWARE SUPPORT FAX PAGE 127
OTHER MOTION SOFTWARE PRODUCTS 128

DeskTop Dynos
Using Computers To Build Horsepower
1—Introduction & Acknowledgements

This is not a typical "hot rodding" book. Yet it is written specifically for you: The amateur or professional automotive enthusiast. This book may reveal more to you about high-performance and racing engines than you've discovered in all the other "enthusiast" books and magazines you've read. I know this to be true, because I have been an engine and book enthusiast all my life, and the nearly two-year process of writing this book taught me more about high-performance engines than my thirty years of engine building, tinkering, and racing.

Most books, like many products aimed at the consumer, begin with a publisher (the manufacturer) "discovering" a need in the marketplace. Often, that means simply making a list of "best sellers." Then an individual is assigned to write a sequel. A quick glance at the overabundance of smallblock Chevy books clearly indicates the "Hollywood" approach. All of these books do not fill the magazine racks because the world is full of writers enthusiastically ready to reveal new insights about a 40-year-old engine (there are a few notable exceptions, but only a few).

Every once in a while, though, a book is published that falls outside of the typical form. It is not produced because of a publisher's assignment. It is not meant as a shot at the "big bucks." It is born from a unique collaboration—the result of fortuitous events—that could never have been planned. This is one of those books.

Two years ago, this book was simply to be a comprehensive guide for Motion Software's Filling-And-Emptying engine simulation software. What the author failed to realize at first was that there is very little difference between understanding engine simulations and understanding engines themselves. In retrospect, it's obvious: If a simulation is a good one, it must mimic the physics at work inside the IC engine. Understanding engine simulations is simply another approach to understanding IC engines.

But engine simulations have been around for years, and there are many talented engineers, developers, and university professors that understand the physics and math that make the IC engine tick. *What's very rare is the individual who has this knowledge <u>and</u> understands racing engines and the needs of the high-performance engine builder.* That individual is Curtis Leaverton, the developer of Motion Software's engine simulation and my associate in the development of this book. This book is, to a great extent, a transcription of a small portion of his vast knowledge, with my contribution being one of organizer and presenter.

Despite the inauspicious beginnings and its odd evolution, this book has become a true "hot rodders" engine guide. Engine books—the better ones, at least—are a compilation of the learned experiences of the author/racer. They describe what components and procedures are known to work, and they conjecture about what is less understood or what seems to defy logic. This "out-side-in" approach is completely understandable. It is a direct result of the most common method of engine development used by engine builders and racers: Trial-and-error. This book follows a new path. It describes engine function from the "inside-out." You won't find a list of bolt-on parts that work on only a few engines, rather you'll discover information that will help you understand WHY engines "need" parts of a specific design to optimize horsepower.

Admittedly, this book only "scratches the surface" of the vast and complex fields of engine-pressure analysis, thermodynamics, and gas dynamics, but that's actually what makes this book "work." There are many other publications that delve deeply into these subjects, the *Bibliography* on page 126 list a few of these tomes, and many are not especially "approachable."

Hopefully, what you find here will be the right mix of theory and practical application. As you read about the development of engines, dynos, and simulation techniques, you will follow a path that has, until now, been obscured by ponderous technical works. If you are able to gain a deeper understanding of the IC engine from these pages and from using the DeskTop Dyno software, I will consider this project a success.

Larry Atherton

Acknowledgments

This book simply would not have been possible without the technical assistance of Curtis Leaverton. Over the last few years I have spent many enjoyable days with Curtis discussing engines and simulation science. He is one of only a handful of people I've encountered in my life who can explain complicated subjects with such enthusiasm that they not only become clear to the listener, but the sheer joy of being guided toward the understanding becomes an indelible memory! In short, Curtis is a terrific teacher (and I like to think, my friend). Occasionally, he conducts seminars throughout the country, and I encourage every reader of this book to avail themselves of the unique opportunity to be "taught by one of the masters."

I also wish to thank the many manufacturers that provided photos and information for this book, especially Harold Bettes of SuperFlow Corporation. Harold, a lot like Curtis Leaverton, has no shortage of enthusiasm and excitement about engines and performance. He has also been extremely generous with his valuable time, and I have learned a great deal from the many hours of conversation we have had (over some great Chinese dinners!). Thanks Harold.

A heartfelt thanks to all the manufacturers that helped with this publication:

Borla Performance, Bonnie Sadkin
Carroll Supercharging, Sheryl Davis
Childs & Albert, Raymond Akerly
Edelbrock, Tom Dufer
HKS Performance, Howard Lim
Hooker Headers, Jason Bruce
Intel Corporation, Rachel Stewart
Moroso Performance Products, Barbara Miller
Snap-on Tools, David Heide, Tami Valeri
SuperFlow Corporation, Harold Bettes
TPS, Bob Hall
Weiand, Jim Davis

A special thanks to Dave Arnold of CarTech Books for taking an interest in this book, and for allowing me the latitude to produce something unique. Dave, it been a pleasure working with you! Thank you for your support.

Another special thanks to Jim Dennewill for the many fine drawings throughout this book. Jim's talents and patience are both rare and boundless. Thank you for all your help and your friendship.

Finally, a sincere thanks to Paul Hammer. I can't imagine what this book project would have been like without Paul's dedicated help in "putting out the fires" around me (and I can imagine some pretty awful stuff!).

DeskTop Dynos
Using Computers To Build Horsepower
2–Engine & Dyno Basics

As widely used and as highly developed as the internal combustion (IC) engine is today, it is a remarkable fact that the IC engine "took its first breath" in the early 1860s, a mere 135 years ago. This first primitive engine, built by the French inventor, Etienne Lenoir, and several others who soon followed, burned a coal-gas and air mixture at atmospheric pressure. Instead of the now critical compression stroke before combustion, these engines used a variation of the two-cycle design. The first "cycle" was a combination intake and power stroke. The piston, starting at the top of the cylinder, would draw in fuel during the first half of the stroke, then a valve would close and the charge was ignited. The expanding gasses would drive the piston down during the second half the stroke. The second cycle was a conventional exhaust stroke. This technology did a poor job of harnessing fuel energy, and most engines of the time produced less than 1 horsepower and operated at an efficiency of only about 5%.

While the first IC engines were crude and inefficient, they generated considerable interest and excitement among inventors of the day. The prospect of developing a lightweight engine that would operate without a bulky and dangerous steam boiler was the main catalyst for research. A compact and powerful engine would bring considerable financial reward to the lucky designer, as a ready market existed of almost unlimited potential applications, including water pumps for mines and farms, fac-

tory main shafts to drive lathes and other machinery, or even to propel that odd, new invention: the "horseless carriage."

The Otto-Cycle Engine

The next major steps in IC engine development were made by a man whose name will forever be tied to the modern automobile engine: Nicholas A. Otto (1832-1891) a German inventor. But before we discuss Mr. Otto's most noted development, its predecessor deserves attention, if only for comparison purposes. In 1867 Otto, along with Euben Langen (1833-1885), developed a free-piston engine using a rack-gear assembly that achieved an efficiency of about 11%, a commendable effort since it still operated without compression before ignition. Also a two-stroke variant, the engine displaced a remarkable 4900cid, weighed about 4000lbs, and produced about 2 horsepower at 90rpm.

Then Otto had a *stroke* of genius (no pun intended). He believed that by building an engine with valves timed to produce *four* separate strokes, one for power, one for exhaust, one for induction, and a stroke for compression, and finally combining this design with a precisely timed spark ignition, efficiency and power would be optimized. He was absolutely right, but he only partially understood why his new design was superior.

His prototype ran in 1876 and was a breakthrough

Nicholas A. Otto's (1832-1891) *stroke* of genius was an engine with valves timed to produce *four* separate strokes. His prototype ran in 1876, by 1880 over 50,000 "Otto-cycle" engines were built and sold in the U.S. and Europe. The world-wide acceptance of the new powerplant effectively started the internal combustion engine industry.

design over his previous free-piston engine. The new four-cycle motor produced the same 2 horsepower but with greatly reduced weight (from 4000lbs down to about 1200lbs), reduced volume (it displaced only 310cid), and improved efficiency of about 14%. The new engine was a huge success, and by 1880 over 50,000 "Otto-cycle" engines were built and sold in the U.S. and Europe. The worldwide acceptance of the new powerplant effectively started the internal combustion engine industry.

If you were to ask Mr. Otto why his innovative four-cycle engine was so efficient, he might begin to explain how a dedicated induction stroke ensured strong "suction" of the air-fuel charge for optimum power. Mr. Otto was right. The "intake" stroke is an important step in optimizing volumetric efficiency (known as VE, more on this later) and obtaining high horsepower per cubic inch displacement. Mr. Otto might also mention that the spark-ignition feature of his engine made certain that the combustion of fuel began at precisely the right moment, again optimizing power. On this analysis, Mr. Otto was also correct. But then he might describe how a "stratification of charge" improved combustion efficiency and further improved power. In this case, Mr. Otto, unfortunately, missed the mark. He lacked an understanding of one of the most important elements of his "Otto-cycle" process: the compression stroke. By compressing the charge before combustion, a higher post-combustion pressure drives the piston with greater force and extracts additional energy from the fuel (more on this critical concept later).

An Overview Of The Otto-Cycle Process

Before we continue to delve into engine design and the dyno testing process, it's helpful to have a thorough understanding of Otto's theory. Even though Otto lacked a full understanding of the subtleties of his own design,

the four-cycle concept—sometimes called the "suck, squeeze, bang, and blow" process—was <u>the</u> key breakthrough that made the modern automobile- and racing-engine possible.

In the simplest terms, Otto's four-cycle process begins with the piston at Top Dead Center (TDC) and the intake valve open or starting to open. As the piston moves down the bore, the first cycle—called the *Intake Cycle*—draws air and fuel into the cylinder through the induction system. When the piston reaches Bottom Dead Center (BDC), the intake valve closes and the piston begins to move back up the bore, beginning the *Compression Cycle*. At or near TDC, the fully compressed charge is ignited by a spark plug. This drives the piston back down the bore producing the *Power Cycle*. When the piston again reaches BDC, the exhaust valve opens and burnt gasses are driven out of the cylinder as the piston moves back to TDC, completing the *Exhaust Cycle*. Now the intake valve opens, beginning the next series of four-step Otto cycles. The steady repeating of these cycles, typically 24,000 full Otto cycles per minute in high-speed engines, produces a seemingly smooth flow of power.

Otto's assumption that the intake and exhaust valves should be opened and closed right at TDC or BDC, is based on the belief that the air-fuel mixture and exhaust gasses start and stop instantly. At very low engine speeds—like the 160rpm peak speeds of Otto's original four-cycle engine—this assumption is not far from the truth. However, as engine speeds climb to 2500rpm and higher, gasses develop considerable momentum. In addition, finite amplitude waves are also created within the induction and exhaust systems (more on this later) that carry substantial energy and influence mass flow.

This complex phenomenon changed everything. To a great extent, it is the understanding and harnessing of this phenomenon that determine the success of most engine modifications. Induction design, camshaft profiles,

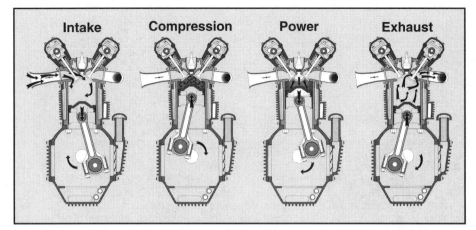

| Intake | Compression | Power | Exhaust |

Otto's four-cycle process begins with the piston moving down the bore on the *Intake Cycle*—drawing air and fuel into the cylinder. At Bottom Dead Center, the intake valve closes and the piston begins to move back up the bore, beginning the *Compression Cycle*. Near Top Dead Center, the fully compressed charge is ignited, driving the piston back down the bore on the *Power Cycle*. When the piston again reaches Bottom Dead Center, the exhaust valve opens and burnt gasses are driven out of the cylinder on the *Exhaust Cycle*. The steady repeating of these cycles produces a smooth flow of horsepower.

cylinder head ports, valve size, exhaust tubing shape and length, and many other engine components must harness the hidden forces in the flow of gasses if they are to produce optimum power and efficiency.

Motion Software engine simulations, and most of the information in this book, are devoted to the efforts of exploring and *exploiting* the energy stored in the "vapors" inside an Otto-cycle engine. Only during the last few years have engine designers begun to use the theories of gas dynamics and advanced computer simulations to create new component designs. Even to this day, a majority of race engine development involves empirical testing, a fancy name for trial and error. Hard to believe, isn't it? Many the world's most successful racing teams build parts, run dyno tests, build more parts, run more dyno tests, and more or less stand around scratching their heads trying to figure out why this worked and that didn't.

Since testing continues to make up a substantial portion of engine development programs, let's take a closer look at the device that has become almost as common as the Snap-on toolbox in professional shops: the dynamometer. With this knowledge, you will be more able to understand and integrate the uses of computer simulations, like those from Motion Software, Inc., into a successful engine design and/or building project.

Modern Engine Development And Testing

Throughout the more than one hundred years that have passed since Mr. Otto designed his original spark-ignition, four-cycle engine, designers and engineers have applied their considerable talents to the task of improving the efficiency and power output of this remarkable powerplant. As each new design enhancement was realized, a careful testing program was implemented that ensured the modified components performed as desired. Without direct feedback from "real world" testing (and lacking adequate mathematical models of engine dynamics), the effects of new designs would remain speculation. In fact, engine-testing programs confirm or refute conjecture, prove or disprove the benefits of component designs, and demonstrate the mechanical reliability of fixed and reciprocating components. Without thorough

testing, IC engine development would not have reached the sophisticated level that is has today (and mathematical engine simulations would never have been developed or would have remained unverifiable theories).

Broadly speaking, piston-engine testing programs fall into two categories: 1) *Reliability Tests* ensure that the engine will provide long service with minimum maintenance, and 2) *Functional Tests* evaluate improvements in power and/or economy over a full range of operating conditions. It is not possible to perform either of these two test programs without a way to operate the engine under load in a "laboratory" environment and carefully measure various temperatures, pressures, and loads. So the evolution and use of sophisticated engine-testing sys-

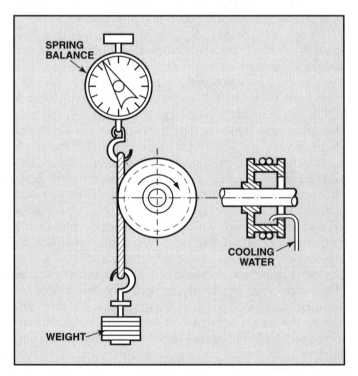

Early dynamometers were basic devices that used a belt, rope, or other friction clutch as an absorber. This rope dyno could be tightened or loosened by varying the weight on one end of the rope. The spring scale measured the absorbed load. To prevent overheating and improve accuracy, early dynos were often water cooled; note cooling tube directing a jet of water to the inside of the drum.

tems, with the dynamometer as the central element, has been a crucial step in the evolution of the internal combustion engine.

The Dynamometer And What It Measures

The need for accurately measuring the power output of an engine existed for many years before the first internal-combustion engine. Throughout most of the early 17th century, the steam engine was applied to an ever-increasing number of tasks, and by the 1850's steam power was in regular daily use for passenger and freight transportation over the roads and waterways in England. Engine designers of the day needed a way to measure power output to help select and improve steam powerplants for specific applications. The machine that provided the solution was the *engine dynamometer*.

Early dynamometers were basic devices that used a belt, rope, or other friction clutch as an absorber. The clutch assembly could be tightened or loosened, varying the braking force on the crankshaft. An arm attached to the clutch was connected to a set of weights or a spring scale that measured the absorbed load.

An early and simple dyno was the Prony Brake. It consisted of a pair of wooden brake shoes mounted in a frame. The shoes rode on a metal drum attached to the engine crankshaft. The brake shoe clamping force, or "drag," was adjusted by tightening or loosening the clamping spring nuts. A weight was hung from the end the torque arm that applied a counterforce, preventing the fixture from rotating with the drum. The absorbed power, as in modern automobile brakes, was converted into heat, and to prevent overheating and improve accuracy, Prony Brakes and similar early dynos were often water cooled.

Before we continue exploring the evolution of dynamometers and engine testing, it's helpful to understand the forces that a dyno must absorb and how these forces are utilized to produce measurements of torque and horsepower.

Torque

The simple structure of the Prony Brake, not unlike modern dynamometers in function, makes it easy to understand the physics behind what "comes out" of an engine and what "goes into" the dynamometer. To begin, let's define the *force* the engine produces as something we will call *torque*. A very unique physicist (Richard Feynman, 1918-1988) once described this concept as: "Force is the stuff that is needed to *make things move* in a straight line, and the stuff that *makes something rotate* is a 'rotary force,' or 'twisting force,' and that is called torque." Now, let's take this concept one step further. When you tighten a bolt with a wrench, it's obvious that the longer the wrench, the easier it is to tighten the bolt. In other words, torque varies with the length of the wrench when the force (the effort applied by your muscles) remains the same. So torque can be described as force (like ounces, pounds, etc.) times the length of the arm (like feet, inches, etc.). Typical torque values are ounce-inches, pound-feet, etc. Let's see how the concepts of force and torque are used in the dynamometer.

Going back to a basic Prony Brake, let's perform a simple dyno test that attempts to measure engine torque at full throttle at 1000rpm. We'll start off by placing a 50-pound weight at the end of the two-foot (24-inch) torque arm. As we tighten the brake springs we'll open the throttle more and more until the 50-pound weight just begins to lift. Now we'll add more weight and continue to open the throttle, all the while maintaining engine speed at 1000rpm. When we reach full throttle, an additional 50 pounds of weight was required, bringing the total weight to 100 pounds. This means that the engine is producing 100 pounds of force acting through a two-foot torque arm, in other words, a torque output of 200 pound-feet. This is the same measurement method used on modern dynos, except instead of crude brake shoes and weights, a precision absorber is used with extremely accurate

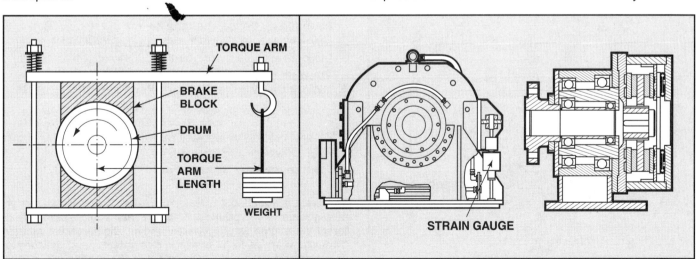

The Prony Brake (left) consisted of a pair of wooden brake shoes mounted in a frame. The shoes rode on a metal drum attached to the engine. The brake shoe clamping force, or "drag," was adjusted by tightening or loosening the clamping nuts. A weight applied a counterforce, preventing the fixture from rotating. A modern version of the Prony Brake (right) used a large disk brake. Like the Prony Brake, the entire dyno was free to rotate, restrained by a precision strain gauge.

load transducers. In either case, the formula for torque is simply:

$$\text{Torque} = \text{Force} \times \text{Torque Arm}$$
$$= 100 \times 2$$
$$= 200 \text{ pound-feet}$$

where, **Force** is the applied or the generated force and **Torque Arm** is the length through which that force is applied.

Work

But engines produce more than static torque. They also generate rotary *motion*. About this, our noted physicist went on to say: "If we maintain the analogy between straight-line and angular motion, force times the distance of movement is work, and force times the swept angle of movement [distance again] is also work." So to produce work, an engine must move something, not simply exert a static force. So while torque measures how much force an engine *can* generate, power is the rate-based measurement of *how fast* that force is producing work.

To begin our exploration of work, let's first calculate the work per revolution produced by the test engine. Start with the applied force at the end of the two-foot torque arm. Then multiply this force by the swept distance through which the equivalent counterforce generated by the engine would rotate the same "weight" one full revolution:

Work Per Revolution = Force x Swept Distance

The force is 100 pounds (it's the weight attached to the arm on the Prony Brake), and swept distance is the circumference of the circle generated by the two-foot torque arm length (the arm is the radius of the circle). To determine the swept distance per revolution, a simple formula for the circumference of a circle is applied:

Swept Distance (Circumference) = 2 x Pi x Radius

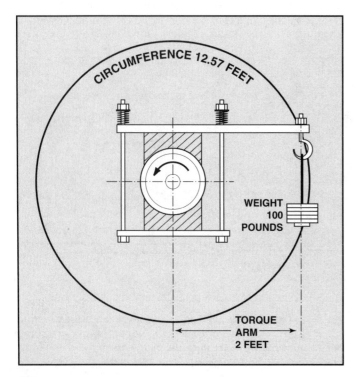

$$= 2 \times 3.1416 \times 2$$
$$= 12.57 \text{ feet}$$

Now we'll substitute the swept distance back into the work-per-revolution formula:

Work Per Revolution = Force x Swept Distance
$$= 100 \times 12.57$$
$$= 1257 \text{ pound-feet}$$

In simple terms, this means the engine "moves" 100 pounds through 12.57 feet during each revolution of the crankshaft. Interestingly, an equivalent amount of work would be performed by moving 1257 pounds one foot, or by moving one pound 1257 feet.

Horsepower

Up to this point, we have found that 1257 pound-feet of work are done during each revolution of the crankshaft. Since the engine is running at 1000rpm and each rev takes only 0.06 seconds, we could say that 1257 pound-feet of work are produced every 0.06 seconds. This is the same *rate-of-work* as 20,950 pound-feet in one second or 1,257,000 pound-feet per minute. All of these values are based on the same uniform rate of power production. They simply measure work over different periods of time. What we need is a common basis for comparison; an identifiable number that will make engine designers "feel warm and fuzzy."

The "number" we're looking for is *horsepower*, and we can thank James Watt (1736-1819), a Scottish engineer and inventor, for dreaming it up. Watt was the first to derive the scientific calculation for power from his practical observations of horse-drawn loads. He initially figured that an average horse could move 200 pounds, 110 feet, in one minute; which is the same as 22,000 pound-feet per minute. Watt later raised this figure to establish the current value for one horsepower: 33,000 pound-feet per minute or 550 pound-feet per second.

Now let's apply Watt's horsepower rating to the Prony Brake test engine. So far, we have determined the work produced during each revolution of the crankshaft (1257 pound-feet). Since the engine on our Prony Brake is running at 1000rpm with the applied load, we'll multiply the per-revolution work by the engine speed to calculate the work (in pound-feet) per minute:

Work Per Minute = Work Per Revolution x RPM
$$= 1257 \times 1000$$
$$= 1,257,000 \text{ pound-feet/minute}$$

To find Watt's horsepower rating simply divide the above pound-feet-per-minute work by 33,000:

Horsepower = Pound-Feet Per Minute / 33,000

The weight attached to the arm on the Prony Brake generates a force of 100 pounds. A torque that would exactly counteract the engine would have to "move" the same 100 pounds through an arc of 12.57 feet (the circumference of the torque-arm circle) during each revolution of the crankshaft, generating 1257 pound-feet of work in 0.06 seconds. This is the same *rate-of-work* as 1,257,000 pound-feet per minute. To find horsepower divide this by 33,000. The result is 38 horsepower.

James Watt, a Scottish engineer and inventor dreamed up what we are all searching for: horsepower. Watt was the first to derive the scientific calculation for power from his practical observations of horse-drawn loads. He eventually settled on the figure that is now the currently accepted standard for one horsepower: 33,000 pound-feet per minute or 550 pound-feet per second.

The days of crude rope- or wooden-brakes dynos are long gone. The modern electric or hydraulic dynos use a precision absorber that directs engine torque through an extremely accurate load transducer. Temperature sensors, automatic throttle actuators, and many other computer controls make dyno testing much easier and more accurate than it was in the "good old days."

$$= 1,257,000 / 33,000$$
$$= 38 \text{ Horsepower}$$

By working backwards through the previous equations (we'll save you most of the trip), a simple relationship between horsepower and torque can be shown. Calculating the horsepower from any known torque is possible with this equation:

$$\textbf{Horsepower} = (\text{Torque} \times 2 \times \text{Pi} \times \text{RPM}) / 33,000$$
$$= (\text{Torque} \times \text{RPM}) / 5,252$$

Remember that **Torque** in this equation is the static force developed by the resistive force times the length of the torque arm. Applying the formula to the Prony Brake test gives the same result:

$$\textbf{Horsepower} = (\text{Torque} \times \text{RPM}) / 5252$$
$$= (200 \times 1000) / 5252$$
$$= 38 \text{ Horsepower}$$

The horsepower being measured by the Prony Brake and calculated by these equations is just one of several ways to rate engine power output. Various "definitions" or "descriptions" for horsepower are commonly used, and each method provides additional information about the engine being tested.

Horsepower By Any Other Name

As you might have guessed, the horsepower calculated so far is *brake horsepower* (bhp). Its name comes directly from the designs of early dynamometers, like the Prony Brake. Brake horsepower (sometimes referred to as *shaft* horsepower) is always measured at the flywheel or crankshaft. However, modern engines are equipped with a myriad of "accessories" that consume power and can substantially lower brake horsepower measurements. Because of this, two common techniques for measuring horsepower have become accepted practice, and the power measured using each method has been given unique names.

Gross brake horsepower describes the power output of an engine in stripped-down, "race-ready" trim. The only drain on power from accessories comes from the oil pump, and possibly the mechanical fuel and water pumps. All other nonessential power-robbing devices have been removed, including exhaust manifolds that are usually replaced with non-muffled tubular headers. Before 1970, virtually all automakers rated their engines using this method, and surely many of you fondly remember the 425+ gross horsepower ratings of the sixties. But beginning in the early 1970's, this rating method was changed to reflect a more representative power level for engines as they are operated in vehicles on the highway.

Net brake horsepower measures the power at the flywheel when the engine is tested with all standard accessories attached and functioning. This includes the cooling system, exhaust system including mufflers and catalytic converters (or a fixed restriction welded in the exhaust pipes to simulate the backpressure of mufflers and cats), plus fuel, oil, water and smog pumps. However, power-steering pumps and air conditioning compressors are difficult to hook up in a dyno-test environment so are often eliminated during net horsepower testing.

While this may muddy the waters of understanding of what is meant by specific horsepower numbers, matters get even worse. There are several additional types of horsepower commonly used by engineers: friction horsepower, indicated horsepower, and rated horsepower are the more common, among others. Each of these values "tells" a unique story about the mechanical design and thermodynamic efficiency of the engine. We'll take a quick look at them here, then we'll revisit them later in this chapter when an important discussion about engine pressures will give you insight into how both engines and computer simulations function.

Friction horsepower is the power absorbed by the mechanical components of the engine during normal operation. Most frictional losses are due to piston ring pressure against the cylinder walls. Combustion gasses during the power stroke force the rings against the cylinder walls and generate an excellent seal. Unfortunately, these high pressures also create substantial drag and frictional heating.

Frictional power losses are not easily measured by direct testing, although some electric dynamometers, as we shall see, have the ability to "motor" an engine and partially measure frictional drag. However, frictional losses can be accurately *calculated* knowing the brake horsepower (from dyno testing) and the indicated horsepower (discussed next). Over countless dyno tests and years of research, accurate frictional models have been developed for piston driven, internal-combustion engines. These mathematical models are usually based on the bore size and stroke length and can predict frictional losses with an accuracy of a few percent throughout a wide range of

Before 1970, virtually all automakers rated their engines using *gross brake horsepower*, a method describing power output of an engine in stripped-down, "race-ready" trim. Beginning in the early 1970's, *Net brake horsepower* was used to reflect a more representative power level for engines as they are operated in vehicles on the highway. *Net brake horsepower* measures the power at the flywheel when the engine is tested with all standard accessories attached and functioning, much like the setup on this LT5 Corvette engine.

engine designs. Without these models, computer simulations would not be possible. Despite their predictive ability, however, if there ever was an area where real dyno testing remains an absolutely necessity, it's in the measurement of friction and losses due to the variations in piston rings, valvetrain components, and lubrication. While the changes are often small, they are virtually "immune" to computer modeling and prediction.

Indicated horsepower is the maximum power that a particular engine can *theoretically* produce. It is calculated from an analysis of the gas pressures in the cylinders throughout the entire four-cycle process. Cylinder pressures are directly measured by installing pressure transducers (usually) into the combustion chambers and accurately recording their readings—along with exact crankshaft positions—at very small increments throughout the full combustion process. Once measured, these pressures determine not only how much power is being produced, but the "health" of the engine under test.

There is a direct relationship between brake, friction, and indicated horsepower values. Simply stated, if you start with the maximum indicated horsepower and subtract the losses due to friction, you wind up with brake horsepower:

Indicated HP - Friction HP = Net Brake HP

These principles are discussed in more detail in the next chapter on engine pressures and how computer simulations work.

Horsepower And Torque In The Real World

We have nearly completed our overview of torque

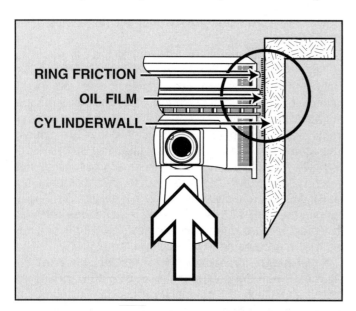

Frictional losses within the IC engine are mainly due to piston ring pressure against the cylinder walls. Combustion gasses during the power stroke force the rings against the cylinder walls and generate an excellent seal. Unfortunately, these high pressures also create substantial drag and frictional heating.

and horsepower. There is just one more relationship that should be discussed before we continue to explore dynos and engine testing systems. Remember that torque measures how much force an engine *can* generate, power is the rate-based measurement of *how fast* that force is producing work.

When any IC engine is tested, presumably at wide open throttle, it initially produces increasing amounts of torque as engine speed rises. This increasing torque is generated from proportionally larger amounts of fuel and air being drawn into the engine and converted to high pressures that drive the pistons and crankshaft. Horsepower also rises quickly because not only is torque increasing (the capacity to perform work), but so is engine speed (the rate at which work is being done). Most automobile engines reach peak torque output somewhere between 3000 and 6000rpm, beyond this speed, torque "noses over" and begins to fall off at higher engine speeds. This happens because the pathways that air and fuel pass through in the engine are no longer of sufficient volume to accommodate the ever-increasing flow demands of the cylinders.

When torque first begins to fall off, it does so gradually. This allows the horsepower to continue to increase since engine speed is increasing faster than torque is declining. As long as the *torque decrease rate* is slower than the *speed increase rate*, horsepower will continue to rise. At high engine speeds, the induction system becomes an overwhelming restriction to airflow, and engine efficiency falls off rapidly. This drives torque downward faster than engine speed can increase, forming a horsepower peak and then decline.

As you will find in your further exploration of the IC engine, many factors affect airflow, torque, and therefore horsepower, including cylinder head design, valve size, carburetion/fuel-injection flow capacity, valve timing, and intake/exhaust wave tuning effects. All of these factors, and more, interact with one another to make up a complex, seemingly unpredictable system—unpredictable until now, that is! Motion Software engine simulations take all these factors into consideration using a complex mathematical model to determine precise induction and exhaust system flow; an essential element in predicting cylinder pressures that ultimately determine torque and horsepower levels.

Now let's return to our discussion of dynamometers and continue to explore the testing machine that was an essential factor in the turning Otto's basic engine into the prime mover it is today.

Other Types Of Dynos

Engine testing with early dynos, like the Prony Brake, must have been interesting to watch. The test engine was brought up to the desired rpm, the clutch or brake was tightened to apply some load, engine power was increased, more was load applied, and so on. When the engine was running at "full throttle" with the friction absorber and weight stack adjusted to "hold back" the en-

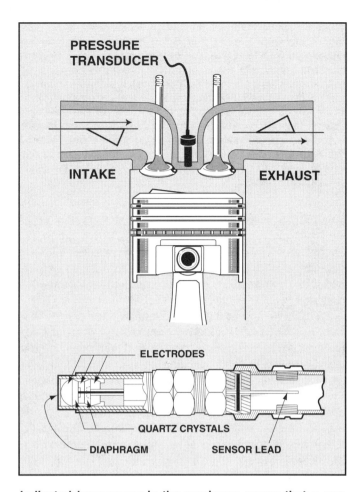

Indicated horsepower is the maximum power that a particular engine can produce. It is calculated from an analysis of the gas pressures in the cylinders throughout the entire four-cycle process, along with a precise record of crank position. Cylinder pressures are directly measured with pressure transducers. Once measured, these pressures determine not only how much power is being produced, but the "health" of the engine under test.

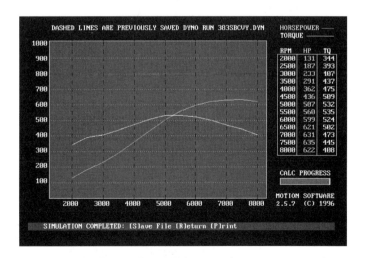

Most automobile engines deliver peak torque somewhere between 3000 and 6000rpm. Beyond this, torque "noses over" and begins to fall off at higher engine speeds. This happens because the pathways that air and fuel pass through in the engine are no longer of sufficient volume to accommodate the ever-increasing flow demands of the cylinders.

William Froude invented the hydraulic-absorber dyno consisting of an outer casing supported by bearings at each end. Otherwise free to rotate, the casing was retained by a torque arm attached to a scale or balance weights. Engine power was transmitted to impellers (rotors) inside the casing that forced or pumped a liquid, usually water, against another set of impellers (stators) fixed to the interior of the casing. This design is quite similar to a torque converter used in modern automatic transmissions. The amount of load transmitted from the rotors to the exterior casing was adjusted by sliding in or out a pair of "dividing walls" or sluice gates between the rotors and stators.

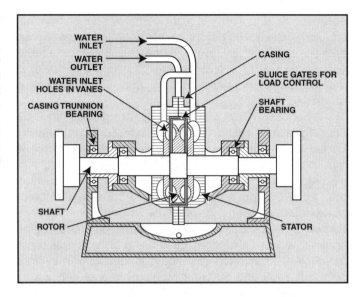

gine at the desired rpm, a quick reading of the rpm gauge was taken before the friction materials overheated or caught fire! While this activity must have been a crowd pleaser, early friction absorbers were difficult to use, inaccurate, and needless to say, required constant maintenance.

To solve this problem, a dynamometer design was required that would absorb power reliably without overheating. An absorber was needed that was easily adjustable, repeatable, and provided an unvarying load even at high power levels. The answer came from William Froude (1810-1879). Primarily a civil engineer and naval architect, Mr. Froude was the first to perform scale-model testing of ship hulls in an effort to evaluate the flow of water and determine the sources of drag (he found it to be friction between the hull and water and the formation of waves). Froude understood liquid dynamics. He knew that friction from water and other non-compressible fluids was a very effective power absorber. He believed that a hydraulic absorber held potential for use as a dynamometer. Furthermore, if a steady flow of liquid was fed into the absorbing unit it would carry away absorbed heat and maintain stable temperatures and braking characteristics.

The Hydraulic Dynamometer

Froude's idea of a "hydraulic" dyno consisted of an outer casing supported by bearings at each end. Otherwise free to rotate, the casing was retained by a torque arm attached to a scale or balance weights. Engine power was transmitted to impellers (rotors) inside the casing that forced or pumped a liquid, usually water, against another set of impellers (stators) fixed to the interior of the casing. This design is quite similar to a torque converter used in modern automatic transmissions. The amount of load transmitted from the rotors to the exterior casing was adjusted by sliding in or out a pair of "dividing walls" or sluice gates between the rotors and stators.

Froude's design worked very well, and modern versions of this early design are widely used in engine development shops throughout the world. Their overwhelming acceptance is due to one, clear-cut advantage over other methods of power absorption and measurement: low cost. The water dyno offers other significant advantages as well: 1) high power absorption capacity for a small physical size, 2) high reliability, 3) stability

Modern water-brake dynos, like this one from Superflow, Inc., have become very sophisticated in both operation and data analysis. A dyno test on a modern dyno involves the operator simply entering the desired engine speed range, fully opening the throttle, and pressing a button to begin the test. A built-in computer directs the dynamometer throughout the test. The computer records the torque absorbed and displays a complete test analysis. Remarkably, even with considerable computer instrumentation included, a basic 1000hp water dyno sells for only about $10,000.

This is just one of several sophisticated dyno test cells at Edelbrock, Inc., the world's largest manufacturer of intake manifolds and related induction equipment. The engine under test is a 350hp smallblock Chevy designed for smog-legal street operation. This dyno "cell" provides dyno water circulation and cooling, engine water and heat radiation, adequate flow of clean outside air for engine induction, and precision instrumentation. The total cost: over $75,000.

and accuracy, 4) rapid heat dissipation from steady water flow, and 5) a wide range (envelope) of operation from low speed and torque absorption to high speeds and high loads.

Modern water-brake dynos have also become very sophisticated in both operation and data analysis. A dyno test on a modern dyno involves the operator simply entering the desired engine-speed range, fully opening the throttle, and pressing a button to begin the test. A built-in computer directs the dynamometer absorption unit to draw the engine down to the lowest test speed, hold it there for a second or so, then increase engine speed to the next test point, hold it, and so forth throughout the selected speed range. The computer records the torque absorbed at each power level then displays a complete test analysis, including calculated horsepower, immediately after the test is concluded.

Remarkably, even with considerable computer instrumentation included, a basic 1000hp water dyno can be purchased from several sources, including the well-known manufacturer Superflow, Inc., for only about $10,000. However, a fully equipped dyno testing cell (room) that provides dyno water circulation and cooling, engine water and heat radiation, adequate flow of clean outside air for engine induction, and precision instrumentation can cost $40,000 to $75,000. While these costs may seem high at first, until recently it was not possible to set up a sophisticated dyno testing facility for less than a multiple six-figure investment.

Modern "mass-produced" water dynos have contributed, in no small measure, to the outstanding advances

in race-engine power levels over the past 15 years. David Vizard, a noted engine expert, recently said, "There have been more dyno tests on modern water-brake dynos over the last 10 years than in all the previous years since the IC engine was invented. And now with engine simulation programs, you can run a 'dyno test' in only a few minutes that would otherwise have taken all day or even several days on a real dyno. It's hard to predict what effects this will have on engine development, but it's safe to say that it will be as significant as the contribution from the of the water dyno itself."

The Electric Dynamometer

While the water-brake dyno has become the common testing tool for most race-engine shops, the electric dynamometer was, and still is, widely used for engine development throughout the world. The electric dyno harnesses a generator to convert rotational power into electricity that is then dissipated as heat by liquid- or air-cooled resistors. The electric dyno is almost always more expensive than a water-brake system due to the use of sophisticated components required to control the high electrical currents produced during testing. But in the past at least, electric dynamometers were considered the "Rolls Royce" of testing systems, providing optimum control and high accuracy. Recent design improvements in water-brake systems, however, have raised their accuracy to a level now on par with many electric absorbers.

There are several types of electric dynos, including direct-current, regenerative alternating-current, and eddy-current absorbers. The first two, as previously mentioned, use generators to convert engine power into electrical energy. The eddy-current system also converts rotational power to electrical energy, but instead of dissipating the energy with resistors, it's absorbed by the rotor assembly inside the "generator." Because power is generated and absorbed in such a small space, the rotors of eddy-current absorbers are always water cooled.

While it is theoretically possible to determine engine power by measuring the current generated in an electric dyno, most electric dynos operate on the same direct-measurement principle as the water brake. The electric generator or absorber is supported by trunnion bearings at each end of the casing. The absorbed load is measured by the force generated at the end of a torque arm attached to the casing. As always, the torque is equal to the effective length of the lever arm times the net force exerted by the arm on a load or strain gauge. In these designs, the electric current generated during the test is simply considered "waste heat."

Measuring Friction Horsepower With Electric Dynos

Electric dynos offer a feature that is unavailable in water-brake systems. Since most electric absorbers are really electric generators, and many electric generators function as motors when fed with electrical power, elec-

Many "hot rods" have been bolted together from available components, a touch of ingenuity, and a good dash of visceral esthetics. This is finally changing as the performance industry moves into the "modern era" of electronics, computers, and sophisticated simulations.

tric dynos can often "motor," or rotate the test engine. In addition to making an excellent starter motor, this feature can be used to directly measure internal engine friction. By spinning the engine with the ignition turned off, the kilowatts of power required to maintain a fixed engine speed are determined. Kilowatts are converted to horsepower (by multiplying by 1.341) to reveal the *Friction Horsepower* absorbed by engine "internals."

A typical motoring test begins by running the engine with the ignition on. A moderate load is applied to allow all components, lubricating oil, and cooling water to reach full operating temperatures. Modifications are made to the engine cooling system so that during the motoring test, water is recirculated within the engine, rather than fed through an external radiator, to help maintain a steady temperature. At this point the ignition is switched off and power is applied to the dyno generator to maintain the same engine speed. In an effort to duplicate actual operating conditions as closely as possible, the power consumption required to rotate the engine is recorded within seconds after the ignition is turned off.

Measuring friction horsepower by this method produces very good results. However, several factors reduce the accuracy, including: 1) temperatures inside the motoring engine are lower than those inside a running engine, 2) the pressures on the engine bearings, piston rings, and valves are much lower in the motoring state, and 3) since interior temperatures are lower, internal clearances (particularly piston-to-cylinderwall) are greater. While the measurement of motoring friction may not produce exact results, it has been proven to be a good method to evaluate the frictional properties of the entire mechanical engine assembly. A more accurate determination of friction horsepower can be made, as described earlier, by subtracting the measured *brake horsepower* from the calculated *indicated horsepower*. However, the data required to calculate indicated horsepower from a test engine requires the precise measurement of cylinder pressures throughout the rpm range. That can only be done using the best laboratory-grade dynamometers equipped with state-of-the-art instrumentation.

The Schizophrenic Course Of Engine Development

Since the invention of the internal combustion engine, scientists and engineers have made remarkable progress in explaining the physical processes that take place during each of Otto's cycles. Using the laws of physics as a framework and mathematics as the precise instrument of examination, they have probed inside ports, cylinders, and manifold systems. They have quantified much of the thermodynamics of combustion. They've developed equations that describe concepts given odd

names like finite pressure waves, flow reversion, and indicated mean effective pressures.

This methodical development, undertaken by some of the largest firms in the US, was primarily driven by a single overriding factor: Profit. It was essential for aircraft, automobile, and industrial engine manufacturers to understand the dynamics of the internal combustion engine, because without this understanding, they could not build reliable powerplants to meet their customers' demands.

Substantial additional strides were made during WWII when combat pilots needed more horsepower to outrun the German Luftwaffe with their piston-driven fighter aircraft. The war provided a powerful incentive that drove IC engine research to new heights of understanding, sophistication, and performance.

However, the "big-scale" programs within business, science, and the government have not been the only venues for piston-engine development. Throughout the past 100 years and continuing to this day, engine development has followed another distinctly different road. An alternate path began almost as soon as the *second* automobile was built. Efforts here were not driven by science as much as ego; more by muscle than math. It was the simple desire to go faster than the next guy; to win a race.

By the 1930's hundreds of small shops sprung from nowhere to begin selling cams, heads, manifolds, carburetors, and other bolt-on accessories to improve performance. By the 1950's an entirely new culture had developed around fast cars, now known as "The Hot Rodding Scene." Many "hot rods" were bolted together from available components, a touch of ingenuity, and a good dash of visceral esthetics. There was no desire to review the nearly 50 years of compiled research into the internal combustion engine. In fact, many members of this new counterculture had a disdain for the "establishment," and the establishment included the automakers. The feeling was, to some degree, that only the Hot Rodder could unleash the "hidden" power the auto manufacturer's were unable to discover. This attitude maintained a schism between the established body of knowledge about IC engines and what racers designed for the race track. A parallel arena of development, driven by trial-and-error testing combined with the sheer determination of will, drove engine development in a separate universe that only a few noted racers would bridge with established research.

The Dynamometer:
The Ultimate Trial-And-Error Tool

While this "less scientific" approach may have taken a more circuitous route to horsepower and high-speed reliability, racers are very driven people and not easily discouraged. One by one, as each component would fail or not perform as required, new pieces were designed and substituted for inferior "stock" parts. New cam designs, valve contours, port designs, and a thousand other components were installed and tested. This entire process of trial-and-error testing was driven into high gear as the cost to purchase and setup a dyno declined. Today, in the 1990's, a majority of racers, even most of the successful professional teams, still perform engine testing using the same trial-and-error (or "empirical," if you prefer) methods pioneered nearly 100 years ago. Many have discovered "winning" combinations consisting of groups of parts that produce certain horsepower or torque levels, but most (by far) lack a full understand of _why_ those parts work in concert. They may change one element (valve timing, say) and find that exactly the opposite of the expected effect was produced. This is a sure

Computer simulation programs, like the PC series from Motion Software, are merging the scientific and practical paths of engine development. Racing experts have been stunned by the predictive ability of these high-end mathematical simulations and are taking a new look at the body of academic knowledge on the IC engine. While the dyno will always be needed to perform real-world testing, in the future its use will shift more toward a tool of confirmation rather than brute experimentation.

sign that the underlying physics was never really understood.

But things are finally changing. Today, we are just beginning to observe the merging of the scientific and practical paths of engine development. Changes are being driven by, among other things, the growing use of computer simulation programs, like the PC series from Motion Software, by professional engine builders. Racing experts have been stunned by the predictive ability of these high-end mathematical simulations and are taking a new look at the body of academic knowledge on the IC engine. While the dyno will always be needed to perform real-world testing, in the future its use will shift more toward a tool of confirmation rather than brute experimentation.

Now that you understand dynamometer basics and how dynos are used by racers and engine builders, we will turn our focus toward the science of engine modeling. The next chapter will answer a fundamental question posed by many enthusiasts: How can a computer predict the power output of a device as complex as the IC engine? We'll explore how the pressures within each cylinder dictate power output, and how these same pressures can be understood by combining the physics of gas dynamics, thermodynamics, and time-based analysis. And if we've done our job right, you will be able to understand all of this without taking time out to "brush up" on physics or calculus.

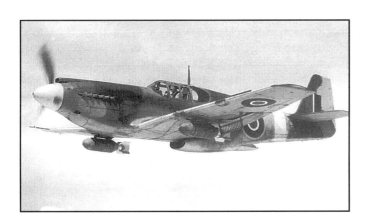

Substantial strides in engine development were made during WWII when combat pilots needed more horsepower to outrun the German Luftwaffe with their piston-driven fighter aircraft. The war provided a powerful incentive that drove IC engine research to new heights of understanding, sophistication, and performance.

Engine Pressures

You've probably heard someone say the IC engine is "just an air pump." This oversimplification is more true than you might imagine. Air is drawn in during the intake stroke, raised in pressure during the compression stroke, and pumped out during the exhaust stroke. If you attached all the exhaust ports to a suitable tank, removed fuel from the picture (and slightly adjusted valve timing), the IC engine would make a functional air compressor. But an air compressor *consumes* power in order to pump air; the IC engine *produces* power while it pumps air through its ports and cylinders. This crucial difference is due to the cylinder pressures generated when the air/fuel mixture is ignited. In fact, understanding how both an air compressor and an IC engine function more or less boils down to measuring and understanding the various pressures that exist in the ports, cylinders, and exhaust system. This concept is so crucial to the understanding of how engines *and engine simulation programs* work that a brief discussion of the pressures found in the IC engine is in order.

Perhaps the engine pressure that most automotive enthusiasts recognize is measured with a compression gauge. Compression pressure is created when the piston moves toward top dead center (TDC) after the intake valve closes, trapping the induced charge (normally a

fuel/air mixture) within the cylinder. This pressure is commonly measured by installing a dial-type pressure gauge in the cylinder in place of the spark plug. The engine is cranked over by the starter with the ignition switched off. To improve measurement accuracy, the throttle is usually held wide open, and the remaining spark plugs are removed to minimize cranking loads and optimize pressures in the cylinder under test. As each compression stroke occurs, the gauge will jump to indicate the pressure. Most compression gauges have a one-way valve that retains pressure in the gauge, so after a few crank cycles, the gauge will home in on, and then stay at, the highest recorded cylinder pressure.

Compression pressure is directly related to the volume of air drawn into the cylinder just before the intake valve closes, and that is directly related to intake valve timing. If the intake valve doesn't close until the piston moves a substantial distance up the bore (as is the case with racing camshaft profiles), a portion of the induced air will be pushed back out of the cylinder into the intake port, reducing the trapped volume and the compression pressure. Remember that compression pressures are measured at cranking speeds, and the amount of charge pushed backwards will change dramatically as engine speed increases. At slow speeds gasses act like lightweight vapors, but as engine and gas speeds increase, the momentum of the air/fuel mixture and generated pressure-wave dynamics make otherwise insubstantial gas-

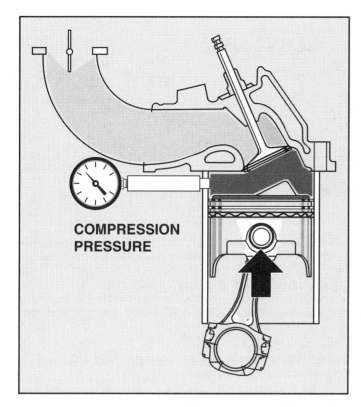

COMPRESSION PRESSURE

Compression pressure is created when the piston moves toward top dead center (TDC) after the intake valve closes, trapping the induced charge (normally a fuel/air mixture) within the cylinder. This pressure is commonly measured by installing a dial-type pressure gauge in the cylinder in place of the spark plug. Compression pressure is directly related to the volume of air drawn into the cylinder just before the intake valve closes, and that is directly related to intake valve timing.

ses act like "thick" liquids. In this case, charge momentum can drive more mixture in the cylinder, even as the piston moves up the bore. Combustion pressure is also related to the space that remains in the cylinder—called combustion volume—when the piston reaches TDC (this is not *combustion-chamber volume*, although they are directly related; more on the differences later). The smaller the combustion volume, the higher the compression pressure (and the compression ratio) will be.

This most familiar of all pressures is—like virtually every other element of the IC engine—dynamically linked to a number of other variables, including engine speed, valve timing, charge density, temperature, intake system flow, and so on. But that doesn't reduce the value of measuring it at cranking speed. At these low speeds, it can reveal the "health" of each cylinder. Ring wear, valve seat quality, and even head gasket condition can be evaluated by measuring cranking compression. An engine that develops very consistent cranking compression pressures (between cylinders) is likely to be in good mechanical condition.

Indicated Cylinder Pressures

While cranking compression pressures vary from

about 100 to 300psi, the pressures in the cylinder of a *running engine* can vary from below atmospheric (a partial vacuum) to several thousand psi (in a top-fuel dragster generating 5000hp). The measurement of these pressures offers a direct way to mathematically determine the power produced and consumed by the engine at each point in crankshaft rotation. The indicated cylinder pressures are the sum total, or net effects, of all engine variables taken together (*indicated horsepower*, briefly mentioned in the last chapter, is calculated from the measurements of indicted cylinder pressures). For example, when cylinder head flow is improved, more air/fuel mixture can be drawn into the cylinders. This can both reduce the vacuum in the cylinders during the intake stroke (since air and fuel flow into the engine with less restriction) and increase <u>peak</u> pressures since more air and fuel are burned in the same, fixed space. A change in cam timing can provide another example: Measured cylinder pressures reveal the net effects of the change in valve events, their effect on flow, and the net changes in power production throughout the rpm range.

Just as the simple measurement of compression pressure revealed the health of the mechanical components in the cylinder, the more complex analysis of cylinder pressures in a running engine—throughout the complete four-cycle process—reveals the combined effects of all mechanical components, plus the thermodynamic effects of heat transfer, and the fluid dynamics of mass flow. Indicated cylinder pressure is the "master" measurement of engine performance.

Before cylinder pressures in a running engine can be analyzed, they have to be measured. And that's not an easy task. Any measuring device must operate in a very

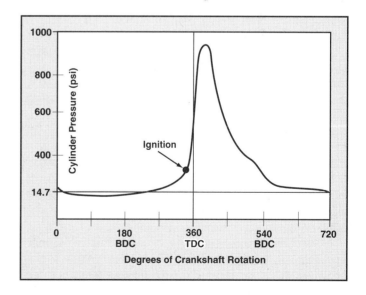

The pressures in the cylinder of a *running engine* can vary from below atmospheric (below 14.7psi) to over one thousand psi in a racing engine. The measurement of these pressures provide the "raw material" to calculate the power produced and consumed by the engine at each point in crankshaft rotation. These indicated cylinder pressures are the sum total, or the net effect, of all engine variables taken together.

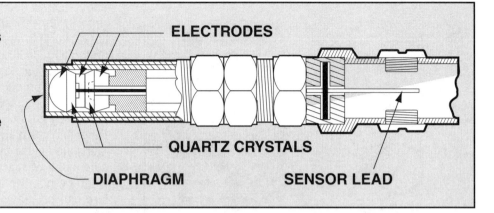

Cylinder Pressure Sensors Must Have:
1) **Linear Output**
2) **Fast Response**
3) **Temperature Resistance**
4) **Shock Resistance**
5) **Repeatability/Long Life**

ELECTRODES

QUARTZ CRYSTALS

DIAPHRAGM

SENSOR LEAD

The cylinder pressures sensor directly measures pressure inside a running engine. It must meet a laundry list of requirements: 1) The voltage output from the sensor should be linear, 2) it must be able to react very quickly to pressure changes, 3) the sensor must be very *insensitive* to temperature changes, 4) and it must work reliably under the high acoustic and vibrational conditions that exist in a test engine. Most sensors use a quartz crystal that is sensitive to pressure changes (the piezoelectric effect generates a voltage under pressure) but are relatively insensitive to temperature variations. The quartz transducer offers the engine designer a remarkably accurate "look" inside the cylinders of a running engine.

demanding environment. If you were assigned the task of designing a "cylinder pressure sensor," here is a list of the requirements that your final instrument would have to meet: 1) The voltage output from the sensor should be linear, that is, if it sends out 1 millivolt at 100psi, it should output 2 millivolts at 200psi. 2) It must be able to react very quickly to pressure changes. In an engine running at 8000rpm, each cylinder takes less than fifteen one-thousandths of a second to complete the four-cycle process. So the pressure sensor must react to changes that happen at least 100 times more quickly (about .000015, or fifteen millionths of a second) if we are to record enough data points to accurately map pressures throughout the four-cycle process at high engine speeds. And finally, 3) the sensor must be very *insensitive* to temperature changes. Cylinder temperatures can vary from nearly ambient during the intake cycle to over 6000 degrees (F) during the power stroke. If the sensor output varied as the temperature changed, we wouldn't know to what degree it was measuring temperature or pressure. So variations in sensor reading of less than ten one-thousandths of one percent per degree are needed to maintain an overall pressure-measurement accuracy of approximately 1%. Building a sensor that will meet these design requirements, and working reliably under the acoustic and vibrational conditions that exist in an engine under test, is no small accomplishment. Any ideas?

Surprisingly, pressure transducers used to test modern engines meet all of these demanding requirements. Most are designed around quartz crystals that are sensitive to pressure changes (the piezoelectric effect generates a voltage under pressure) but are relatively insensitive to temperature variations. All in all, the quartz transducer offers the engine designer a remarkably accurate "look" inside the cylinders of a running engine. But what does he see? The typical output from one of these sensors is pictured on the previous page.

The Pressure Crank-Angle Diagram

There are two common ways that cylinder pressures are illustrated, and each reveals unique information about the engine. The first, a *pressure crank-angle* diagram, plots cylinder pressure against the position of the crankshaft during the four cycles. Top Dead Center (TDC) at the beginning of the intake stroke generally forms the zero point on the horizontal axis labeled "Degrees of Crankshaft Rotation." Ambient or atmospheric pressure forms the baseline for the vertical "Cylinder Pressure" axis, below which vacuum levels are plotted. As the intake stroke begins, cylinder pressure decreases to zero as exhaust venting concludes. Pressures then change to a slight vacuum during the intake stroke (or a much stronger vacuum at part-throttle) until the cycle ends with the closing of the intake valve. Now the trapped charge is compressed and cylinder pressures rise to 100 to 300psi. Typically, a few degrees before the piston once again reaches TDC, the spark plug fires, igniting the mixture and sending cylinder pressures up to thousands of pounds per square inch within about 45 degrees of crank rotation. If the ignition point was timed properly, peak cylinder pressure will occur about 12 to 14 degrees after TDC. This timing allows cylinder pressures to be most efficiently converted to rotational force or torque. As the piston continues to move down the cylinder and pressures decrease, the exhaust valve opens, beginning a dramatic drop in pressure. Finally, cylinder pressures stabilize at a few psi during the exhaust stroke when burnt gasses are forced out of the cylinder.

The Pressure-Volume Diagram

The pressure crank-angle diagram provides an easily understood view of the widely varying pressures in the cylinder. While it's easy to see "what's happening and where it's happening" with a crank-angle diagram,

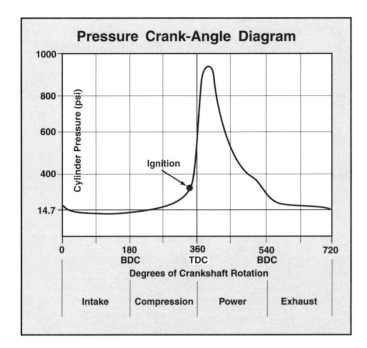

Pressure Crank-Angle Diagram

Cylinder Pressure (psi)

1000
800
600
400
14.7

Ignition

0   180   360   540   720
     BDC   TDC   BDC

Degrees of Crankshaft Rotation

Intake   Compression   Power   Exhaust

The *pressure crank-angle* diagram is one of two common ways that cylinder pressures are illustrated. This method plots cylinder pressures against the position of the crankshaft during the four cycles. Top Dead Center (TDC) at the beginning of the intake stroke generally forms the zero point on the horizontal axis labeled "Degrees of Crankshaft Rotation." Ambient or atmospheric pressure (14.7psi) forms the baseline for the vertical "Cylinder Pressure" axis, below which vacuum levels are plotted.

another method of plotting the identical cylinder pressures offers a very different look and unique insight into the same data. This plot, known as a *pressure-volume* (*PV*, called a *Pee-Vee* or *indicator*) *diagram*, is very helpful in understanding the work produced and consumed by the engine.

The PV diagram plots pressure against the displaced volume in the cylinder. Notice in the accompanying drawing that the curve tends to wrap around and reconnect with itself, forming a complete path. This curve represents cylinder pressures throughout the entire Otto cycle process. It begins at the same point as the previous crank-angle diagram—just after the intake valve opens—marked as a **1** on the graph. The cylinder and piston below the graph illustrate the position of the piston and the volume in the cylinder at each point on the curve. As the intake stroke continues, the piston moves down the bore and the plot indicates pressure below atmospheric continuing to point **2**. Here the piston begins to move back up the bore and pressure rises as the compression cycle begins. At point **3**, the fuel is ignited, rapidly increasing cylinder pressure. The piston reaches TDC at point **4** and the power stroke begins. Cylinder pressure continues to rise to point **5**, ideally about 15 degrees after TDC. The exhaust valve opens at point **6**, just before BDC, assisting in cylinder depressurization. The piston reaches BDC at point **7**. The exhaust cycle continues as the piston moves back up the bore maintaining some

positive pressure in the cylinder until, at point **1**, the piston once again reaches TDC.

Notice that the pressure curve has directional arrows that indicate the same sequence of events as just described. Trace along the curve from the starting point **1** around part of the "bottom loop" marked with a minus sign. Notice that you are moving in a slightly counterclockwise direction. As you move from point **2** through **7** and a bit beyond, you trace out the "upper loop," marked with a plus sign, in a clockwise direction. Finally, as you move from just past point **7** back to **1**, you trace out the upper half of the "bottom loop," again in a counterclockwise direction. What does all the "clockwise stuff" have to do with anything? You may be amazed by the relationship. A PV diagram has the remarkable feature of isolating the *work consumed* from the *work developed* by

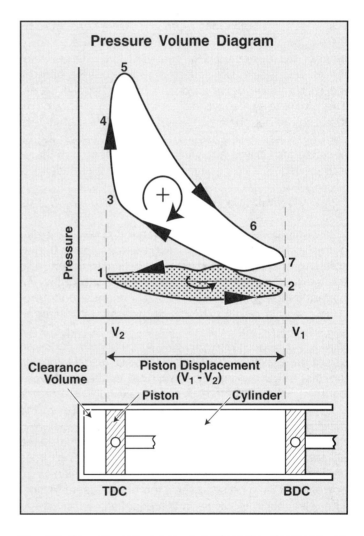

Pressure Volume Diagram

Pressure

V_2 V_1

Clearance Volume

Piston Displacement
($V_1 - V_2$)

Piston   Cylinder

TDC   BDC

The PV diagram plots pressure against the displaced volume in the cylinder and illustrates the same cylinder pressures displayed in the pressure crank-angle diagram. The PV diagram has the remarkable feature of isolating the *work consumed* from the *work developed* by the engine. The area within the lower loop, drawn in a counterclockwise direction, represents the work consumed by pumping losses. The upper loop area, drawn in a clockwise direction, indicates the work produced by expanding gasses after combustion.

the engine. The area within the lower loop, drawn in a counterclockwise direction, represents the work consumed by the engine "pumping" the charge into the cylinder and forcing the exhaust gasses from the cylinder. The upper loop area, drawn in a clockwise direction, indicates the work produced by the engine from pressures generated by expanding gasses after combustion.

Remarkable, isn't it? Look again the previous crank-angle diagram on the previous page. Would you have thought the relatively "simple" curves in that plot would contain so much more information?

Let's test the work-isolating concepts of PV diagram with a cylinder misfire. In this case, the air/fuel mixture is drawn into the cylinder as usual, but it fails to ignite and boost cylinder pressure. The PV diagram of this event still consists of two loops (more or less), an upper and a lower. However, if we start at point **1** and trace through the sequence of pressures, we outline two counterclockwise loops. So both loops represent power consumed by the engine. The upper loop encloses very little area since most of the power used to compress the charge is returned when the piston is forced back down the bore by the compression pressure on the "power" stroke. (Note: The pressure in the cylinder as the piston moves down the bore on the "power" stroke of a misfire is slightly less than the measured pressure on the compression stroke because the charge has given up some heat, and therefore pressure, to the cylinderwall and other surfaces.)

Calculating Horsepower: The Basics

At this point you might be wondering what PV diagrams have to do with predicting horsepower or understanding how Motion Software simulations function. And the answer is: A lot. You've just learned one of the important things quality engine simulations must do to produce accurate results: They must generate (simulate) an internal PV model and subtract counterclockwise-pressure loops, also called pumping losses, from clockwise power-generating loops. The net result is *indicated power*, the theoretical maximum power that can be produced from the pressures measured in the cylinder.

When an engine is tested on the dyno, however, the measured power is always lower than the indicated power. If the test engine is equipped with the minimum required accessories—typical configuration for measuring gross brake horsepower—the difference between the indicated power and brake horsepower is the power lost to friction. The relationship is shown in this equation:

Brake HP = Indicted HP - Friction HP

For the dyno operator, brake horsepower is easy to determine; it's the power directly measured by the dyno. And if the cylinder pressures are also measured during the test run, indicated horsepower can be calculated and frictional losses determined from the above equation. But the engine simulation programmer is trying to *calculate* brake horsepower, and the only way to do that is to simulate both indicated <u>and</u> friction horsepower. The basic steps to accomplishing this are: 1) the simulation

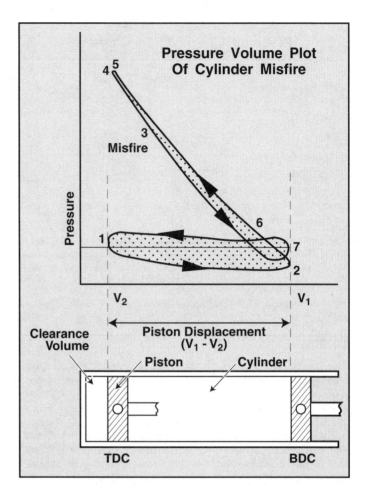

The work-isolating concepts of a PV diagram are evident with a cylinder misfire. In this case, the air/fuel mixture is drawn into the cylinder as usual, but it fails to ignite and boost cylinder pressure. The PV diagram of this event still consists of two loops; however, if we start at point 1 and trace through the sequence of pressures, we outline two counterclockwise loops. Both loops represent power consumed by the engine.

must calculate the pressure in the cylinder throughout the four-cycle process (the real "heart" of the simulation; more on this next), 2) the indicated horsepower is calculated from these pressures, 3) another mathematical model must be applied that accurately predicts frictional losses (luckily, this is somewhat easier than it sounds), and finally, 4) brake horsepower is calculated by subtracting indicated power from the power needed to overcome friction.

From this explanation, it is clear that the measure of any engine simulation lies in its ability to calculate cylinder pressures and frictional losses. With this accomplished, the rest of the simulation is relatively straightforward. The next few sections provide an overview of some of the techniques used by engine simulations to predict indicated and friction horsepower.

Calculating Cylinder Pressures

If a simulation technique is to accurately predict the

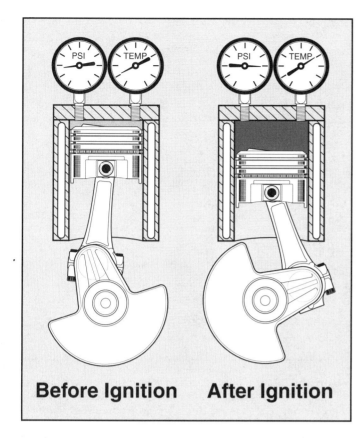

Before Ignition   **After Ignition**

When the initial charge volume and the burning characteristics of the fuel are known, accurately calculating the heat released and the resulting cylinder pressures for each position of the piston throughout the power stroke is a straightforward, although not necessarily simple, thermodynamic problem. A crucial step, however, is to accurately calculate the *initial air/fuel volume in the cylinder* just after the intake valve closes.

power produced by an IC engine, it must precisely calculate the pressures acting on the piston throughout the power stroke. At first this might seem to be an impossible task. But the high pressures in the cylinder are directly related to the *increase in temperature* from combustion. If you know the initial charge volume and the burning characteristics of the fuel, accurately calculating the heat released and the resulting cylinder pressures for each position of the piston is a straightforward, although not necessarily simple, thermodynamic problem. However, a crucial step is to accurately calculate the *initial air/fuel volume in the cylinder* just after the intake valve closes.

This chapter began with the observation that an IC engine is "just an air pump." And once again this analogy provides useful insight, for it's the pressure *differences* generated by the pumping characteristics of the engine that are the basis of solving the problem of charge flow into the cylinder. In the simplest case, if you want to know how much "stuff" will move through a passage from point **A** to point **B**, you need to know the pressure at both points and the effective size of the passage. Knowing these variables (and a little about the flow characteristics of the "stuff" you're measuring), you can calculate

the volume that flows from point **A** to point **B** over any period of time.

Intake Cycle Pressures

Let's take a simplified look at how this can be applied to the IC engine by focusing on the intake cycle. When the piston moves down the bore on the intake stroke, the increasing volume lowers the pressure within the cylinder. Calculating this change in pressure involves applying the appropriate pressure-volume formulas for compressible gasses. The next step is bit more tricky: To determine the amount of air/fuel mixture flowing into the cylinders we must calculate the "restriction" caused by the intake valves. In other words, we need to know the effective size of the passageways. One solution starts with the diameters of the valves and how far they are held off of the valve seats to determine the exposed areas. These "hole sizes" (known as the curtain areas) are compared with flow-bench data to develop "discharge coefficients" for the cylinder head. These flow coefficients help the simulation accurately model the "true" or effective valve sizes.

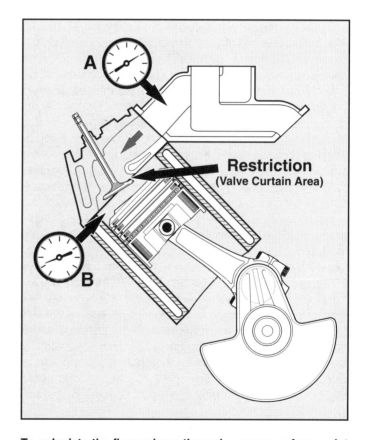

Restriction
(Valve Curtain Area)

To calculate the flow volume through a passage from point A to point B, you need to know the pressure at both points and the effective size of the passage, in this case the "restriction" caused by the intake valve. Restriction is based on the diameter of the valve and how far it is held off of the valve seat. This "hole size" (known as the curtain area) is compared with flow-bench data to develop a "discharge coefficient" for the cylinder head. This, in turn, helps the simulation accurately model the "true" effective valve size.

Now that we know the cylinder pressures and effective valve sizes, the next step in determining how much air/fuel mixture moves into the cylinders is to pinpoint the pressure drop across valves. To do that, the pressure in the port and intake manifold runners must be found. Finding runner pressure is another application of the same pressure-drop problem. Since all outside air is drawn through a carburetor or throttle body of a known flow characteristic, the pressure drop across the induction system can be calculated. From this pressure drop and the outside atmospheric pressure, the manifold/port pressure (or vacuum) can be found. As the simulation runs, it "zeros in" on the pressures and volumes flowing in the engine passageways at each degree of crank rotation under consideration. The process of pressure drop and mass-flow calculation, repeated many times through a process called *time-step iteration*, accurately determines the total air/fuel mixture drawn into each cylinder during the time the intake valves are open.

Power Cycle Pressures

Now that a method has been found to accurately determine the air/fuel density in the cylinder, the energy required to compress the mixture during the compression stroke can be calculated (by the same application of Pressure-Volume-Temperature [PVT] formulas). Furthermore, with a known mixture density, the heat released during combustion can also be found. By applying a model that "burns" the fuel at the appropriate rate (dependent on engine speed, air/fuel mixture, etc.), we can accurately calculate the pressure pushing against piston throughout the power stroke. If a engine simulation is working properly, the <u>calculated</u> pressures throughout the compression and power strokes will look nearly identical to the upper loop of a PV diagram taken from actual pressure measurements.

As mentioned earlier, the lower loop of the PV diagram represents the pumping losses of the engine during the intake and exhaust strokes. The simulation techniques we've discussed so far have calculated cylinder pressures during the intake stroke—required to simulate mass flow into the cylinder—so the lower loop on the PV diagram that describes intake pumping losses already can be plotted. But the other half of the loop represents pressures during the exhaust cycle. The simulation of these pressures is an essential step in building an accurate model of engine power output, but unfortunately, this is often the most difficult step in engine simulation.

Exhaust Cycle Pressures

A pressure transducer located in the cylinder during the exhaust cycle measures a complex series of changing pressures. Here's what is typically found: 1) Just before the exhaust valve opens (several degrees before BDC—Bottom Dead Center), high pressures from the power stroke are still present in the cylinder. When the exhaust valve lifts off the seat and the exhaust cycle

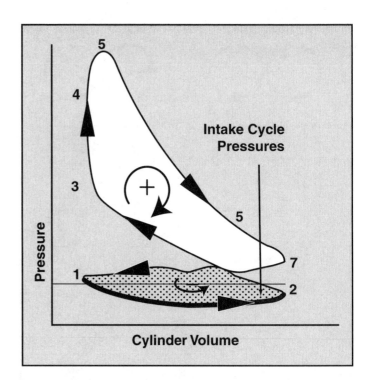

When the piston moves down the bore on the intake stroke, the increasing volume lowers the pressure within the cylinder. Calculating this change in pressure involves applying the appropriate pressure-volume formulas for compressible gasses. The valve restriction is calculated as a "discharge coefficient" that adjusts flow based on valve diameter, lift, and flow efficiency.

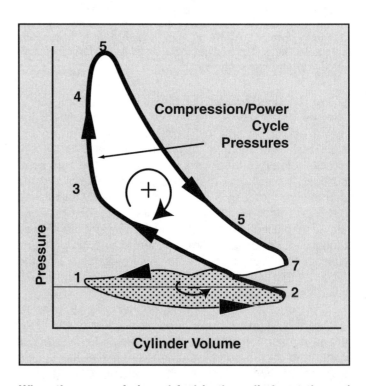

When the mass of air and fuel in the cylinder at the end of the intake cycle has been calculated, cylinder pressures during the compression stroke can be found by the application of Pressure-Volume-Temperature [PVT] formulas. Applying a model that "burns" the fuel at the appropriate rate determines the pressure pushing against the piston throughout the power stroke.

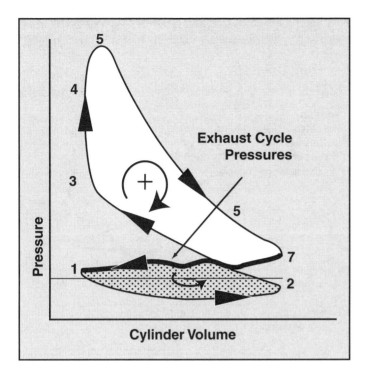

Pressure / Cylinder Volume

Exhaust Cycle Pressures

The hodgepodge of changing cylinder pressures that exist in the cylinder throughout the exhaust cycle presents a serious challenge for the simulation programmer. Since pumping work represents a significant source of power consumption, especially at higher engine speeds, simulating pressures during the exhaust cycle is an important element in a quality simulation.

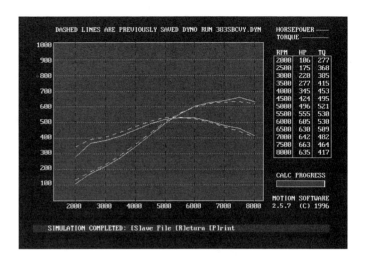

DASHED LINES ARE PREVIOUSLY SAVED DYNO RUN 383SBCVY.DYN   HORSEPOWER ——
TORQUE ——

RPM	HP	TQ
2000	106	277
2500	175	368
3000	220	385
3500	277	415
4000	345	453
4500	424	495
5000	496	521
5500	555	530
6000	605	530
6500	630	509
7000	642	482
7500	663	464
8000	635	417

CALC PROGRESS

MOTION SOFTWARE
2.5.7 (C) 1996

SIMULATION COMPLETED: [S]lave File [R]eturn [P]rint

This simulation—using Motion's Filling And Emptying software—shows the effects of earlier exhaust valve opening timing. "Depressurizing" the cylinder has reduced low-speed power, but at higher engine speeds—when exhaust pumping work becomes much greater—early cylinder blowdown reduces pumping losses and boosts horsepower. Accurate power predictions involving exhaust cycle pressures require complex simulation techniques.

technically begins, a powerful "pulse" or pressure wave blasts through the port and down the exhaust/header pipe. 2) Pressure declines rapidly during this blowdown phase until the piston reaches BDC. 3) After Bottom Dead Center the piston begins to move up the bore, so residual gas pressure will push against the piston, increasing pumping losses. 4) At about 70 degrees before TDC—Top Dead Center—piston speed reaches a maximum point. At this peak velocity, pumping work reaches a maximum value and cylinder pressures begin to rise as the exhaust valve and port become a restriction to outward flow. Finally, 5) the intake valve opens just before TDC (usually) and, if the exhaust system is tuned properly, a negative-pressure wave arriving from the header system will reduce cylinder pressure and assist in both exhaust scavenging and in beginning the flow of fresh air/fuel mixture into the cylinder. This negative pressure wave reduces cylinder pressures, typically to below atmospheric levels.

This hodgepodge of changing cylinder pressures throughout the exhaust cycle presents a serious challenge to the simulation programmer. In fact, most engine simulation programs don't even attempt to reconstruct the pumping-loss loop, instead making a "guess" at the losses based on stroke, valve size, and other variables. But pumping losses represent significant power consumption, especially at higher engine speeds, so simulating pressures during the exhaust cycle—and fully reconstructing the counterclockwise pumping loop—is an important

element in a quality simulation.

The complete description of the techniques used to accurately predict exhaust cycle pressures is beyond the scope of this book. However, several separate methods are included in Motion's Filling And Emptying model, and each one improves the accuracy of the final pressure curve prediction. First of all, since the simulation has already determined the mass flow into the cylinder during the intake cycle and has applied a "burn" model to predict cylinder pressures during the power stroke, cylinder pressures just before the exhaust valve opens have been calculated. Next, the simulation begins another mass-flow analysis across a pressure differential, but this time the high-pressure gasses are analyzed as they flow by the opening exhaust valve. Using this method, it is possible to obtain a good approximation of gas flow volume and of the residual cylinder pressures at each crank degree throughout the exhaust cycle. But because cylinder pressures are quite high at the beginning of the exhaust cycle, both positive and negative pressure waves are created that travel through the exhaust system. These powerful waves change the way gasses move and affect the pressures in the cylinder. To compensate for these effects, a "mini wave-dynamic" model is applied to improve cylinder-pressure prediction. Finally, valve timing has a profound effect on cylinder pressures and pumping losses. For example, *early exhaust valve opening* improves exhaust scavenging but can reduce power-stroke efficiency, since some of the pressure in the cylinder that could otherwise drive the crankshaft and produce horsepower is dispersed into the exhaust system. On the other hand, *late exhaust-valve opening* extracts more power from expanding gasses, but also increases pumping losses because there is less time to force the same volume of exhaust gas from the cylinder. So the exact point at which the valve opens, the rate at which it opens, and the precise closing point must be carefully included in the model. All of these important elements, and others, are taken together to "fine tune" exhaust-cycle pressure prediction.

With the simulation of exhaust-cycle pressures, the entire PV curve has been reconstructed. While this is a considerable accomplishment, our final goal is to predict brake horsepower. To move closer to this objective, the next step involves separating gross power (upper PV loop) from pumping losses (lower PV loop), then converting these constantly varying pressures into a term that simplifies the calculation of brake horsepower.

Indicated Horsepower And Mean Effective Pressure

The PV diagram illustrates the continuously varying pressures in the cylinder throughout the four-cycle process. As described earlier, the upper loop records the pressures produced within the cylinder that contribute to power, while the lower loop indicates cylinder pressures during the intake and exhaust "pumping" cycles.

In the previous chapter we found that power is defined as a force applied through a distance. The PV diagram plots pressure in the cylinder on the vertical axis and volume in the cylinder on the horizontal axis. The cylinder pressure axis is a direct measurement of the force applied to the piston and the volume axis directly measures the "sweep" of the piston from TDC to BDC. Therefore, the <u>area</u> contained within the upper loop accurately represents the *power produced* throughout the compression and power strokes, and the <u>area</u> within the

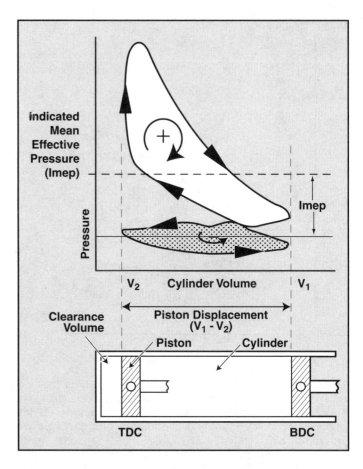

The PV diagram plots pressure in the cylinder on the vertical axis and volume in the cylinder on the horizontal axis. The **area** contained within the upper loop represents the *power produced* and the **area** within the lower loop indicates the *power consumed*. If the pumping-loss area is subtracted from the power-production area, the theoretical maximum potential horsepower will be found. This maximum power level is called *indicated power.*

Since cylinder pressures reflect the total effect of all engine components, except frictional losses, they can be extremely helpful during engine development. The shape of each pressure curve reveals subtle details of engine function to the experienced researcher.

lower loop indicates the *power consumed* during the intake and exhaust strokes. If the pumping-loss area is subtracted from the power-production area, the theoretical maximum potential horsepower that each cylinder can deliver to the crankshaft will be found. This maximum power level is called *indicated power.* The following equation describes indicated horsepower and its relationship to the PV diagram:

Indicated Power = (upper loop) - (lower loop)
= Gross Power - Pumping Power

While indicated power is the maximum possible power that each cylinder can produce, it is much more than a "theoretical" number. Remember that indicated power is derived directly from cylinder pressures—either measured or simulated—so it is <u>directly related</u> to power delivered to the crankshaft. The losses from incomplete combustion, improper air/fuel ratios, and many other "real-world" factors change cylinder pressures. Therefore, the influence of these changes has already had its effect on indicated power (quality engine simulations take all of these pressure-altering losses into consideration!). In fact, the only element separating indicated horsepower from

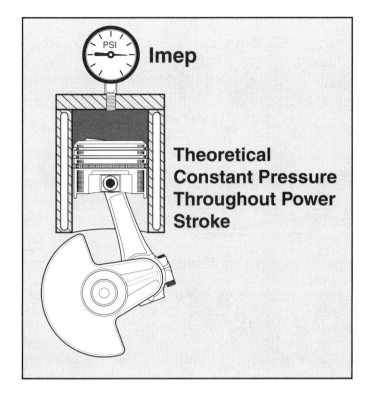

Imep

Theoretical Constant Pressure Throughout Power Stroke

Converting the irregular areas of the PV diagram directly into horsepower poses a complex mathematical problem. By finding the *average pressure* within the net diagram volume, the computation of indicated horsepower becomes considerably easier. This average pressure, called the indicated mean effective pressure or Imep, is a hypothetical <u>constant</u> pressure acting on the piston during the <u>entire power stroke</u> that would produce the same net work (net horsepower) as the varying pressures that exist in the cylinder throughout the actual four-cycle process.

our final goal—the determination of brake horsepower—is the power loss from friction. Unfortunately, friction has little effect on cylinder pressure and must be simulated independently (more on this later).

Before indicated power can be calculated, however, a way must be found to measure the area within the upper and lower loops. Engine testers have traditionally copied the PV diagram from the TV-like screen of an oscilloscope (coupled to pressure transducers, it displays cylinder pressures from a test engine) onto a sheet of paper. Then a planimeter is used to measure the area (a planimeter looks like a pocket watch with a small toothed wheel that is traced along the outline of the shape; the area is read directly from the dial). This method is simple but suffers from marginal accuracy and is obviously impractical for computer-driven engine simulations. Luckily, there are several mathematical methods for accurately <u>calculating</u> the area within a closed path when the curve is described by a series of known points. And since the Filling And Emptying model determines cylinder pressures at each crank degree throughout the entire four-cycle process, 720 points are available for the PV diagram area calculations. This provides sufficient resolution to ensure accurate calculation of power- and pump-

ing-loop volumes.

Once the area that *represents* the pumping losses is subtracted from the gross horsepower loop, the result is an area *representing* the indicated horsepower (the net work) of all four cycles. Converting this irregular area directly into horsepower poses a complex mathematical problem. However, by finding the *average pressure* within the diagram, the computation of indicated horsepower becomes considerably easier. This average pressure, called the *indicated mean effective pressure* or Imep, is found by dividing the area of the diagram (net work) by its length (swept volume). This equation describes this relationship:

**Imep = Net Work / Swept Volume
    = Net Area of Diagram / Length of Diagram**

The indicated mean effective pressure is a hypothetical constant pressure acting on the piston during the <u>power stroke</u> that would produce the same net work (net horsepower) as the varying pressures that exist in the cylinder throughout the actual four-cycle process. By simply multiplying the Imep by the displacement of the engine (CID) and the engine speed (RPM), then dividing by a constant to adjust for unit conversions (and to account for the single power cycle for every two crank rotations in a 4-cycle engine), the indicated horsepower can be found:

Indicated HP = (Imep x CID x RPM) / 792,000

With the calculation of indicated horsepower, we've come a long way along the path that engine simulations must take to determine actual engine output. Indicated horsepower can be considered the power generated by the pressures exerted on the surface of the piston before the losses due to friction have been taken into consideration. Since our final goal is to determine brake horsepower—the power available at the crankshaft and measured by a dynamometer—one important step remains.

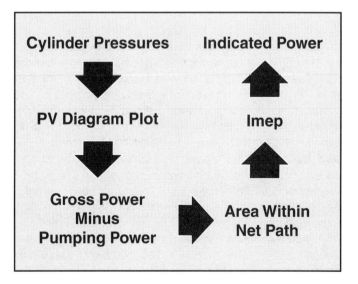

The path to Indicated Power is complex. Cylinder pressures are used to draw the PV plot, which separates Gross Power from Pumping Work. Since directly converting the irregular net-work area into power is quite difficult, Imep is used to simplify the calculation of Indicated Power.

Frictional and pumping losses make up a vast majority of the non-thermodynamic losses within the IC engine. Among frictional losses, the piston/crank assembly accounts for about 80% of all losses. Pistons and rings do a remarkable job of sealing high pressure gasses, but a substantial price must be paid, principally due to ring-to-cylinderwall friction and heating. Pumping losses, occurring primarily from the exhaust cycle, also consume considerable power. While there isn't a lot than can be done about friction, pumping work can be minimized with optimum cam timing and a properly-tuned exhaust system.

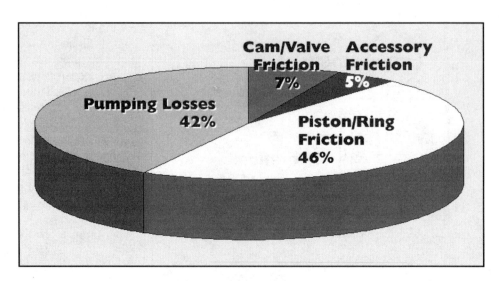

Several methods of *measuring* friction have been used by engine designers and test engineers. The most common method is using a motoring dynamometer to directly measure the power required to rotate the engine. During these tests, engine operating conditions are duplicated as much as possible, including maintaining operating temperatures. To eliminate pumping losses from the measurements, pistons with open tops and valves without valveheads are sometimes used. Frictional power is also determined by carefully measuring indicated power at each test speed (by measuring cylinder pressures) then subtracting the brake horsepower absorbed by the dyno during a full-throttle test at the same rpm. This latter method produces very accurate results when cylinder pressures are carefully recorded. However, neither of these methods are suitable for *calculating* frictional losses. An engine simulation program must resort to less direct methods of determining engine friction.

Simulating Frictional Losses

As described above, not all power applied to the pistons is delivered to the flywheel. The power consumed by the engine is called *frictional power*. This loss can be as small as 10% during full load at lower engine speeds, to as high as 100% at idle (a stable idle speed is the result of a balance between indicated power and frictional losses). Frictional power consists of the power to overcome the resistance to motion of all moving parts, and the power required to drive essential engine accessories, usually the oil and water pumps and sometimes the fan and alternator. All work lost to friction is eventually converted into heat and most is dissipated through the engine cooling system.

Frictional losses *within* the engine occur between every moving component. Friction occurs at the crankshaft and camshaft bearings, within the valvetrain, at the cam sprockets and chain, in the oil pump, and within distributor and drive gears. All of these internal frictional losses taken together, however, amount to only about 20% of the total power consumed by friction. The balance is due to rubbing contact between the pistons, pis-

A dynamometer capable of "motoring" an engine—rotating the engine with outside power—can be very useful in measuring frictional losses. This supercharged engine consumes considerable power from friction and pumping losses during motoring. However, when the engine is running under its own power, the payback from forced induction is impressive!

ton rings and the cylinderwalls.

The accompanying chart shows the relationship between all frictional losses and dramatically illustrates both the degree of power loss due to cylinderwall friction and the relatively insignificant losses elsewhere in the engine. Looking at this chart gives one pause about the efforts commonly found to reduce valvetrain friction with exotic needle-bearing components while considerably less effort seems to be directed at the major source of frictional loss: the cylinderwall surfaces, pistons, and rings.

Despite the fact the most frictional losses occur during rubbing contact with the cylinderwalls, the complexity

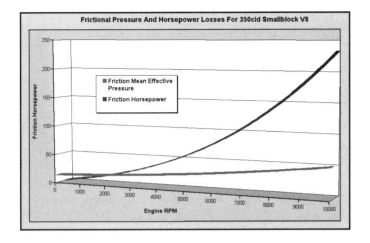

This chart shows the Friction Mean Effective Pressure (Fmep) and the horsepower consumed by friction in a high-performance 350cid smallblock Chevy engine. At 10,000rpm about 230 horsepower is converted to heat primarily through ring friction. With that much power used to simply "drag" the rings over the cylinderwall surface, it's remarkable that the rings don't instantly turn to dust!

of calculating the friction at each contacting surface, combined with the various properties of lubricants and temperature effects, plus other factors, makes the *simulation* of friction extremely difficult. In fact, efforts to simulate friction by calculating the losses at each point of contact often produce *less accurate* results than simpler empirical techniques.

Empirical methods involve gathering data from a large number of real-world tests, then finding a relationship between the data and the components under test. Fortunately, because frictional losses principally occur during rubbing contact with the cylinderwalls, empirical models based on bore diameter and stroke length have emerged that are able to predict friction to a remarkably high degree of accuracy. The following empirical equation is used in Motion's engine simulation programs to determine frictional mean effective pressure:

$$Fmep = (12.964 + (Stroke \times (RPM / 6))) \times (0.0030476 + (Stroke \times (RPM / 6) \times 0.00000065476))$$

While there are other models, this empirical formula has proven to be accurate throughout a wide range of stock and high-performance engine configurations. Once the friction mean effective pressure has been calculated, the following equation, virtually identical to the previous equation used to calculate indicated horsepower, will determine the horsepower lost to friction:

Friction Horsepower = Fmep x CID x RPM / 792,000

Now that the simulation of both indicated and friction horsepower is complete, our final goal is one simple step away. By removing the losses due to friction from indicated power, the brake horsepower can be calculated at last.

Brake HP = Indicted HP - Friction HP

Obviously, the previous descriptions of how PV diagram pressures, mean effective pressures, frictional losses, and finally brake horsepower are calculated have been simplified. The simulation programmer also must carefully consider a number of additional factors, including charge momentum (forces of fast-moving gasses), pressure-wave dynamics in both the intake and exhaust systems, flow reversion during valve overlap (the flow of exhaust gasses into the induction tract), charge heating as it moves through the induction system, air/fuel ratios, spark timing, and much more. Like the pressure-predicting models that we've discussed up to this point, taken as a whole these additional issues seem extremely complex and insoluble. But broken down and understood one at a time, mathematical models for the physics that take place within the internal combustion engine have been devised and are included in the best engine simulations. It is probably now clear why very few computer programs currently on the market perform a complete engine simulation: It is a complex task involving dozens of sub-simulations carefully integrated together. While possible (and some simulation experts may even say straightforward), as you discovered in this chapter, it is far from a trivial accomplishment.

An Overview Of Simulating And Calculating Horsepower

1—Determine Port And Valve Restrictions

2—Calculate Pressures For All Cycles

3—Calculate Initial Mass Flow Rates

4—Iterate Over Each Degree Of Crank Rotation

5—Calculate Gross Power

6—Calculate Pumping Losses

7—Determine Area Of Indicated Power Loop

8—Calculate Indicated Mean Effective Pressure

9—Calculate Indicated Horsepower

10—Calculate Friction Horsepower

11—Calculate Net Horsepower

12—Repeat Entire Process For Next Engine Speed

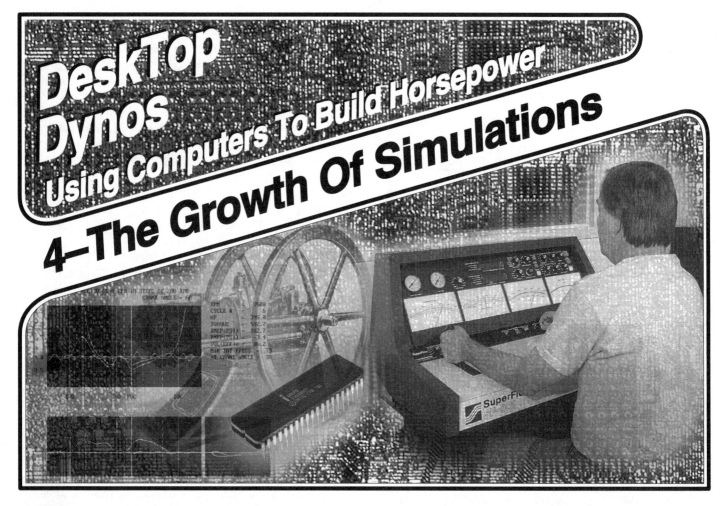

DeskTop Dynos
Using Computers To Build Horsepower
4—The Growth Of Simulations

T he DeskTop Dyno is not the first program to simulate a part of the "real world." Simulations are used everywhere! Cars, planes, trains, and virtually every other complex machine is designed with the help of mathematical simulations. The simulation of dynamic motion is commonplace in computer games and other eye-catching animation. Complex simulations form the basis for the special effects used in many Hollywood films to ensure that the created scene has believable motion. Elaborate manufacturing or design projects are first simulated on a computer to reduce costs, improve quality, and catch design mistakes before they become reality. Large buildings are subjected to computer-simulated weather and earthquakes to reveal design weaknesses that cannot be found in any other way, except during real disasters when it's too late. Even complex software programs, like computer operating systems and software that controls aircraft in flight, are subjected to simulations to help designers shorten development time, reduce costs, and improve reliability. And perhaps the most complex simulations being performed today involve the 3-dimensional analysis of airflow at supersonic speeds to aid the development of fighter aircraft, and the extremely complex job of simulating the effects of aging on the nuclear weapon stockpiles that exist in too many places throughout the world.

These simulation methods all have one thing in common: They are so computationally intensive that they require high-speed electronic computers to perform the countless mathematical operations essential in rendering nearly all "real world" models. Some can run on a simple PC, others require months of computer time on the fastest computers on earth performing trillions of mathematical operations per second. In this age of a PC on every desktop, performing simulations by hand is unthinkable, and for good reason: Many simulations would take longer to do by hand than the average human life span!

This close association between mathematical simulations and computers is a relatively recent development. Over the past 40 years, the computational speed of the computer has made the science of simulations a practical, almost "basic" scientific tool. But the need to develop mathematical models to help predict the outcome of otherwise expensive and time-consuming processes has been on the minds of designers for hundreds of years. In fact, it has been the dream of engine builders—for as long as there have been engines—to be able to assemble a "paper" engine, an accurate model developed through mathematical simulations. This "paper" model could quickly evaluate new ideas, shorten development times, save money, and give a competitive edge to any engine manufacturing company.

Early Modeling Efforts

The history of how the desire to build a "paper" en-

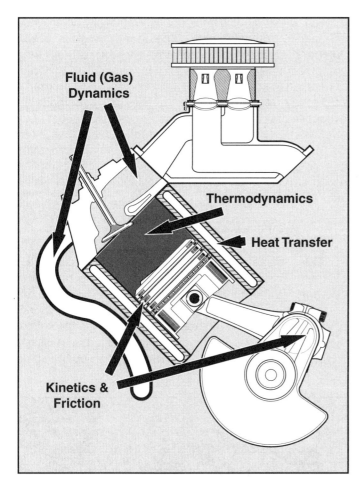

Theoreticians of the late 1800's and early 1900's focused on one or two of the basic four models (fluid-dynamic, thermodynamic, heat-transfer, and kinetic). Often just a thermodynamic analysis of the heat released during combustion, and the subsequent pressure rise in the cylinder, would make up the main modeling element. This analysis, capable of being performed by hand with slide rules, used the well-understood laws of conservation of mass and energy to predict cylinder pressures and power output. These *zero-dimensional* methods ("zero" here means based on a *single* model) lacked adequate burn, kinetic, and fluid-dynamic models, and they offered only limited predictive ability. As additional real-world factors were incorporated, such as combustion-burn and frictional-loss modeling, the basic zero-dimensional models were elevated to *phenomenological* models that offered greater and greater accuracy as each engine "phenomenon" was added to the model. Phenomenological models eventually evolved into relatively complex systems that incorporated thermodynamic burn models, heat-transfer equations, and good kinetics simulations. These "advanced" models, sometimes referred to as *quasi-dimensional* ("quasi" alluding to the fact that these models were "almost but not quite" true multidimensional systems), still lacked a geometric description of inlet and outlet passages and a dynamic model of induction and exhaust flow. Since the behavior of gasses within the induction and exhaust systems has a substantial effect on cylinder filling and emptying, all phenomenological and quasi-dimensional models were less than reliable predictors of cylinder pressures and engine performance. The best that can be said of these relatively "simple" models is that they could be calculated by hand, without requiring the yet-to-be-invented electronic com-

IC engine simulations are based on one or more of the following models: fluid-dynamics (mass flow through passages and restrictions), thermodynamics (energy conversion into heat during combustion), heat-transfer (energy loss to cylinder walls, the exhaust system, etc.), and kinetics (losses in mechanical systems, e.g., friction, etc.).

gine became the simulation science of today is not well documented. But the first attempts date back to before Mr. Otto first applied the 4-cycle process to the internal combustion engine in 1867. From these earliest days in the development of the IC engine, it has been understood that analysis would be based on one or more of the following models: fluid-dynamics (mass flow through passages and restrictions), thermodynamics (energy conversion into heat during combustion), heat-transfer (energy loss to cylinder walls, the exhaust system, etc.), and kinetics (losses in mechanical systems, i.e., friction, etc.). However, by the late 1800's, engine developers were only just beginning to acquire a detailed knowledge of these processes, particularly as they applied to the four-cycle engine. Combined with the lack of powerful mathematical tools to analyze wave motion, describe combustion, and predict other physical phenomenon, the attempts at fundamental engine modeling were limited to very simplified models.

Zero- And Quasi-Dimensional Models

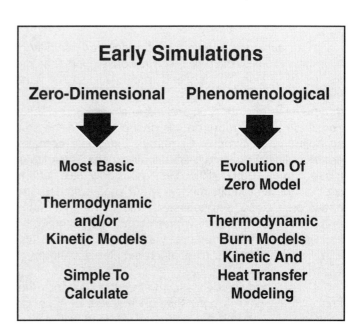

Early Simulations

Zero-Dimensional	Phenomenological
⬇	⬇
Most Basic	Evolution Of Zero Model
Thermodynamic and/or Kinetic Models	Thermodynamic Burn Models Kinetic And Heat Transfer Modeling
Simple To Calculate	

IC engine simulations of the late 1800's and early 1900's focused on the one or two of the basic four models. These methods lacked adequate burn, kinetic, and fluid-dynamic models, and they offered only limited predictive ability.

Instead, these models "look up" an empirically determined VE (usually from a table) to come up with "realistic" power numbers. Quasi-steady methods are conceptually and computationally simple, and for this reason they continue to be used in several power-predicting software programs sold today. Models based on quasi-steady methods inevitably suffer from a lack of accuracy. This is most obvious when engines are tested that fall outside their internal models and look-up tables. These computer programs can be identified by their capacity to display complete power curves on screen almost instantly after the "simulation" has begun.

Filling-And-Emptying Models

Quasi-steady models are not able to calculate the changing pressures and gas volumes in the ports and cylinders. Without this information it is impossible to accurately predict the effects of variations in cam timing, heat transfer to the charge, back flow into the intake system (reversion), and flow friction with the passage walls. All of these effects vary with engine speed. Some

More sophisticated engine simulations incorporate port, runner, and manifold modeling, and include a complex analysis of *finite-amplitude waves* that travel within these passages. Techniques that use this modeling require extremely complex math to predict mass flow. The Filling And Emptying and the powerful gas dynamic Method Of Characteristics techniques (used in the Dynomation program) are examples of multidimensional models.

puter, within a reasonable period of time.

Multidimensional Models: Quasi-Steady Flow

In an quest to improve the accuracy and usability of IC engine models, the next step took developers first into the world of port, runner, and manifold modeling, and then into a complex analysis of *finite-amplitude waves* that travel within induction and exhaust passages. Finite-amplitude waves (more on this phenomenon in the next section and in Chapter 6) require extremely complex mathematical models to predict their actions. Because of these computational difficulties, mass-flow calculations used in the first multidimensional IC engine models are based on a steady or quasi-steady flow through a series of "restrictions." These flow restrictions, representing the air cleaner, throttle, runners, valves, and exhaust system, lend themselves to a much simpler mathematical analysis.

Quasi-steady models assume that the flow of air/fuel and exhaust gasses pass through a series of separate volumes—defined by the ports, valves, and cylinders—with no accumulation of mass within any single volume. By nature, quasi-steady models do not incorporate a means to calculate the dynamic changes in volumetric efficiency (VE) that occur as engine speed increases.

The Filling And Emptying model used in the DeskTop Dyno divides intake and exhaust passages into a finite series of sections. This method accurately predicts average pressures within sections of the intake and exhaust system. This technique produces substantially more accurate and information rich modeling than quasi-steady models. The improvements are also due to a *time-step analysis* that calculates pressures at each degree of crank rotation throughout the full four-cycle process.

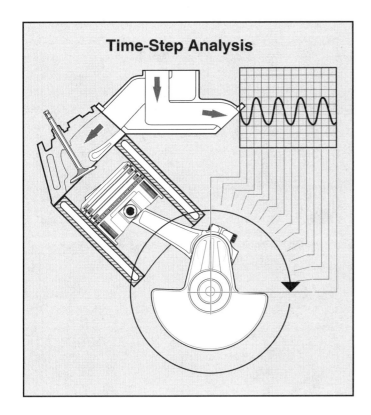

Time-Step Analysis

Simulations that use a time-step method, like the Filling And Emptying model in the DeskTop Dyno, repeat an instantaneous flow analysis for each rpm point. Horsepower and torque curves are "built up" one power point at a time. While the math needed to predict each power value involves several million calculations, modern PCs can develop an entire multi-point power curve in only seconds.

are more important at low speeds, such as charge heating, and others have a more pronounced effect at high speeds, like resistance to flow (and the consequent decrease in VE). By dividing the intake and exhaust passages into a finite series of sections, and analyzing the mass flow into and out of each section at each degree of crank rotation, a clearer picture of the pressures within the system can be obtained. This method, called *Filling-And-Emptying*, can accurately predict average pressures within sections of the intake and exhaust system, but cannot account for variations in pressure *within* these sections due to gas dynamic effects.

Despite their inability to predict gas-dynamics, filling-and-emptying techniques are substantially more accurate and information rich than quasi-steady models. These improvements are due, in most part, to the *time-step analysis* used to predict pressures and flow volumes. This technique requires emptying-and-filling models to perform their computations over and over, in a process called *iteration*, calculating pressures at each degree (typically) of crank rotation throughout the full four-cycle process. This degree-by-degree analysis accounts for the model's sensitivity to changes in cam timing, volume in the intake and exhaust systems, and valve and port configurations. The models can even analyze transient effects that occur when the throttle is opened and closed.

Filling-and-emptying models repeat this entire flow

analysis for each rpm point at which horsepower and torque are to be predicted. As a result, computer programs that use this technique, like those from Motion Software, commonly "build up" engine power curves by calculating and then drawing them one power point at a time. The math needed to predict each power value involves several million calculations. Despite these oppressive computational requirements, a modern PC equipped with a math co-processor can develop an entire power curve, consisting of 10 to 15 data points, in only a few seconds. Beyond the emptying-and-filling technique, the next step in accuracy requires wave-dynamic analysis (discussed next and in Chapter 6), but unfortunately this method increases mathematical complexity by a factor of 100 to 500, extending computation times. So, if reasonably fast answers are needed in response a series of "what-if" questions, the filling-and-emptying technique currently represents the highest level of sophistication that can be used on commonly available PC systems.

Gas-Dynamic Models

Surprisingly, all of the modeling methods described thus far had been discovered by 1900, although their use beyond scientific circles was limited; this was particularly true for calculation-intensive methods. Despite the lack of wide acceptance and application of even the simple modeling systems, scientists realized that an accurate description of the IC engine would only be possible when the pressure waves that moved within the engine's internal passages could be described and predicted mathematically. As race engine development continued through the first half of the 20th century, it became obvious that induction and exhaust tuning were contributing more and more power and complexity to component design. Without a model to accurately describe how these systems worked—precisely, at each degree of crank rotation—designers would forever be tied to endless and expensive testing, a good deal of which would produce inexplicable results. Power gains, when found, were closely guarded secrets that were rarely transferable to even similar engines. And the more an engine relied on induction and exhaust system tuning, the more difficult it became to explain subtleties in the power band or to modify or "fine tune" the system to meet specific requirements.

A first step toward a solution to this problem was made as early as 1860, when the Reverend F. Ernshew published a paper called the *Mathematical Theory of Sound* that analyzed compound wave systems. Despite the name of his paper, Ernshew was not much concerned with low-pressure sound waves. Rather, he attempted to mathematically describe the unusual and much more complex motion of high-pressure waves, the same phenomenon found in the intake and exhaust systems of the IC engine. Called finite-amplitude waves, these pulses of energy are several thousand times as powerful as sound waves, and they don't act anything like simple sound waves as they travel through engine passages.

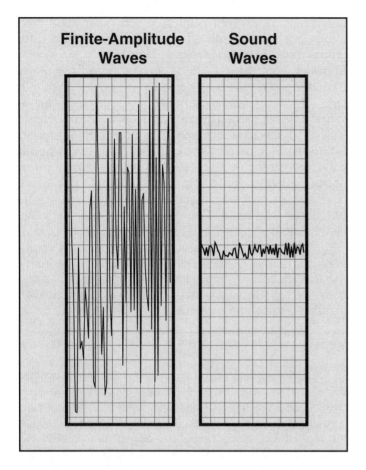

Finite-Amplitude Waves   Sound Waves

The high-pressure waves found in the intake and exhaust systems of the IC engine are called finite-amplitude waves. These pulses of energy are several thousand times as powerful as sound waves, and they don't act anything like simple sound waves as they travel through engine passages.

Before we delve into finite-amplitude wave dynamics, by contrast let's examine the actions of familiar sound waves. Picture a group of people discussing the events of the day. Sound moves through the air from various speakers to listeners without interacting or distorting. That is to say, sound waves leave a speaker's mouth, pass through the morass of other sounds in the room, reach a listener's ears and remain fully understandable. This seems to everyone to be a very "normal" event. But when you consider that many different sound waves *occupied the same physical space* as they traversed the room, without having any detectable effect on each other, it is a truly remarkable event!

Now picture what life would be like if sound waves weren't so cooperative and interacted like waves on a pond. The pressure waves of one voice would "bump into" another and each would distort into a completely new shape. When the sound reached the other side of the room it would have a completely unique character; it wouldn't "sound" like the original voices at all! Now let's assume that sound waves are even more troublesome and that they "mutate" simply by moving through the air. So, even if there is no other sound waves or other objects for them to "bump" into, the characteristics of the

Typical Sound Waves Pass Through Each Other With No Distortion

Finite-Amplitude Waves Interact With Each Other Distorting Original Character Of Waves

To explore finite-amplitude waves, picture people in a room discussing the events of the day. Sound moves through the air from various speakers to listeners without interacting or distorting. Despite a number of conversations going on at the same time, all sound remains fully understandable. On the other hand, if people spoke with finite-amplitude waves, one voice would "bump into" another and distort into a completely new shape. When it reached the other side of the room it wouldn't "sound" like the original voices at all!

sound would change, transforming like ocean waves rolling ashore.

While this has been simply an exercise for the imagination where sound waves are considered, it is very much an accurate description of reality for the finite-amplitude waves that move within engine passages. If you could yell loud enough to generate these waves, the sound of your voice would continue to change as it moved further away from your mouth. And if these high pressure waves interacted with other finite-amplitude waves or fixed objects, the resulting wave soon would be completely unintelligible. Finally, imagine how difficult it would be to design a "receiver" that would convert these seemingly random wave distortions back into the original intelligible signal. Now you have a glimpse of the incredible complexity involved in analyzing and predicting wave motion in the intake and exhaust systems of the modern high-speed IC engine.

Despite this complexity, Reverend F. Ernshew's early work took the first solid steps toward a mathematical model of finite-pressure waves. In 1910 Taylor published a book titled *The Conditions Necessary For Discontinuous Motion In Gasses.* His work provided a methodology to solve the thermodynamic equations first postulated by Ernshew. But practical applications of these methods were extremely challenging (involving hyperbolic, partial-differential equations) and without a breakthrough to further simplify the solutions (and without electronic computers to run through the math), there was little hope for any practical application or experimental verification of Ernshew's theories.

While the application of Ernshew's theories would lie several decades in the future, others continued work on related finite-amplitude problems. In 1940, Giffen, in his paper *Rapid Discharge Of A Gas To Atmosphere,* proved that the well-accepted theory of "Kadenacy" (that attempted to explain gas flow in the exhaust system) was incorrect. Up until this time, it was widely accepted that when the exhaust valve opened, a high pressure "slug" of gas blasted out of the port and down the header pipe. As this slug moved, it was believed that a low-pressure "wave" was created behind it, similar to the way a compression wave travels through a "Slinky" coil-spring toy; a tight group of coils (representing high pressure) moves along the spring followed by a more open group of coils (representing low-pressure). While this easy-to-visualize theory seems to make sense, Giffen demonstrated that finite-amplitude waves to not act in this manner. Despite

his mathematical proof delivered nearly 60 years ago, the Kadenacy effect is still widely believed by engine "experts" to this day!

It was about this time that IC engine development got its biggest boost in history: World War II. The IC engine was a strategic element in the transportation of goods, in all forms of combat vehicles, and it was the most crucial element in fighter aircraft of the day. Aerial combat during WWII, much like today, was fast, furious, and very dangerous. Pilots needed every advantage to defeat their opponents. If the enemy plane was more powerful and could outmaneuver, out-climb, or outrun his aircraft, he was at a serious disadvantage. And that was too often the case for many British fighters early in the war; they were simply out-horsepowered by the Germans. On top of this, the process of engine development, to a large extent still dependent on empirical testing, was taking considerable time and that was costing more lives. Attention was turned in earnest toward building practical mathematical models that could be used to reliably evaluate "paper engine" concepts.

A great deal of effort was applied to the problem of IC engine modeling during the war years. Unfortunately, the breakthroughs that were made contributed little to the war effort because of three factors: 1) A method was not found to simplify the complex equations and perform actual component testing, 2) the digital computer, desperately needed to solve iterative calculations, had only just been invented and was still an impractical, unreliable, and slow processing device, and 3) the jet engine, almost instantly after it became a practical powerplant, replaced the piston-driven engine in high-performance aircraft. However, the theoretical and practical work done during the war would prove to have a substantial impact on IC engine design and modeling work for many years

Incorrect "Kadenacy" Theory For Exhaust Gas Dynamics

High Pressure "Slug" (similar to compressed spring)   Low Pressure Follows (similar to expanded spring)

In an effort to explain gas flow in the exhaust system, it was believed that when the exhaust valve opened, a high pressure "slug" of gas blasted out of the port and down the header pipe. As this slug moved, it created a low-pressure "wave" behind it, similar to the way a compression wave travels through a Slinky™ coil-spring toy. While this easy-to-visualize theory seems to make sense, it was conclusively disproved nearly 60 years ago. Despite this, the Kadenacy effect is still widely believed by engine "experts" to this day!

This is the world's first operational jet fighter aircraft: the German Me-262. Although it contributed very little to the German war effort, it started a chain of events that lead, by the mid-1940s, to a radical slowdown of the development of the 4-cycle IC engine. However, the research performed during the early years of the war would have a substantial impact on IC engine design for many decades to come.

to come. Hundreds of mechanical components and power-optimizing techniques, such as roller cam followers, turbocharging, and nitrous-oxide injection systems, had become reliable methods of adding considerable horsepower to fighter aircraft. Many of these were later rediscovered by auto enthusiasts and racers; the most successful applications of this "new" technology often drew on the research performed between 1930 and 1945—the frenetic years of World War II.

The next breakthrough in the analysis of finite-amplitude waves came from Rudinger in 1949, and later in 1953, when he introduced and then perfected a practical analysis of wave motion using a graphical approach he called *Wave Diagrams*. Since finite-amplitude wave equations were still unsolvable throughout the 1950's, Rudinger's approach, although somewhat inelegant, allowed the limited analysis and prediction of complex wave motion. While this early attempt produced some answers, the underlying gas-dynamic equations still remained unsolvable.

Then, in 1964, the most important advance since Reverend Ernshew's early work was made by Roland Benson. In a work titled *A Numerical Solution Of Unsteady Flow Problems*, he presented a comprehensive numerical solution to the Method Of Characteristics for the solution of the complex finite-amplitude wave equations (his method transformed unsolvable hyperbolic partial-differential equations into "ordinary" solvable differential equations). Called the Mesh Method, his technique was a distinctly superior to earlier Wave Diagrams and even extended the analysis to multicylinder models. Benson was also the first to develop a Mesh-Method

The simulation software of the early 1960s was developed by corporate engineers working in cooperation with university research staff. The software was written for mainframe computers at a cost of hundreds of thousands to millions of dollars. Even with "heavy iron" like this UNIVAC LARC, it took considerable time to grind through the complex calculations. Despite the computational limitations, for the first time IC simulations were powerful enough to build a "paper engine"; a practical and quintessential step in the development of any modern powerplant.

During the early years of World War II, the IC engine was subjected to an intensive development program. Hundreds of mechanical components and power-optimizing techniques were perfected, including roller cam followers and rockers, turbocharging, and nitrous-oxide injection systems. Many of these were later rediscovered by auto enthusiasts and racers.

computer program and use a high-speed digital computer (a mainframe system of the day) to run calculations and complete the analysis that was originally envisioned nearly 100 years earlier.

Within a few years, Roland Benson's wave-dynamic solutions were fashioned into engine modeling programs and used by auto and motorcycle manufacturers throughout the world. Virtually all of these initial efforts were developed by corporate engineers working in cooperation with university research staff. The software was written for mainframe computers at a cost of hundreds of thousands to millions of dollars, and it featured the addition of accurate and comprehensive thermodynamic, combustion, kinetic, and frictional models to the Mesh-Method of analysis. For the first time, computer models existed that were powerful enough to build a "paper engine"; a practical and quintessential step in the development of any modern powerplant. Computer analysis using these and other advanced methods have made possible the impressive power, wide torque bands, and low emissions that are commonplace in modern IC engines.

Modern Engine Modeling Meets The PC

By 1972, an event had paved the way for an explosion in the development and widespread application of engine simulations, vehicle dynamic analysis, and numerous other mathematical models. This event, seemingly insignificant at the time, was the invention of the microprocessor; the entire "thinking core" of computer on a single chip of silicon. This innovation occurred shortly after similar reductions in the size of memory and other logic circuits that are needed to build an entire computer

Described as "the world finest personal computer" in this ad of the mid-1970s, the IMSAI—along with the Altair manufactured by MITS—was mostly an empty box with a series of flashing lights on the front panel. It used an 8-bit Intel 8080 or Zylog Z-80 microprocessor running at 2 or 4 Mhz. Programming involved flipping a series of switches on the front panel. Despite a lack of practical applications, these systems generated a firestorm of in-terest among many enthusiasts who dreamed of "owning their own computer."

system. The stage was set.

In 1974, the curtain opened for the introduction of the world's first "personal" computer. It was called the Altair; it was manufactured by Micro Instrumentation Te-lemetry Systems (MITS); it retailed for slightly less than $400; it was only available as a mail-order, assemble-it-yourself kit; and it did little more than flash a series of lights on the front panel. But the public demand to "own your own computer" was overwhelming, and throughout the next seven years the microcomputer developed into a tool that found widespread use in business and engi-neering establishments throughout the world. These early systems were slow by today's standards, but they pro-vided processing power hundreds of times faster than desktop calculators of the day. And they easily could be programmed to perform math-intensive, repetitive tasks.

Arguably, the second most momentous development in the history of the personal computer (with due respect to Stephen Wozniak and Steven Jobs of Apple Com-puter fame, perhaps the *third* most momentous event) occurred in 1981 when IBM introduced its own micro-computer, called the IBM PC. While not a technical mile-stone, it contributed tremendous credibility to the desk-top computer concept, and within a few years, the PC

was a standard fixture in many businesses, schools, and laboratories. The original PC used a 4-Mhz, 16-bit micro-processor (the Intel 8088) that could be equipped with a *numeric coprocessor*. This add-on math powerhouse sped up calculations by 20 to 100 times. A coprocessor-equipped PC could now grind through the complex math required for engine simulations that just 10 years previ-ously required a multimillion dollar mainframe; an amaz-ing accomplishment for an innocuous-looking box sitting on a desktop! Now, for the first time in history, incredible computing power was available to the general public.

By 1982, IBM's PCs had transformed into ATs equipped with Intel's 32-bit 80286 processor. Then in 1985, the 80286 was replaced by a more efficient and powerful 80386DX processor. The 80486DX chip was introduced in 1989 and was the first PC processor to included a numeric coprocessor integrated with the CPU. This all-in-one design set a new math-computing stan-dard for PC systems, and was a clear indication that the 1990's would be a decade of math-intensive applications for the desktop.

Dynomation: Gleam In A Young Man's Eye

The wide availability of inexpensive computing power

This is the original 1981 IBM PC. While not a technical milestone, the PC soon became a standard fixture in many businesses, schools, and laboratories. It used a 4-Mhz, 16-bit microprocessor (the Intel 8088) that could be equipped with a *numeric coprocessor*. This add-on math powerhouse sped up calculations by 20 to 100 times. For the first time in history, incredible computing power was offered to the general public.

Curtis Leaverton's early fascination with wave dynamics resurfaced in 1991 after college. Motivated by the desire to start a business that would produce racing motorcycle components, he dove into the University engineering library and read everything on wave dynamics he could find. He soon discovered the Method Of Characteristics solutions developed by Roland Benson, and that began the long process of writing a computer program to apply, for the first time, this complex and powerful tool to the world of high performance and racing engines.

takes us to the next major step in the development of engine simulations. Actually, it began almost 10 years earlier in 1980, when a notably wild 16 year old, Curtis Leaverton, had his first experience with exhaust tuning. He had just installed a custom expansion chamber on his Ossa motorcycle and was stunned by the increase in power produced by this deceptively simple, *hollow tube*. As a teenager, though, he didn't yet possess the mathematical skills or the knowledge of gas dynamics needed to "look inside" the contrivance and figure out what produced such a dramatic increase in horsepower. For the time being, he simply enjoyed taking his Ossa on hair-raising rides over back roads of Des Moines, Iowa.

His early fascination in wave dynamics resurfaced in 1991 when Curtis, now a college graduate just returning to off-campus life, took stock of his interests and decided to try once again to understand the mysteries of expansion chambers. Motivated by the desire to start a business that would produce racing motorcycle components, he dove into the University engineering library reading everything on wave dynamics he could find. His engineering and math training helped him understand the solutions to finite amplitude waves, but their immense complexity took him by surprise. If he was ever to manufacture components based on unsteady wave dynamics, he needed a way to resolve the hyperbolic partial-differential equations required to analyze the effects of various chamber dimensions. He soon discovered the Method Of Characteristics solutions developed by Roland Benson and began the long process of writing a computer program that would apply, for the first time, this complex and powerful tool to the world of high performance and racing.

Curtis had not spent his college years entirely isolated in study and campus life. His avid attraction to motorcycles and racing technology drove him to build and maintain his contacts with people within the racing community. And there lies the key to his success! Although applications of wave-dynamic theory had been done before, but this was the first time that anyone who understood the theory *also* understood racing technology. For the next several years, Curtis worked methodically on a computer program and compared the results he generated with the data he received from professional racers. Slowly, he began to understand how the complex science of pressure waves applied to the racing engine. Despite his initial objectives, it became obvious that the goal for his program should not be to produce "ideal" pressure waves that would make any Ph.D. in his gas dynamics class smile, but rather to accurately reproduce the effects seen in the non-laboratory world of the race track.

Months of work stretched into years. The initial focus on 2-cycle expansion chambers evolved into a dedicated effort to model 4-cycle multicylinder engines, due in part to the wealth of dynamometer results he received from his racing contacts who primarily tested four, six, and eight-cylinder, 4-stroke engines. Curtis finally developed a functional computer program that began to predict the power levels that engines *would make* with certain induction and exhaust system designs. His colleagues were amazed when they ran the tests he described and found

In 1993, Curtis introduced the world's first PC program that applied the Method Of Characteristics to the design of the 4-stroke racing engine. He christened it Dynomation, and it became the inaugural product from V.P. Engineering, his newly formed company. Dynomation, containing functionality previously valued at over one million dollars, could now be purchased for under $600, run on a $1500 PC, and used to develop winning combinations for just about anyone!

exactly the results his program predicted.

In 1993, Curtis introduced the world's first PC program that applied the Method Of Characteristics to the design of the 4-stroke racing engine. He christened it *Dynomation*, and it became the inaugural product from V.P. Engineering, his newly formed company. Theories that had been conceived 130 years ago, advanced during World War II, solved in the 1960's, and limited to a few scientists and engineers ever since, could now be easily used by engine builders and automotive enthusiasts to analyze and predict power. Even more importantly, from this author's perspective at least, no one before had ever "fine-tuned" these powerful mathematical tools specifically for high-performance and racing engines. Dynomation, containing functionality previously valued at over one million dollars, could now be purchased for under $600, run on a $1500 PC, and be used to develop winning combinations for just about anyone!

If Dynomation had a drawbacks, they were the time required to calculate a complete power curve, the various technical inputs needed to "build" an engine model, and the knowledge required by the user to understand the results and make the appropriate component modifications. It was clear to Curtis that some enthusiasts would not be able to use Dynomation to its full capacity. So in late 1993, in cooperation with Motion Software, Inc., Curtis began development of a simulation program that would incorporate an easy-to-use interface, have quicker processing times, and maintain high predictive accuracy. Now known as the *DeskTop Dyno*, and other brand names, this new model is based on a technique called Filling And Emptying. The new program would also in-

corporate a "mini-version" of Dynomation's wave-action analysis. The Filling And Emptying technique would trade-off some accuracy for an increase in computational speed. The first release in 1994 (version 1.5) ran about 100 times faster than Dynomation and had a power prediction accuracy within 93% (Dynomation often predicted actual dyno power figures within 97% to 98% accuracy). The new program, priced at under $50, provided tens of thousands of enthusiasts the opportunity to run "dyno tests," compare various component combinations, and experience the latest breakthroughs in engine simulation technology on their home PCs.

From 1994 to present, both the Dynomation and Motion's Filling And Emptying programs have grown in power and accuracy (the Desktop Dyno predictive accuracy—as of mid 1996, with version 2.5 scheduled for release in October 1996—is rated at 95%). These programs still remain the only time-based, iterative engine simulations available to public.

The Future Of IC Engine Modeling

A quick visual comparison of the technology found in

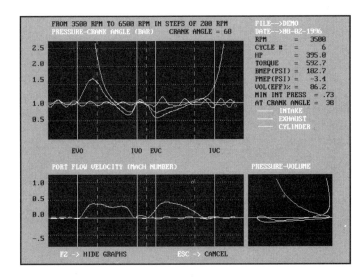

The Dynomation program reveals the entire spectrum of pressures and flow velocities within the simulated engine. Displaying a pressure crank-angle diagram for intake, exhaust, and cylinder pressures, and a pressure-volume (PV) diagram, let's anyone "look inside" a running engine as never before. In addition, particle velocities are shown for both intake and exhaust flow. Studying the pressure curves can help professional engine builders or racers locate inefficiencies and diagnose performance problems, saving considerable time and money.

Curtis spends a good deal of his time working with professional racers, engine builders, and dyno testing facilities throughout the world. The feedback that he receives allows him to continue to fine tune his simulation software, while his collaborators are able to utilize the latest in simulation science.

Winston Cup stock car racing, like virtually all forms of professional motorsports today, is extremely competitive and extraordinarily expensive. Many pro teams are turning to engine simulation software to keep their dyno testing programs moving in the right direction. The days of strictly trial-and-error testing are slowly coming to a close thanks to professional simulation packages like Dynomation. However, even the best simulation software can only help the top-level racers to a limited degree, since their engines are so close to optimum tune. Simulation software is most helpful in evaluating new engine combinations; in these cases, it can reduce development time considerably.

engine compartments of typical 1970's versus 1990's vehicles is clear proof that auto manufacturers are using the once-unsolvable theories of wave dynamics as just another "tool" to improve Otto's remarkable 4-cycle design. As of today, it can be unequivocally stated that *everyone involved in engine design* (for subsequent manufacturing) *is using computer-aided simulation technology.* Top racing teams competing in NHRA, Nascar, and many other forms of racing have also begun to use advanced engine modeling tools, like Dynomation, along with data acquisition systems to thoroughly analyze *and* predict engine and chassis function. All of this innovation just represents the beginning. The leading edge in engine simulation is continuing to move into more efficient, complete and complex models. As these tools are refined—and made more practical by the ever-increasing power of both large and small computers—still higher levels of sophistication and accuracy will be possible.

Some leading-edge engine simulations of the 1990's have incorporated a more flexible method for solving the flow equations that predict intake and exhaust wave dynamics. Called the *Finite Difference Method*, this technique is a time-step (or crank-angle) interative method offering improved efficiency over the Method Of Characteristics for one-dimensional unsteady gas flow. Finite Difference, however, is not perfect. It is prone to instabilities, especially from shock waves that can exist in the exhaust system. Despite these drawbacks, the Finite Difference method currently represents state-of-the-art in solutions to one-dimensional fluid/gas flow.

Advanced simulations currently running on mainframes may also employ Engine Cycle Simulation. This technique refers to models that, to some degree, follow the changing chemical and thermodynamic state of the intake and exhaust charge throughout the 4-cycle process. These methods attempt to describe the properties of burned and unburned gasses, heat transfer to the cylinderwall, piston, port, surrounding gasses, and rate of charge burning. These models generally include some three-dimensional geometric features of the cylinderhead, valves, ports, and properties of combustion. Sufficiently-detailed Engine Cycle Simulations can predict preignition, detonation, and engine emissions.

When you need to match an engine combination to a race vehicle, simulation software can run through several possibilities and help pro teams find the optimum combination. This 430cid smallblock for off-road truck racing features many specialized and expensive components that can be quickly tested with IC engine simulations.

This brings us to the "bleeding edge" of engine simulations. All flow-dynamics solutions included in the models discussed thus far, with the partial exception of Engine Cycle Simulations, restrict flow to one dimension. This means that the pressure waves are assumed to move along a straight line down the port or passage. This technique enormously simplifies the math and, for the most part, produces reasonably accurate results. However, when finite-amplitude waves encounter a turn, meet a junction, or even transition into rapidly changing volumes, they no longer exhibit one-dimensional properties; they become highly multidimensional in nature. The junction between ports and valves, between the valves and the enlarging volumes of the ports, and passage intersections in the intake manifold are examples of situations where one-dimensional assumptions break down.

The analysis of these areas requires a much more rigorous three-dimensional technique.

Multidimensional models attack the problem by subdividing an area, such as the combustion chamber or port junction, into a series of volumes (or cells) through which the model solves the differential equations of thermodynamics and fluid flow. A time-step mesh analysis is repeated (through a process called a *continuum*) to evaluate how each volume affects its neighbor. One cell may increase the temperature of the next or transfer gas volume into or from adjacent cells. The smaller and more numerous the volumes, the more accurate and the more computationally intensive the solution. In order to apply this to an IC engine, complete three-dimensional "patterns" of the passages, chambers, runners, manifolds, and headers would have to be made available to the program. Then, reproducing the dynamics throughout the entire induction and exhaust system, a series of models would calculate the changes in each of the millions of cells, as mass, heat, and pressure waves move through the engine. The interaction of these cells would reveal the idiosyncrasy of each part of the overall system. Needless to say, you will need a PC 1000 times faster than the quickest Pentium Pro systems to even consider performing these simulations on your desktop. But when it's possible (and it will happen!), you will be able to design very subtle features within the induction and exhaust systems and thoroughly test their effect on horsepower, fuel efficiency, and emissions throughout the rpm range.

While the engine simulation models under development today will set standards for sophistication and accuracy, where is this technology headed? The ultimate goal will be to build virtual vehicles, including the engines, drivelines, chassis, and all the electrical and hydraulic components. The mathematical models of a complete vehicle, you might call it a "paper vehicle," would be built, tested, refined, and perfected entirely within the virtual world of the computer. These simulations will provide the new car buyer thoroughly debugged models that offer an unprecedented level of reliability, performance, economy, safety, and comfort. The reality of this dream lies in the future. However, considering the rate at which advances are now proceeding, many of you reading this book may have the unique experience of buying and driving a vehicle that, while the odometer reads nearly zero, was already "road tested" by a computer several million miles before a single bolt was tightened.

Auto makers are currently using computer-aided design systems, but the ultimate goal is to build <u>virtual</u> vehicles, including the engines, drivelines, chassis, and all the electrical and hydraulic components. The mathematical models of a complete vehicle, you might call it a "paper vehicle," would be built, tested, refined, and perfected entirely within the virtual world of the computer. The vehicle would be thoroughly "road tested" by a computer for several million miles before a single bolt was tightened.

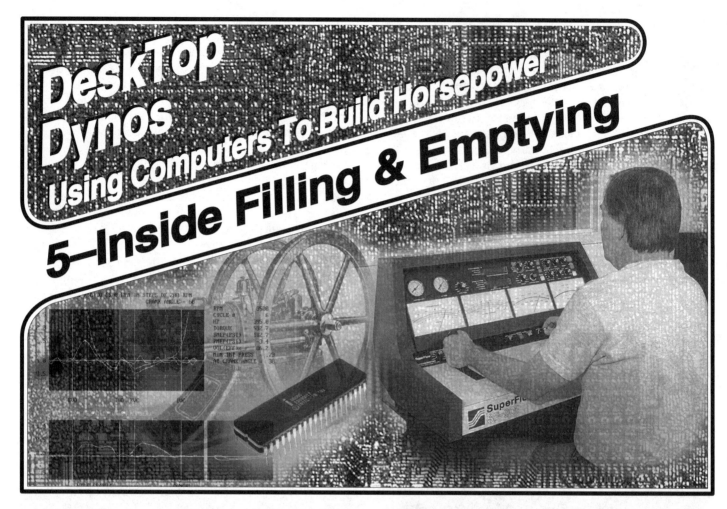

NOTE: *If you purchased software with this book, you will find step-by-step installation instructions and troubleshooting in Appendix–A on page 108. You will also find a helpful resource for program operation, and discover optimization techniques, printing methods, mouse and keyboard tips, and answers to frequently asked questions.*

Filling & Emptying By Any Other Name

s described in the previous chapters of this book, Motion Software recently released engine simulation software for IBM-compatible "PC" computers. These simulation programs are based, as of the writing of this book, on the *Filling-And-Emptying* method of full-cycle analysis as applied to the 4-stroke IC (internal combustion) engine. These software packages are available under various names, including the *DeskTop Dyno* (available from Mr. Gasket Corporation and from Motion Software, Inc. and its distributors) the *GM PC Dyno Simulator* (available from GM Performance Parts) and others. Each of these packages has individual functional differences, but all of these products use the same simulation methodology and many of the menu choices are comparable. Because of these similarities, the information in this chapter applies equally to version 2.0, 2.5, and later simulation software releases. Minor functional differences will be discussed as required. Most screen illustrations in this book depict the latest

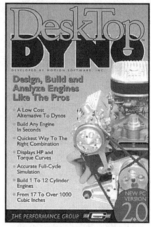

Motion Software, Inc., has recently released engine simulation software for IBM-compatible "PC" computers. These programs are based on the *Filling-And-Emptying* **method of full-cycle analysis. They are available under various names, including the** *DeskTop Dyno,* **the** *GM PC Dyno Simulator* **and others.**

version of the software (version 2.5.7 was in development when this book was published). This chapter is intended to help you obtain a clearer understanding of overall program function, what is covered by each menu group, the implications of individual choices within the menus, and how to interpret simulation results. In addition, we will illustrate what can and cannot be modeled and why, the drawbacks of the current simulation software, and what advances may be possible in the near future.

Motion Engine Simulation Basics

Motion engine simulations have been optimized for rapid "what if" testing. Engine component parts are grouped in menus along the top of the screen. One or more selections from each menu group effectively "builds" a test engine (called a "paper engine" in simulation parlance). Then, simply pressing "RUN" begins a full-cycle analysis of cylinder pressures. The simulation plots a graphic, on-screen representation of horsepower and torque for easy visual analysis. It is a simple procedure to save the test, select a new part or component dimension from one of the menus, and rerun the simulation to perform back-to-back testing. The changes in power and torque that would occur if a "real" engine were built and tested with the components at hand are clearly displayed in the graphic curves. Remarkably, this entire process often takes less than one minute on most computer systems.

Ease of use has always been an important design element. Without it, many of the tens of thousands of automotive enthusiasts that have successfully "assembled and tested" engines would not have been able to use our simulation programs. Imagine if one of the necessary inputs requested: "Enter the intake port flow at each 0.010-inch of the valve lift up to the maximum valve lift." Yet this information is absolutely necessary to perform a true engine simulation. To make this software technology available to as wide an audience as possible, the information requested by the program is straightforward and generally known by most enthusiasts. The program uses this "basic" information to derive flow curves, cam profiles, frictional models, induction characteristics, and other "technical details." While the widely understood terms in the menus have made these programs accessible, their less-than-exact wording has left some experienced users scratching their heads. Engine builders and other advanced users are often very aware of the "internal complexities" of the IC engine and may not realize at first glance how Motion's simulations handle many of these important considerations.

Furthermore, some performance enthusiasts are disappointed when they realize that engine simulations do not include some of the components they were expecting to test. A short list of these might include: block and head metallurgy, piston types and dome shapes, head-gasket thickness, combustion-chamber shapes, oils, oil-pan designs, ignition timing, bolt torque loads, and many

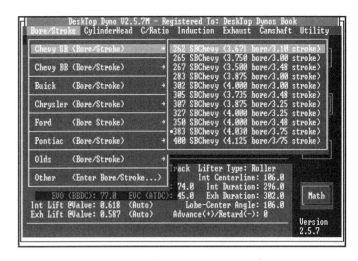

Motion's Filling And Emptying simulation offers an inexpensive and rapid way to select component combinations that produce power and torque generally accurate to within 5% of actual dyno figures. The various choices in the Bore/Stroke menu are shown here (version 2.5.7—in development when this book was published—includes expanded menu choices and several other enhancements, plus a *Cam Math Calculator* that makes working with cam timing much easier).

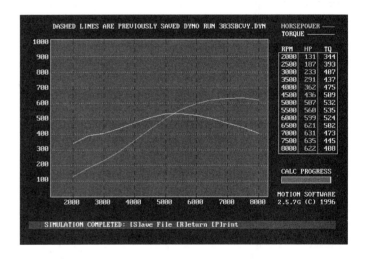

The simulation described in this chapter is easy to use and provides a remarkable level of predictive power. If you have a tendency to "dismiss" Motion simulations because they seem to consist only of simple pull-down menu choices, we encourage you to take a second look. We believe this software, at under $50, offers the greatest value of any product in the performance marketplace!

more. Modeling many of these elements would require very complex techniques (with concomitant complex inputs from the user, not to mention extend calculation times) and would reveal only relatively small power differences. These limitations are discussed throughout this chapter, but a good example of complexity vs. practicality can be found in oil pan testing. In order to simulate the conditions inside an oil pan, here are a few of the inputs that the user would have to address: dimensions of pan and lower crank/block contours, position of oil pump, positions and sizes of baffles, trays and screens, oil viscosity and temperature, level of oil in pan, acceleration and directional vectors (and how these vectors change over time), and more. Simply gathering together the needed information would be quite a project!

While it would be wonderful if an inexpensive computer program could simply and quickly zero-in on the optimum combination of all components for any intended application, that time has not yet come. However, most of the engine components that play a major role in power production *are* modeled in Motion's Filling-And-Emptying simulations. Cam timing, compression ratio, valve size, cylinderhead configuration, bore and stroke, induction flow, and manifold type are just some of the modeled elements that have major effects on engine power.

The simulation discussed in this chapter is easy to use and provides a remarkable level of predictive power. The designers have purposely avoided complex areas that would either make data entry difficult or greatly extend computational times. If you have a tendency to "dismiss" these simulations because they seem to consist only of simple pull-down menu choices, we encourage you to take a second look. Motion's Filling And Emptying simulation offers an inexpensive and rapid way to select component combinations that produce power and torque curves often within 5% of optimum for applications that lie within the range of the simulation. We believe that's quite an accomplishment for a software program you can load in your PC for under $50!

That brings us to the main purpose of this chapter (and this book in general). The information presented here revolves around detailed descriptions of every item listed in the on-screen component menus. You'll discover the assumptions made by Motion programmers with respect to each of the possible choices and combinations. Within sections that discuss each menu category, you'll also find substantial background information that can be helpful for both your simulated and real-world engine building projects. This information was compiled from the feedback of thousands of users, hundreds of beta testers, and countless hours of testing and exploration. We are confident that what you find here will make using Motion engine simulation software easier and your engine analysis more productive.

THE ON-SCREEN MENU CHOICES:

After starting Motion's engine simulation, the user can follow two paths of engine testing: To recall a previous test (using the **UTILITY** menu discussed later) or to "build" an engine from scratch. Assuming the latter selection, a common choice is to start with the leftmost **Bore/Stroke** menu then work, menu-by-menu, from left to right. While there are no restrictions dictating the order in which menus must be opened, the upcoming sections in this chapter follow the "natural" left-to-right progression taken by most "engine builders."

THE BORE/STROKE MENU

The **Bore/Stroke** menu is located on the left end of the menu bar. By opening this menu, you are presented with a variety of "pre-loaded" engine configurations. If any one of these choices is selected, the appropriate bore, stroke, and number of cylinders will be loaded in the SHORTBLOCK section of the on-screen Component Selection Box. In addition to selecting an existing engine configuration, you can scroll to the bottom of the Bore/Stroke menu and choose the "Other..." option. This closes the menu and positions the cursor in the Component Selection Box, permitting direct entry of bore, stroke (in inches to three decimal places) and number of cylinders. At each data input position, a range of acceptable values is displayed at the bottom of the screen. As with all numerical input, only values within the range limits will be accepted by the program.

What's A "Shortblock"

When a particular engine combination is selected from the Bore/Stroke menu, the bore, stroke, and the number of cylinders are "loaded" into the on-screen Component Selection Box. These values are subsequently used in the simulation process of predicting horsepower and torque. The Bore/Stroke menu choices should be considered a "handy" list of common engine cylinder-bore and crankshaft-stroke values, not a description of engine configurations (e.g., V8, V6, straight 6, V4, etc.), material composition (aluminum vs. cast iron), the type of cylinder heads (hemi vs. wedge) or any other specific engine characteristics. The Bore/Stroke menu only loads **bore**, **stroke**, and the **number of cylinders** into the program database.

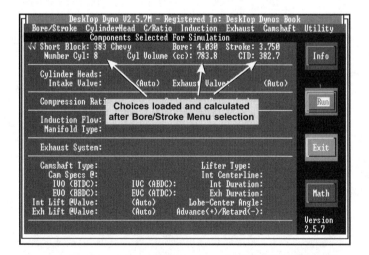

When a selection is made from the Bore/Stroke menu, the bore, stroke, and the number of cylinders are "loaded" into the on-screen Component Selection Box. In addition, the swept cylinder volume (in cubic centimeters) and the total engine displacement (in cubic inches) will be calculated and displayed. These values are subsequently used in the simulation process of predicting horsepower and torque.

Bore, Stroke, & Compression Ratio

After making a selection from the Bore/Stroke menu, or when the individual bore, stroke, and number of cylinders have been entered manually, the swept cylinder volume (in cubic centimeters) and the total engine displacement (in cubic inches) will be calculated and displayed in the on-screen Component Selection Box. The swept cylinder volume measures the volume displaced by the movement of a single piston from TDC (top dead center) to BDC (bottom dead center). This "full-stroke" volume is one of the two essential elements required in calculating compression ratio. We'll discuss compression ratio in more detail later in this chapter, but for now it's helpful to know that compression ratio is determined with the following formula:

$$\frac{\text{Swept Cyl Vol} + \text{Combustion Space Vol}}{\text{Combustion Space Vol}} = \text{CR}$$

In other words, the total volume that exists in the cylinder when the piston is located at BDC (this volume includes the Swept Volume of the piston and the Combustion Space Volume) is divided by the volume that exists when the piston is positioned at Top Dead Center. For the time being, it's important to keep in mind that your selections of bore and stroke dimensions greatly affect compression ratio. When the stroke, and to a lessor degree the bore, is increased while maintaining a fixed combustion-space volume, the compression ratio will rapidly increase. And, as is the case in Motion's simulation software, if the compression ratio is held constant—because it is a menu selection and, therefore, fixed by the user—the combustion space volume must increase to maintain the desired compression ratio. This may seem more understandable when you consider that if the combustion-space volume did not increase, a larger swept cylinder volume (due to the increase in engine displacement) would be compressed into the same final combustion space, resulting in an increase in compression ratio.

One example of how bore and stroke can have a significant affect on compression ratio is demonstrated in a destroked racing engine. Engine designers have realized for many years that shorter-stroke engines waste less power on pumping-work (more on this later), leaving more horsepower available for rotating the crankshaft. Furthermore, if engine displacement is held constant (by a concomitant increase in bore size), a larger cylinder diameter will accommodate larger valves, and increasing valve size is one of the most effective ways to improve breathing and horsepower. All of these changes taken together can produce considerable power increases, *providing the compression ratio is maintained or increased.* Unfortunately, it is difficult to maintain a high compression ratio in short stroke engines because: 1) Overall swept volume is often reduced, 2) combustion space volume is proportionally larger, and 3) short stroke engines move the piston away from the combustion chamber more slowly requiring increased valve-pocket depth to maintain adequate piston-to-valve clearance.

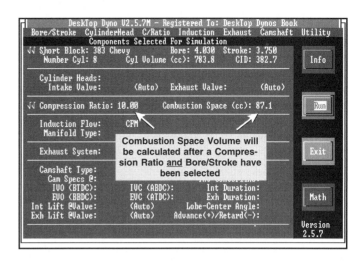

Bore and stroke have a direct effect on combustion space and compression ratio. (Remember, combustion space volume is rarely equal to combustion chamber volume. Combustion space is the total volume in the cylinder when the piston rests at Top Dead Center—see page 59.) When the stroke, and to a lessor degree the bore, is increased while maintaining a fixed compression ratio—because it is a menu selection and, therefore, fixed by the user—the combustion space volume must increase to maintain the desired compression ratio.

It is easy to use your PC to simulate a 1-inch stroke, 5-inch bore, 8-cylinder engine of 157 cubic inches with an 11:1 compression ratio that produces over 500hp at 8000rpm (with the power continuing to climb rapidly!). Unfortunately, it may be nearly impossible to build this engine with much more than 9 or 10:1 compression because the volume needed for the combustion chamber, valve pockets, and head gasket on a 5-inch bore is large compared to the swept volume produced by the short 1-inch stroke. If we installed typical smallblock race heads on this short-stroke configuration and great care was used in machining the valve pockets, a total combustion space of about 55cc's might be possible. Unfortunately, this would only produce 7:1 compression. The entire combustion-space volume would have to be less than 32 cubic centimeters to generate a compression ratio of 11:1 or higher!

Bore And Stroke Vs. Friction

You know that selecting stroke length will determine, in part, the cubic-inch displacement of the engine. And from the previous section you now realize that obtaining high compression ratios with shorter stroke engines can be quite difficult. What you may not realize is that setting the stroke length determines, to great extent, the amount of power lost to friction. The stroke fixes the length of the crank arm, and that determines how fast the piston and ring packages "rub" against the cylinder-walls at any given engine speed. And here's another rub (pardon the pun): *70% to 80% of all IC engine frictional losses are due to piston and ring-package "drag" against the cylinderwall!* If a 1-inch stroke engine running at

8000rpm looses 10 horsepower due to cylinderwall friction, the same engine will loose 25hp with a 2-inch stroke, 40hp with a 3-inch stroke, 70hp with a 4-inch stroke, 90hp with a 5-inch stroke, and 120hp with a 6-inch stroke at the same 8000rpm crank speed. That means this 6-inch stroke engine consumes 110 more horsepower than its 1-inch stroke counterpart just to drive the pistons and rings up and down their bores!

Try this simulation on your PC to demonstrate frictional losses. Build a 603.2 cubic-inch engine, we'll call it a very "Long-Arm" smallblock, with the following components:

Bore: 4.000 inches
Stroke: 6.000 inches
Cylinderheads: Smallblock/Stock Ports And Valves
Valve Diameters: 2.02 Intake; 1.60 Exhaust (Valve diameters must be manually selected to disable the "Auto Calculate" function. This keeps the valve size fixed when the bore size is changed—required for the next test.)
Compression Ratio: 10.0:1
Induction Flow: 780 CFM
Intake Manifold: Dual Plane
Exhaust System: Small-Tube Headers with Open Exhaust
Camshaft: Stock Street/Economy
Lifters: Hydraulic

This combination produces the power and torque curves shown in the accompanying chart (Long-Arm). Note that the power drops to zero above 5500rpm. Translated, this means that at 5500rpm the engine is using all the power it produces to overcome internal friction!

Now build the same displacement engine, but change the bore and stroke combination to:

Bore: 5.657 inches
Stroke: 3.000 inches

This "Short-Arm" configuration displaces the same 603.2 cubic inches, but it produces over 100hp at 5500rpm and maintains a "non-zero" power level until about 6500rpm. Where was the "extra" horsepower hiding? The majority is "freed" by lower piston speeds and reduced bore-wall friction from the 3-inch shorter stroke.

As mentioned in an earlier chapter, Motion simulations use an empirical equation to calculate frictional mean effective pressure (Fmep):

Fmep = (12.964 + (Stroke x (RPM / 6))) x (0.0030476 + (Stroke x (RPM / 6) x 0.00000065476))

And you may also recall that once the Fmep is known, the horsepower consumed by friction can be calculated with the following equation:

Friction HP =
= (Fmep x CID x RPM) / 792,000

Applying these equations to the two previous test engines reveals the following:

Power consumed by friction with the 6-inch stroke engine @ 5000rpm: **120.7hp**

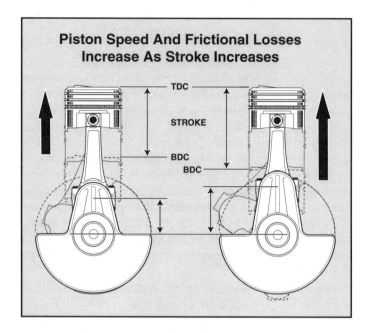

Piston Speed And Frictional Losses Increase As Stroke Increases

The stroke length determines, to great extent, the amount of power lost to friction. *70% to 80% of all IC engine frictional losses are due to piston and ring-package "drag" against the cylinderwall!* A longer stroke increases the length of the crank arm, and that increases the speed of piston and ring contact with the cylinderwall.

Power consumed by friction with the 3-inch stroke engine @ 5000rpm: **44.8hp**

So far we've discussed how stroke length affects displacement, compression ratio, and frictional losses within the engine. In addition to these effects, bottom-end configuration can have a measurable effect on power consumed by the processes of drawing fresh fuel/air mixture into the engine and forcing burned exhaust gasses

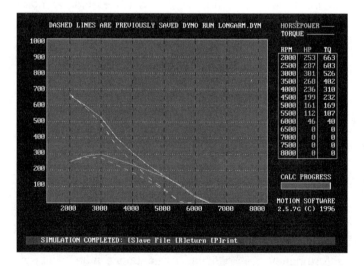

This "Short-Arm" configuration (solid lines) displaces the same 603.2 cubic inches as the "Long-Arm" test (dotted lines), but it produces nearly 100hp more at 5500rpm and maintains a "nonzero" power level until about 6500rpm. Where was the "extra" horsepower hiding? The majority is "freed" by lower piston speeds and reduced bore-wall friction from the 3-inch shorter stroke.

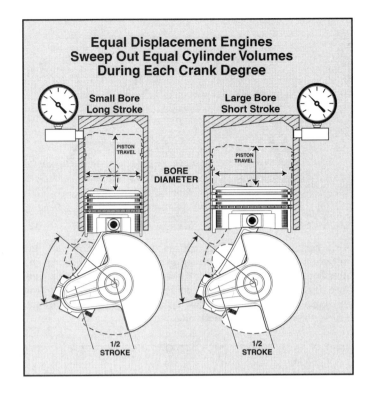

**Equal Displacement Engines
Sweep Out Equal Cylinder Volumes
During Each Crank Degree**

Small Bore
Long Stroke

Large Bore
Short Stroke

PISTON TRAVEL

PISTON TRAVEL

BORE
DIAMETER

1/2
STROKE

1/2
STROKE

While it's true that shorter-stroke engines consume less frictional horsepower, it is not true (as believed by some) that shorter-stroke engines, with their slower piston speeds, generate less pumping work. For equal displacements, equal cylinder volumes are swept out at each increment of piston travel from BDC to TDC. Short-stroke/large-bore engines pump just as much air as long-stroke/small-bore engines.

from the cylinders (a process called *pumping,* consuming what is termed *pumping work*). However, the IC engine is a remarkably complex mechanism that can sometimes fool nearly anyone into believing that they have discovered subtle, "secret" power sources. The logic behind the discovery may seem to make perfect sense, but eventually turn out wrong or misleading. This is the case with the belief purported by some "experts" that: 1) Shorter-stroke/larger-bore engine configurations have the potential to be more efficient high-speed air pumps, and 2) Shorter strokes are the key to producing high-speed horsepower. Let's take an in-depth look at how bore, stroke, and rod length affect piston speed and pumping work.

Fallacy One:
Stroke Length Vs. Pumping Work

The concept of pumping work is more easily understood when you remember that the IC engine is, at its heart, an air pump. Air and fuel are drawn into the cylinders during the intake cycle, and burned exhaust gasses are pumped from the cylinders during the exhaust cycle. The power required to perform these functions is called *pumping work* and is another source of "lost" horsepower.

The intake stroke begins with the piston accelerating from a stop at TDC. As it begins to move down the bore,

the swept volume within the cylinder increases, creating a lower pressure. This drop in pressure causes an inrush of higher pressure air and fuel from the intake system to compensate or "fill" the lower pressure in the cylinder. As the piston continues to accelerate down the bore, the speed of the induced charge also increases, until at about 70-degrees after top dead center, the piston reaches maximum velocity. At this point, the greatest pressure drop exists within the cylinder, drawing outside charge with the greatest force. It is this "force" that is the key element in understanding pumping work. The differences in pressures that cause the inrush of air and fuel are not a freebie from nature; they consume work. The greater the difference in pressure between the intake manifold and the cylinder, the more pumping work will be required to move the piston from TDC to BDC. Any increase in pumping work directly reduces the power available at the crankshaft.

Let's consider various techniques that can reduce pumping work on the intake stroke and potentially increase power output. First of all, pumping work can be substantially reduced by lowering cylinder volume. A smaller cylinder takes less work to fill it. Unfortunately, reducing cylinder volume also reduces the amount of air and fuel that can be burned on the power stroke, lowering power output more than any possible gains from a reduction in pumping work. So if power is the goal, reducing pumping work must be accomplished without decreasing the swept volume of the cylinder.

The question is how can we fill the same space using less work? This can be translated to read: How can

While pumping work is not directly affected by bore or stroke, larger displacement engines, like this 600cid big block, generate tremendous pumping work at high engine speeds. The pumping losses are due to restrictions at the valves, ports and runners, and throughout the intake and exhaust systems. At some point in engine speed, there no longer exists enough <u>time</u> to move the necessary gasses through passages of fixed sizes. When this happens, power takes a nose-dive.

we move the same or more air/fuel volume into the cylinder while inducing less pressure drop between the cylinder and the intake system? Solutions to this problem are widely used by racers and include larger intake valves, freer-flowing ports and manifolds, larger carburetors or injector systems, and tuned-length intake runners. All these techniques allow the same or more air/fuel mixture to flow into the cylinder while consuming less pumping work.

While it's true that shorter-stroke engines consume less frictional horsepower to drive the pistons up and down the cylinders (as described in the last section), it may also seem logical that a shorter stroke engine, with its slower piston speeds, can reduce pumping work. Here's how this concept is often described and how the underlying thread of truth often remains undiscovered: First, picture a 6-inch stroke, small-bore engine. When the piston begins to move away from TDC, the long stroke sends it quickly towards a maximum velocity (maximum volume change) that occurs about 70 degrees ATDC. At this point, the long stroke has accelerated the piston to very high speeds that generate a strong pressure drop in the cylinder. It is claimed that this low pressure generates flow velocities so high that the cylinder heads, valves, and the induction system become a significant restriction to flow. The rapid buildup in flow and high peak flow rates lower pumping efficiency, and the overall picture gets worse as engine speed and piston speed increase. Now consider a 1-inch stroke, large-bore engine. Because the stroke is much shorter, peak piston speed—and therefore peak pressure drop—are believed to be considerably lower. The reasoning continues that induction flow never reaches as high a rate but is spread out more evenly across the entire intake cycle. The shorter stroke is believed to allow the induction system to more efficiently fill the cylinder, consuming less pumping work. As engine speed increases, this improved efficiency lets the engine produce higher power levels at greater speeds than a longer-stroke engine.

The accompanying **Chart-A** (drawn from a simulation based on the underlying physics) illustrates the actual differences in incremental flow between an engine with a long stroke and the same displacement engine with a "destroker" crank and a larger bore. Notice how the shorter stroke engine develops less peak flow and spreads the same total flow volume slightly more evenly across the entire intake stroke. This reduction in peak flow allows the induction system to operate more efficiently, slightly improving cylinder filling and reducing pumping work. So that would seem to prove it, right? The chart shows that a shorter stroke pumps more efficiently. While that may seem to be the case, take a look at **Chart-B**. Here's a plot of the same two engines, but this time the rod lengths have been adjusted so that they have exactly the same rod ratio, that is, the length of all connecting rods are now equal to 1.7 times the length of the strokes. With identical rod ratios, the cylinders in both engines pump exactly the same volume at each degree of crank rotation. The "proven benefits" of a short

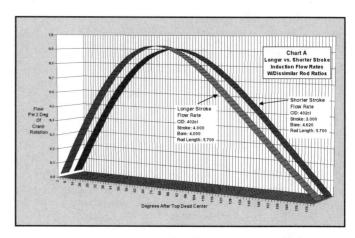

This graph illustrates the differences in incremental flow between an engine with a long stroke and the same displacement engine with a "destroker" crank. Notice how the shorter stroke engine develops less peak flow and spreads the same total flow volume slightly more evenly across the entire intake stroke.

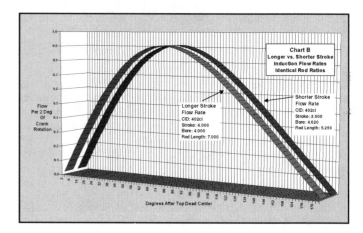

Here's a plot of the same two engines, but this time the rod lengths have been adjusted to have exactly the same rod ratio of 1.7 times the length of the strokes. With identical rod ratios, the cylinders in both engines pump exactly the same volume at each degree of crank rotation.

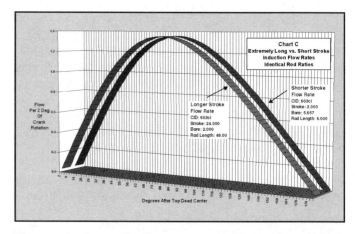

The graph shows the flow per crank degree for a 3-inch stroke, 5.67-inch bore engine vs. a 24-inch stroke, 2-inch bore engine. Both engines have the same 603ci displacement and sweep out the same volume at each 2-degree increment of crank rotation throughout the entire intake stroke, despite the *21-inch difference in stroke lengths*!

stroke disappear.

The misunderstanding that longer stroke engines are less efficient breathers probably occurs because during dyno tests of various combinations, identical rod ratios are not maintained when stroke lengths are changed. So measured differences in power are mistakenly attributed to changes in stroke, rather than the real cause: Variations in rod ratio. If you have any doubts about this, take a look at the simulation depicted in **Chart-C**. Here's a test of a 3-inch stroke, 5.67-inch bore engine compared to a very long 24-inch stroke engine having a 2-inch bore. Both engines have the same total displacement of 603ci and the same rod ratios (2.0 times the stroke length). The graph shows that the pistons in both engines sweep out the same volume at each 2-degree increment of crank rotation throughout the entire intake stroke, despite the *21-inch difference in stroke lengths*!

So it's not stroke, but rather rod ratio, that has subtle, measurable effects on pumping work and peak flow rates. The longer the rod ratio, the more spread out the induction flow and, potentially, the greater the high-speed power. The shorter the rod ratio, the higher the peak flow and the earlier in the intake cycle the flow peak is reached. Considering these flow changes, short-rod combinations could show potential gains on engines that benefit from a strong carburetor signal at lower engine speeds, like short-track and street engines. But even rod ratio cannot be considered in isolation. When the rod length is changed it also affects lateral loads on the pistons, and it can change the way the pistons "rock" in their bores and the way the rings "flutter" or seal against the cylinder walls. So, depending on the lubricants used, the cylinder block and piston configurations, and several additional factors, the "theory" of rod ratio and the power changes that are predicted may or may not be found on the dyno. At least you now have an understanding of the underlying theory, even though it makes its predictions in isolation of many other interrelated variables.

While we're on the subject of rod ratio, many readers may be wondering why this variable was not included in one of the pull-down menus in Motion Software's engine simulation. There are two reasons for this: 1) As just stated, the effects of varying rod length are very subtle and often masked by other variables within the engine (such as piston side loads, bore-wall friction, etc.) making accurate modeling extremely difficult, and 2) The subtle changes in swept volume primarily require wave-action dynamics for rigorous analysis (a process discussed in the next chapter). So rather than add a component that could not be modeled as accurately as the other variables in the program, rod length is not presented as a "tunable" element (although it is included within the simulation process).

Fallacy Two:
Long-Stroke Torque Vs.
Short-Stroke Horsepower

Another remarkably widespread belief has to do with stroke length vs. engine speed and torque vs. horsepower. A great many performance enthusiasts believe that long-stroke engines inherently develop more low-speed torque and short-stroke engines generate more high-speed horsepower. This understanding (probably as the result of reading various magazine articles over the years) is almost completely incorrect, and some enthusiasts are quite defiant when confronted with the fact that stroke, by itself, has little to do with high-speed or low-speed power potential. But, like the fallacy that short-stroke engines are more efficient air pumps, there is a thread of truth lying hidden under the surface.

To start off, long- and short-stroke engines of equal displacement will produce the same cylinder pressures during the power stroke for the same swept volumes (assuming that they have consumed equal quantities of air and fuel; and we've already demonstrated that stroke, by itself, has almost nothing to do with induction efficiency). While the pistons in a longer-stroke engine are smaller in diameter and, therefore, experience less force from the same cylinder pressure (force on the piston is directly related to the surface area of the piston and pressure in the cylinder), the crank arms are longer and have a greater mechanical advantage. The result, believe it or not, is that *equal displacement engines of unequal stroke lengths—experiencing the same cylinder pressures—will produce the same torque at the crankshaft* (see illustration on page 47). Stroke, however, is not an isolated variable; it affects the design of many other engine components. It's in this interrelatedness that we find the roots of misunderstanding about stroke vs. horsepower.

Probably the most direct reason for the belief that longer-stroke engines are lower-speed "torque generators," not capable of producing as many horsepower per cubic inch, is that many longer-stroke engines have smaller bores. An engine with smaller bores almost always has smaller combustion chambers, and smaller combustion chambers have smaller valves. So most longer-stroke engines are forced, by the design of the cylinder heads and the entire induction system, to produce less power at higher engine speeds. It's not the length of the stroke that limits power potential, its reduced flow from smaller valves, ports, and runners.

For more concrete proof, refer back to the simulation we performed in the earlier section on stroke vs. friction. In that test, we compared identical displacement engines of 603ci, one with a 6-inch stroke (dotted lines on graph) to one with a 3-inch stroke (solid lines). Both engines used the same size valves and the same 780cfm induction flow capacity. As previously demonstrated, the increase in horsepower from the shorter-stroke engine is due to a reduction in bore-wall friction, adding about 100 horsepower at 5500rpm. But look at the *shape* of the solid-line curves. They match the *shape* of the dotted-line curves for the longer-stroke engine. There is no noticeable boost in low-speed torque from the engine with a 6-inch stroke. A steadily-increasing power loss from additional cylinderwall friction is clearly visible, but notice

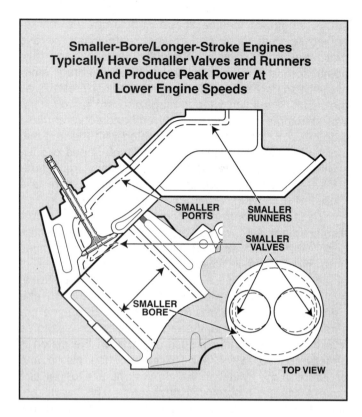

Smaller-Bore/Longer-Stroke Engines Typically Have Smaller Valves and Runners And Produce Peak Power At Lower Engine Speeds

SMALLER PORTS

SMALLER RUNNERS

SMALLER VALVES

SMALLER BORE

TOP VIEW

Many people believe that longer-stroke engines are lower-speed "torque generators," not capable of producing as many horsepower per cubic inch as shorter-stroke engines of equal displacement. What is often overlooked is that most engines with smaller bores almost always have smaller combustion chambers, smaller valves, and smaller runners. It's not the length of the stroke that limits power potential, its reduced flow through the induction system.

that *the short-stroke engine produced no less torque between 2000 and 2500rpm*, a range that many believe the longer-stroke engine should easily out-torque its short-stroke counterpart.

From a "real-world" mechanical standpoint, longer-stroke engines have drawbacks that limit their high rpm potential. As can be seen in our simulation, bore-wall friction becomes a substantial power robber. Ring seal also becomes a serious problem. As the stroke increases, higher and higher piston speeds cause the rings to "flutter" against the cylinderwalls decreasing their sealing ability. It's also possible that at very high piston speeds during the power stroke, the piston moves so quickly that the rings can't maintain a seal between the bottom of the ring and the ring land in the piston, increasing blowby and further decreasing horsepower. The mechanical loads on the piston and rod assembly in long-stroke engines also become a serious factor. As the piston is accelerated from TDC down the bore, extremely high tension loads are imparted to the rods and pistons, and added component weight to compensate for the additional loads further increases stress.

While there are good reasons why longer-stroke engines are ill suited to high-rpm applications, don't confuse these ancillary problems with the basic design rela-

tionships between bore and stroke. And don't fall into the trap of believing, like thousands of enthusiasts, that selecting a longer stroke will automatically boost low-speed power.

THE CYLINDERHEAD AND VALVE DIAMETER MENUS

The **Cylinderhead** pull-down menu, located just to the right of the Bore/Stroke menu, contains two submenus that allow the simulation of various cylinderhead designs and a wide range of airflow characteristics. The first submenu, **Head/Port Design**, lists general cylinder head characteristics, including restrictive ports, typical small- and big-block ports, and even 4-valve cylinder heads. Each category includes several stages of port/valve modifications from stock to all-out race. A selection from this menu is the first part of a two-step process that Motion simulations use to accurately model cylinder head flow characteristics. This initial selection determines the airflow restriction generated by the ports. That is, a selection from the first submenu fixes *how much airflow less than the theoretical maximum peak flow will pass through each port*. And what determines peak flow? That's selected from the second *Cylinderhead* submenu: **Valve Diameters**. Valve size fixes the theoretical peak flow (called *isentropic* flow—more on that later). Most cylinder heads flow only about 50% to 70% of this value. The Valve Diameter submenu allows the direct selection of valve size or **Auto Calculate Valve Size** may be chosen, directing the simulation to calculate the valve diameters based on bore size and the degree of cylinder head porting/modifications.

While it may seem as if the various *Cylinderhead* menu choices simply refer to ranges of airflow data stored within the program, that is not the case. If each menu selection fixed the flow capacity of the cylinder heads to

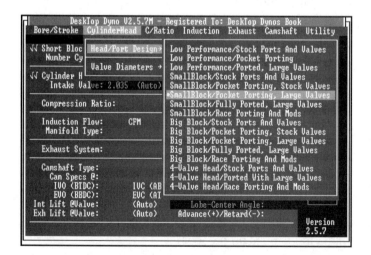

The Head/Port Design menu, under the Cylinderhead main menu, lists general cylinder head characteristics, including restrictive ports, typical small- and big-block ports, and even 4-valve cylinder heads. Each category includes several stages of port/valve modifications from stock to all-out race.

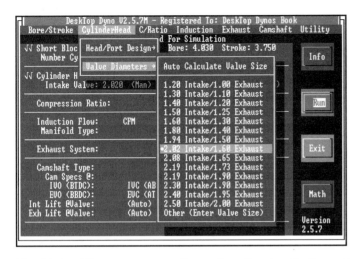

The Valve Diameter menu allows the direct selection of valve size or you can select *Auto Calculate Valve Size*, directing the simulation to calculate the valve diameters based on bore size and the degree of cylinderhead porting and modifications.

a specific range of values (like typical flow bench data measured at a standardized pressure drop), the simulation would be severely limited. While a simulation based on this technique might adequately calculate mass flow for engines that used nearly identical cylinder heads, accuracy would diminish rapidly for engines with even modestly larger or smaller ports and valves.

There are several reasons why the determination of port flow in sophisticated engine simulations can not be based strictly on flow-bench data. First of all, flow generated in the ports of a running engine is vastly different than the flow measured on a flow bench. Airflow on a flow bench is a steady-state, measured at a fixed pressure drop (it's also dry flow, but a discussion of that difference is beyond the scope of this book). A running engine will generate rapidly and widely varying pressures in the ports. These pressure differences directly affect— in fact, they directly cause—the flow of fuel, air, and exhaust gasses within the engine. An engine simulation program, as described in previous chapters, calculates these internal pressures at each crank degree of rotation throughout the four-cycle process. To determine mass flow into and out of the cylinders at any instant, you need to calculate the flow that occurs as a result of these changing pressure differences. Since the variations in pressure, or pressure drops, within the engine are almost always different than the pressure drop used on a flow bench, flow bench data cannot directly predict flow within the engine.

Before we delve deeper into the differences between flow-bench data and the mass flow calculated by an engine simulation program, let's permanently put to rest the idea of *storing* the needed airflow data within the program. Consider for a moment an engine simulation program that's based on internally-stored airflow data. If you assume that the program is capable of modeling a wide a range of engines (like Motion Software simulations), then it must also store a wide range of cylinder head flow

data. Flow would have to be recorded from a large number of engines, starting with single-cylinder motors and working up to 1000+ cubic-inch powerplants. If it were possible to accumulate this much data, there are additional shortcomings in a lookup model. Since the pressures inside the IC engine are constantly changing, a lookup program would have to contain <u>ranges of flow data</u> measured from zero to the maximum pressures differentials developed within the running engine. Even if this much data could be assembled and filed away, additional data for each engine and cylinder head would be needed to predict the flow changes when larger valves were installed; and even more data would be needed to model port modifications. It soon becomes clear that the sheer bulk of flow data needed for a comprehensive lookup model would probably consume more space than exits on your hard drive (and that's considering that most of us now own gigabyte and larger drives)!

Cylinderhead Choices And Discharge Coefficients

While it is impractical to <u>base</u> an engine simulation on extensive flow-bench data, measured cylinder head flow figures are, nonetheless, commonly used in sophisticated engine simulations. Rather than stored in extensive "lookup" tables within the programs, flow-bench data can be used as a means to <u>compare</u> the measured flow of a particular port/valve configuration against the calculated isentropic (theoretical maximum) flow. The resulting "ratio," called the **discharge coefficient**, has proven to be an effective link between flow-bench data and the simulated mass flow moving into and out of the cylinders throughout a wide range of valve openings and pressure drops. Furthermore, the discharge coefficient can be used to predict the changes in flow for larger or smaller valves and for various levels of port modifications. In other words,

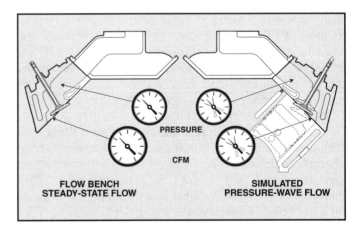

Airflow on a flow bench is steady state, but Motion's engine simulation program calculates internal pressures and mass flow at each degree of crank rotation throughout the four-cycle process. Since the variations in pressure, or pressure drops, within the engine are rarely equal to the pressure drop used on a flow bench, flow bench data cannot directly predict flow within the engine.

it's the discharge coefficient, not flow bench data, that provides a practical method of simulating mass flow within a large range of engines. Since this is such a powerful and often misunderstood concept, the following overview should prove helpful in understanding what's happening "behind the scenes" when various choices are made from the Cylinderhead pull-down menu.

The choices in the Cylinderhead menu are purposely generic. This can be frustrating if you are interested in modeling only one engine or a single engine family. In these cases it would be ideal to list the exact components you wished to test, in name or part-number order. But if you are interested in simulating different engines, including popular 4-, 6-, and 8-cylinder powerplants, the choices provided in the Cylinderhead menu (and many of the other menus) offers considerable modeling power. The menu choices move from restrictive heads to small-block, big block, and finally to 4-valve-head configurations. If each of these choices loaded a higher absolute flow curve into the simulation, they would cover only a very narrow range of engines. Instead, each of the menu choices model an increasing <u>flow capacity and reduced restriction</u>. This makes it possible to accurately simulate a lawnmower engine, a high-performance motorcycle engine, an all-out Pro Stock big block, or a mild street driver, each having different port and/or valve sizes, using selections from the same menu!

The basis for this "universality" is that each menu selection uses a different <u>discharge-coefficient curve</u> rather than airflow curve. While the discharge coefficient data is *derived* from flow-bench data, it is dimensionless (has no length, weight, mass, or time units) and is applicable to any cylinder head of similar flow efficiency. To clarify this concept, picture two large rooms connected by a hole in the adjoining wall. When pressure is reduced in one room, air will flow through the hole at a specific rate. It is possible to calculate what the flow would be if there were no losses from heat, turbulence, etc. This flow rate, called the isentropic flow, is never found in the real world, but is, nevertheless, a very useful term. It's the rate of flow that "nature" will never exceed for the given pressure drop and hole size. If we measure the actual flow through the hole and divide it by the calculated isentropic flow, we will have determined the flow efficiency or *discharge coefficient* of the hole:

Discharge Coefficient (always less than 1) =
Measured Flow / Calculated Flow

Since every orifice has some associated losses, the discharge coefficient is always less than 1. If the calculated discharge coefficient for our hole in the wall was 0.450, this would mean that the hole flows 45% as much air as an ideal hole. In other words, it's 45% efficient.

Let's see how this concept can be applied to cylinder heads. When an intake valve of a specific size is opened a fixed amount, it exposes a flow path for air called the *curtain area*. Through this open area, measured in square inches just like the hole in the wall, air/fuel mixture moves at a specific rate depending the pressure drop across the valve (as you recall, the pressures are calculated by

the simulation software at each degree of crank rotation). If the valve and port were capable of perfect isentropic flow, the simulation equations could calculate the precise mass flow that entered the cylinder during this moment in time. But real cylinder heads and valves are far from perfect, and it's flow bench data that "tells" the simulation how far from perfect the real parts perform. By dividing the isentropic flow by the flow-bench data (both at the same pressure drop) of a comparable head/port configuration at each increment of valve lift, *the simulation software creates a discharge coefficient curve that it can use as a correction factor for port flow at all other pressure drop levels.*

The true power of this method lies in the fact that the cylinder head tested on the flow bench—used to develop the discharge-coefficient curve—may have been designed for an entirely different engine and used different valve sizes. Nevertheless, as long as the head configuration matches the simulated cylinder head, in other words, the ports have similar flow efficiency, the discharge-coefficient curve will closely adjust isentropic flow to real-world corrected flow. So a specific choice in the Cylinderhead menu, say "Pocket Porting With Large Valves" may accurately model a factory performance head for a small-block Chevy, a cylinder head on a 4-cylinder Toyota engine, or even a motorcycle head. <u>With discharge coefficient corrections, it's not the absolute flow numbers that are important, it's how well the valve and port flow for their size that really counts.</u>

As you made selections from the Cylinderhead menu, you may have wondered whether the flow data used to "correct" the isentropic flow in any of the menu items would match the published flow of cylinder heads that

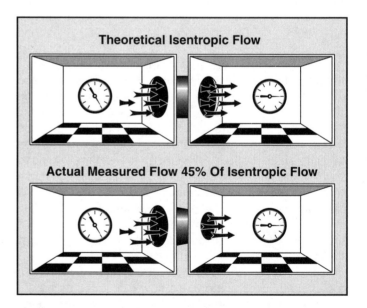

The absolute maximum flow rate through an orifice with no losses from turbulence, heat, or friction is called the isentropic flow. This is the flow rate that "nature" will never exceed for the given pressure drop and hole size. If we measure the actual flow through the hole and divide it by the calculated isentropic flow, we will have determined the flow efficiency or *discharge coefficient*.

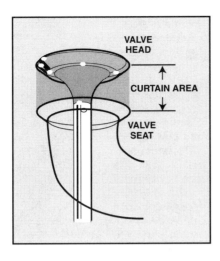

When a valve of a specific size is opened a fixed amount, it exposes a flow path called the *curtain area*. Through this open area (measured in square inches) gasses move at a specific rate depending on the pressure drop across the valve.

you would like to simulate. Considering what you now know about the relationships between cylinder heads of similar efficiencies and how flow data is used by the program, it becomes clear that knowing the flow-bench data used in the program would probably not be helpful. The flow may not have been obtained from the same valve sizes or even the same brand cylinder heads. On the other hand, it is entirely feasible for the simulation to substitute user-entered flow data from tests conducted on a specific set of cylinder heads. This data could then be used to develop custom discharge-coefficient curves that would, in turn, closely model cylinder heads. While this is not currently supported, it will be incorporated in upcoming versions of Motion simulation software (make sure you send in your registration card; you'll receive information on upgrades and new releases).

Ram Tuning And Pressure Waves

Up to this point our discussion has centered around airflow, valve size, and discharge coefficients. The assumption has been that reducing restriction and increasing flow efficiency will allow more air/fuel mixture to enter the cylinders and produce more horsepower. Initially this is true, but when port and valve sizes are increased, power begins to fall off at lower speeds, then at higher speeds, and finally very large passages reduce power throughout the entire rpm range! At first, this may seem quite mysterious. If minimizing restriction was the key to improved airflow and power, this phenomenon would indeed be inexplicable. But as we've discovered throughout this book, the IC engine does not function by simply directing the flow of air and fuel as a hose pipe directs the flow of water. Powerful wave dynamics take control of how air, fuel, and exhaust gasses move within the inlet and exhaust passages. Because of these phenomena, there is an optimum size for the ports and valves for any specific application, from street economy to all-out drag racing.

Consider what happens after the intake valve opens and the piston begins moving down the bore on the intake stroke. As pressure drops, air/fuel mixture enters

the cylinder. During this portion of the induction cycle, any restriction to inlet flow reduces cylinder filling and power output. So, while the piston moves from TDC to BDC, the rule of thumb for the ports and valves is "the bigger the better." After the piston reaches BDC and begins to travel back up the bore on the early part of the compression stroke, the intake valve remains open and the cylinder continues to fill with air/fuel mixture. This "supercharging" effect, caused by the momentum built up in the moving column of air and fuel in the ports and inlet runners, adds considerable charge to the cylinder and boosts engine output. However, as soon as the piston begins to move up the bore from BDC, it <u>tries</u> to push charge back out of the cylinder. Larger ports and valves not only offer low restriction to incoming charge, but they make it easier for the piston to reverse the flow and push charge back out of the cylinder. Furthermore, a low restriction induction system has a large cross-sectional area and allows the incoming charge to move more slowly (in feet per second), so the charge carries less momentum and, once again, is more easily forced back out of the cylinder. So the rule of thumb to optimize power for the period of time between BDC and intake-valve closing is "smaller ports that produce high airflow speeds are better." Since it's not possible to rapidly change the size of the ports as the engine is running, a compromise must be found that minimizes restriction and optimizes charge momentum.

As it turns out, optimum port and valve sizes for performance applications at a specific engine speed must

When the piston moves from TDC to BDC on the intake stroke, "the bigger the better" is the rule for ports and valves. After the piston reaches BDC and begins to travel back up the bore, it <u>tries</u> to push charge back out of the cylinder. Now the rule of thumb to optimize power is "smaller ports and high airflow speeds are better." A compromise must be found that minimizes restriction and optimizes charge momentum. This race engine finds that critical balance with large runners that generate 700-ft/sec peak port velocity at very high engine speeds.

be small enough to allow the charge to reach speeds of about 700 feet per second during the intake stroke. Then, as the piston moves from BDC to the intake valve closing point, the momentum generated by these speeds continues to force air and fuel into the cylinder, optimizing charge density. Typically, the best port size and cam timing for performance allows a slight "reversion" of fresh charge just before the intake valve closes.

Unfortunately, the smaller port cross-sectional areas required to generate optimum flow velocities create a restriction to airflow and increase pumping work. If port cross-sectional areas were smaller and flow velocities increased much beyond 700 feet/second, the added restriction and increased pumping work would reduce overall cylinder filling and engine output would suffer. The "magic" balance found at about 700 feet per second between charge momentum, inlet restriction, and pumping work allows the cylinders to fill with the greatest mass of air/fuel mixture throughout the complete induction cycle from IVO (intake valve opening) to IVC (intake valve closing).

What is the best cross-sectional area for any specific engine; the area that generates about 700 feet/second peak flow velocities? That is a very tough question to answer. In fact, optimum port shapes and cross-sectional areas are so interrelated with other engine variables, like engine displacement and rpm, cam timing, exhaust system configuration, intake manifold design, compression ratio, and more, that engine simulation software is needed to sort through the complexity and find the "magic" combinations. Furthermore, a full wave-action modeling program, like *Dynomation* discussed in the next chapter, is required for this task since it's the dynamics of finite-amplitude wave motion that are responsible for the recorded changes in horsepower.

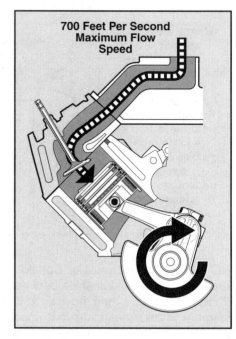

The best cross-sectional area for any specific engine, one that generates about 700 feet/second peak flow velocity, is difficult to find. Optimum port shapes and cross-sectional areas are so interrelated with engine displacement and rpm, cam timing, exhaust system configuration, intake manifold design, compression ratio, and more, that engine simulation software is needed to sort through the complexity and find the "magic" combinations.

Despite these complexities, there are some "rules of thumb" that can be helpful in selecting a workable port for common applications. If the area of minimum cross section in the ports is equal to 0.9 times the areas of the valves for race application and 0.85 times the valve areas for street use, the heads will probably provide good performance. This rule applies to typical automotive engines, not to high-rpm motorcycles or low-rpm aircraft. However, for typical powerbands between 5000 and 8500rpm, this rule should be reasonably close, providing the valve diameters are not too small or too large for the application.

These same relationships between port cross-sectional areas and valve diameters are used in Motion Software's Filling And Emptying simulation. As you move down the Cylinderhead menu, choices within each section—say within the smallblock or big block categories—the minimum port cross-section increases from 0.85 to 0.9 times the selected valve areas. However, since the current simulation does not incorporate as robust a wave-action analysis as the Dynomation program, port cross-sectional areas are not tunable by the user.

The phenomenon of cylinder filling by charge momentum is often called **ram tuning**, and is commonly thought to be an independent property of induction tuning, separate from the complex theory of wave dynamics that most professional racers only vaguely recognize. Because the concept of ram tuning is easy to grasp, it has been widely "applied" for many years. Long injector stacks, extremely large ports and valves, and other measures have been used to facilitate the free flow of additional charge into the cylinder after BDC on the intake stroke. But now that we have uncovered the fine balance needed between port cross-sectional area, charge momentum, airflow velocity, pumping work, cam timing, and

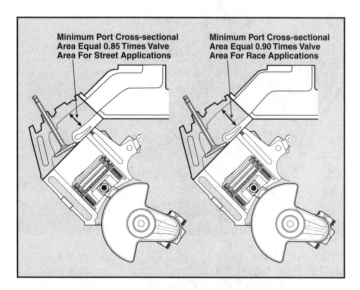

Minimum Port Cross-sectional Area Equal 0.85 Times Valve Area For Street Applications

Minimum Port Cross-sectional Area Equal 0.90 Times Valve Area For Race Applications

Despite the interrelatedness of engine speed, cam timing, exhaust system configuration, and more, there are some "rules of thumb" in selecting a workable port for common applications. Cylinder heads will probably provide good performance if the area of minimum port cross-section is equal to 0.9 times the valve area for race applications and 0.85 for street use.

engine speed, it is more obvious that large ports and valves, by themselves, are not the answer. Unfortunately, the insatiable desire to have large ports and valves seems to drive the cylinderhead market. Most customers simply want larger ports and valves. So head manufacturers and porters turn out droves of heads with ports that are too large for the application. While they reduce restriction during the intake stroke, low charge momentum during the majority of the rpm range of the engine reduces overall cylinder filling and power output.

One important thing to learn from this book should be to permanently discard the notion that "bigger is better" when it comes to ports and valves. The right combination is the key.

Sorting Out Cylinderhead Menu Choices

Now that we have covered some of the basic theory behind the choices in the Cylinderhead menus, here's some practical advice that may help you determine the appropriate selections for your application.

Low Performance Cylinder Heads—There are three "Low Performance" cylinder head selections listed at the top of the Head/Port Design submenu. Each of these choices is intended to model cylinder heads that have unusually small ports and valves relative to engine displacement. Heads of this type were often designed for low-speed, economy applications, with little concern for high-speed performance. Early 260 and 289 smallblock Ford and to a lessor degree the early smallblock Chevy castings fall into this category. These choices use the

lowest discharge coefficient of all the head configurations listed in the menu. Minimum port cross-sectional areas are 85% of the valve areas or somewhat smaller and, if Auto Calculate Valve Size has been selected (more on this feature in the next section) relatively small (compared to the bore diameter) intake and exhaust valve diameters will be used.

The first low-performance choice models an unmodified production casting. The second choice "Low Performance/Pocket Porting" adds minor porting work performed below the valve seat and in the "bowl" area under the valve head. The port runners are not modified. The final choice "Low Performance/Ported, Large Valves" incorporates the same modifications and includes slightly larger intake and exhaust valves. Valve size increases vary, but they are always scaled to a size that will generally install in production castings without extensive modifications.

The low-performance choices have some ability to model flathead (L-head & H-head) and hybrid (F-head) engines. While the ports in these engines are considerably more restrictive than early Ford smallblock engines, by choosing Low-Performance and manually entering the exact valve sizes, the simulation will, at least, give you an approximate power output that you can use to evaluate changes in cam timing, induction flow, and other variables. Remember it's not essential that your model produce an absolutely accurate horsepower number. A great deal of useful information can be found by simply looking at the *changes in power* that result from various combinations of parts.

Smallblock Cylinder Heads—The smallblock and

The phenomenon of cylinder filling by charge momentum is often called ram tuning, and optimizing this effect means finding a balance between port cross-sectional area, airflow velocity, pumping work, cam timing, and engine speed. This custom manifold was designed—with the help of simulations, including Dynomation—to find that illusive balance on smallblock Fords.

The "Low Performance" cylinder head choices are intended to model cylinder heads that have unusually small ports and valves. Heads of this type were often designed for low-speed, economy applications, with little concern for high-speed performance. Early 260 and 289 smallblock Ford and to a lessor degree the early smallblock Chevy castings fall into this category.

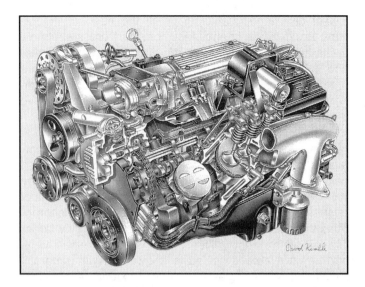

The "Smallblock Cylinder Head" choices model cylinder heads that have ports and valves sized with performance in mind, like these heads on this LT1, 350 smallblock Chevy. The stock selections are not excessively restrictive for high-speed operation, and overall port and valve-pocket design offers a good compromise between low restriction and high flow velocity. The remaining choices in this menu extend to all-out racing configurations.

The "Big-Block Cylinder Head" selections are modeled around heads with canted valve designs. All ports have generous cross-sectional areas for excellent high-speed performance. The first three menu choices model oval-port designs. The final two selections simulate modified rectangular-port heads. The appropriate selection for the L29 big-block Chevy would probably be the second or third menu choice—even though the L29 uses rectangular-ports, the fourth menu choice models an aggressive head with flow capacity beyond the stock L29.

big-block choices comprise the two main cylinderhead categories in the Head/Port Design submenu. Choices from these two groups apply to over 90% of all performance engine applications from mild street use to all-out competition.

The basic smallblock selections model heads that have ports and valves sized with performance in mind. Ports are not excessively restrictive for high-speed operation, and overall port and valve-pocket design offers a good compromise between low restriction and high flow velocity. The stock and pocket-ported choices are suitable for high-performance street to modest racing applications.

The next step is "SmallBlock/Fully Ported, Large Valves" and this cylinder head moves away from street applications. This casting has improved discharge coefficients, greater port cross-sectional areas, and increased valve sizes. Consider this head to be an extensively modified, high-performance, factory-type casting. It does not incorporate "exotic" modifications, like raised and/or welded ports that require custom-fabricated manifolds. "SmallBlock/Fully Ported, Large Valves" heads are high-performance castings that have additional modifications to provide optimum flow for racing applications.

The last choice in the smallblock group is "SmallBlock/ Race Porting And Mods." This selection is designed to model state-of-the-art, high-dollar, Pro-Stock type cylinder heads. These custom pieces are designed for one thing: Maximum power. They require hand-fabricated intake manifolds, have excellent valve discharge coefficients, and the ports have the largest cross-sectional areas in the smallblock group. This head develops sufficient airflow speeds for good cylinder filling only at high

engine rpm.

Big Block Cylinder Heads—All big-block selections are modeled around heads with "canted" valves. That is, the valve stems are tilted toward the ports to improve the discharge coefficient and overall airflow. All ports have generous cross-sectional areas for excellent high-speed performance.

The first three choices are based on an oval-port design. These smaller cross-sectional area ports provide a good compromise between low restriction and high flow velocity for larger displacement engines. The stock and pocket-ported selections are suitable for high-performance street to modest racing applications.

The final two selections simulate extensively modified rectangular-port heads. These choices are principally all-out, big-block Chevy heads, however, they closely model other extremely aggressive high-performance racing designs, like the Chrysler Hemi head. As with the smallblock category, the "Big Block/Fully Ported, Large Valves" heads are not suitable for most street applications. These castings have high discharge coefficients, large port cross-sectional areas, and increased valve sizes. This head is basically a factory-type casting but extensively improved. However, it does not incorporate "exotic" modifications, like raised and/or welded ports that require custom-fabricated manifolds.

The last choice in the big-block group is "Big Block/ Race Porting And Mods." This selection is designed to model state-of-the-art, high-dollar, Pro-Stock cylinder heads. These custom pieces, like their smallblock counterparts, are designed for maximum power. They require

The "4-Valve Cylinder Head" menu selections model cylinder heads with 4-valves per cylinder. These heads can offer more than 1.5 times the curtain area of the largest 2-valve heads. This large valve area, combined with high-flow, low-restriction ports greatly improves air and fuel flow into the cylinders at high engine speeds. These Cosworth heads were designed for the English Ford V6. When they were raced in England several years ago, they regularly beat Chevy V8s.

hand-fabricated intake manifolds, have optimum valve discharge coefficients, and the ports have the largest cross-sectional areas in the entire Head/Port Design submenu, except for 4-valve heads (discussed next). These specially fabricated cylinder heads only develop sufficient airflow for good cylinder filling with large displacement engines at very high engine speeds.

4-Valve Cylinder Heads—The last three selections in the Head/Port Design submenu model 4-valve cylinder heads. These are very interesting choices since they simulate the effects of very low-restriction ports and valves in stock and performance applications. The individual ports in 4-valve heads begin as single, large openings, then neck down to two Siamesed ports, each having a small (relatively) valve at the combustion chamber interface. Since there are two intake and two exhaust valves per cylinder, valve curtain area is considerably larger than with the largest single-valve-per-port designs. In fact, 4-valve heads can offer more than 1.5 times the curtain area of the largest 2-valve heads. This large area, combined with high-flow, low-restriction ports greatly improves air and fuel flow into the cylinders at high engine speeds. Unfortunately, the ports offer an equally low restriction to reverse flow (reversion) that occurs at low engine speeds when the piston moves up the cylinder from BDC to Intake Valve Closing (IVC) on the final portion of the intake stroke. For this reason, 4-valve heads, even when fitted with more conservative ports and valves, can be a poor choice for small-displacement, low-speed engines. On the other hand, the outstanding flow characteristics

of the 4-valve head put it in another "league" when it comes to high horsepower potential on large engines at high engine speeds.

The first choice in the 4-valve group is "4-Valve Head/Stock Ports And Valves." This simulates a 4-valve cylinder head that would be "standard equipment" on a factory high-performance or sports-car engine. These "mild" heads offer power comparable to high-performance 2-valve castings equipped with large valves and pocket porting. However, because they still have relatively small ports, reasonably high port velocities, and good low-lift flow characteristics, they often show a boost in low-speed power over comparable 2-valve heads.

The next choice, "4-Valve Head/Ported With Large Valves" represents a mild rework of "stock type" 4-valve heads. Larger valves have been installed and both the intake and exhaust flow has been improved by pocket porting. However, care has been taken not to increase the minimum cross-sectional area of the ports. These changes provide a significant increase in power with only slightly slower port velocities. Reversion has increased, but overall, these heads should show a power increase throughout the rpm range on medium to large displacement engines.

The final choice, "4-Valve Head/Race Porting And Mods," like the other "Race Porting And Mod" choices in the Head/Port Design submenu, models an all-out racing cylinder head. This selection has the greatest power potential of all. The ports are considerably larger than the other choices, the valves are larger, and the discharge coefficients are the highest possible. These heads suffer from the greatest reversion effects, especially at lower engine speeds on small displacement engines. (These heads, like all head choices, are "scaled" to engine size, so that smaller engines automatically use appropriately smaller valves—providing the Auto Calculate Valve Size option is selected—and smaller ports.) If you would like to know what "hidden" power is possible using any particular engine combination, try this cylinder head choice. It is safe to say that the only way to find more power, with everything else being equal, would be to add a supercharger, nitrous-oxide injection, or use exotic fuels.

When To Choose Smallblock Or Big-Block Cylinder Heads

Making appropriate Head/Port Design choices may be easier now that you are aware of some of the less-obvious issues. However, there are additional aspects of menu selections that should be emphasized to avoid confusion when modeling specific cylinder heads. Perhaps the most "confusing" issue surrounds the selection of heads from the smallblock group for engines that are commonly recognized as big blocks.

Many big-block engines use cylinder heads that are simply "scaled-up" smallblock designs. The valve and port sizes on these heads may be 10 to 20% larger than their smallblock counterparts, but that's about the only difference. The ports remain a tall, rectangular shape,

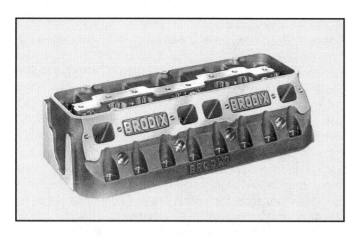

This smallblock Chevy head from Brodix incorporates canted valves and a spread-port intake design, meeting the criterion for a "big-block" for simulation purposes. The second or third menu choices (oval-port) are probably the best models for these heads.

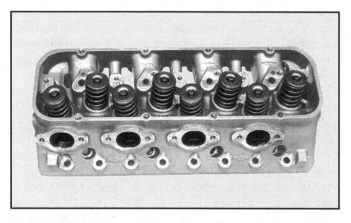

This is another example of a smallblock Chevy with canted valves and spread-port intakes. Developed for the limited IMSA GTP racing program in the early '90s, these Chevrolet splayed-valve heads should be correctly modeled by the fourth big-block menu choice.

The last two choices in the big-block menu will also model Chrysler's 426-Hemi cylinder head. The last menu choice will simulate all-out ProStock configurations.

valve stem angles relative to the port centerline are identical or nearly identical, and combustion chamber shapes are often the same. When proportionally larger heads are installed on engines of proportionally larger displacement, overall flow efficiency remains very similar. So for engines like the big-block Chrysler wedge, Olds, Pontiac and several Ford big blocks, plus many other engines, a selection from the smallblock group, combined with entering (or having the program calculate) larger valve diameters, will closely simulate the power levels of these "big-block" engines.

Some big blocks have cylinder heads of substantially different design. These "true" big block heads are built for higher performance levels and have visibly different ports, valves, and/or combustion chambers. Big-block Chevy heads fall into this category with two common configurations. The first is a milder, "street," oval-port version and the second uses larger rectangular-ports. The larger head is, without question, a high-performance, high-rpm design, even on large-displacement engines. Both of these heads "cant" the valve stems toward the centerline of the port. This shifted valve position improves the discharge coefficient and allows for slightly larger valves.

This same design philosophy is used in Chrysler's Hemi heads. An all-out racing design, the Hemi "cants" the valves even further and uses combustion chambers shaped in a true hemisphere. The ports have large cross-sectional areas with high discharge coefficients. These heads, like all big-block heads with the most "aggressive" designs, come up short on low-speed performance because of poor cylinder filling and high reversion, but produce exceptional horsepower at high engine speeds on large displacement engines.

Finally, there are engines that have smallblock displacements but use cylinder heads that look like they came straight off of a big block. Many 4- and 6-cylinder "sports-car" engines fall into this category, using single- or double-overhead cams, canted valves, and even "hemi" combustion chambers. More rarely, smallblock Chevys even turn up with big-block heads. Chevrolet's maximum performance "splayed-valve" heads for the smallblock Chevy IMSA racing program were released in the early nineties. These cylinder heads are simply a "mini" big-block design, and modeling of this head should be done using the big-block choices in the Head/Port Design submenu.

Valve Diameters And The "Auto Calculate" Feature

The **Valve Diameters** submenu is located in the lower half of the CylinderHead menu. The first selection is "Auto Calculate Valve Size." This powerful feature instructs the simulation software to determine the most likely valve sizes to be used with the current engine based on an assessment of the bore diameter and the Head/Port Design selection. The Auto-Calculate function is active by when selected and by default when the simulation program is started or whenever "Clear Current Component Selections" is chosen from the **Utility** menu. Auto Calculate is especially helpful if you are experimenting with a several different bore and stroke combinations or comparing different engine configurations. Auto Calculate will always select valves of appropriate size for the cylinder heads under test and it will never use valve sizes that are too large for the current bore diameter. If you are using version 2.5 or greater of Motion Software's simulation (version 2.5.7 was under development when this book was published), the program will display the calculated valve diameters in the Component Selection Box along with "(Auto)," indicating that the valve sizes were automatically determined. Earlier versions simply displayed "(Auto)"; calculated sizes were not shown.

While the Auto-Calculate feature is helpful during fast back-to-back testing, it may not "guess" the precise valve sizes used, and therefore, not simulate power levels as accurately as possible. In these situations refer to the second part of the Valve Diameters menu. Here you will find a list of exact valve sizes consisting of common intake and exhaust combinations, or you can choose "Other..." from the bottom of the menu and directly enter any valve diameters within the acceptable range of the program (approximately 0.800- to 2.75-inches). When exact valve sizes are selected by either of these methods, the diameters are displayed in the Component Selection Box along with "(Man)," indicating that the sizes

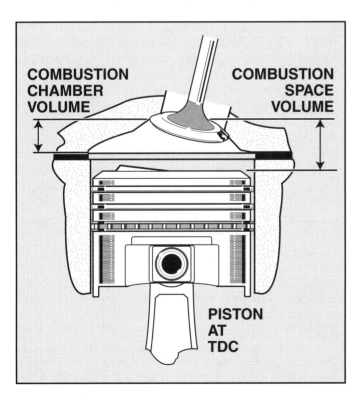

While combustion-chamber volume is simply the volume in the cylinder head, the combustion-space volume is the total enclosed volume when the piston is located at TDC. This space includes the volume in the combustion chamber, plus any volume added by the piston not rising to the top of the bore, less any volume due to the piston or piston dome protruding above the top of the bore.

were manually entered. When "(Man)" is active, the program disables auto-calculation of valve diameters and will not automatically change the displayed values, regardless of the cylinder heads or cylinder bore diameters chosen for the test engine. You can change valve diameters at any time by simply choosing different sizes from the menu or by selecting "Other..." again. You can also re-enable the Auto Calculate feature at any time by re-selecting it from the Valve Diameter submenu.

THE COMPRESSION RATIO MENU

C/Ratio is the third pull-down menu located in the main menu bar. A selection from this menu establishes the compression ratio for the simulated engine from 8:1 to 16:1 (version 2.5.7—under development when this book was published—supports a compression ratio range of 6:1 to 18:1 using the "Other" selection). The compression ratio is a comparison of the geometric volume that exists in the cylinder when the piston is located at BDC (bottom dead center) to the "compressed" volume when the piston reaches TDC (top dead center). As you recall, compression ratio is calculated with the following formula:

$$\frac{\text{Swept Cyl Vol} + \text{Combustion Space Vol}}{\text{Combustion Space Vol}} = \text{CR}$$

Let's take a close look at this relationship to discover exactly what compression ratio is and how compression ratio works inside the IC engine.

Compression Ratio Basics

The above compression-ratio equation contains two variables: 1) swept cylinder volume, and 2) combustion space volume. These volumes are the only two variables

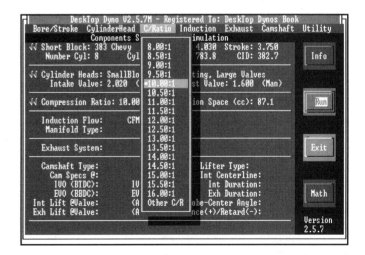

The *C/Ratio* is the third pull-down menu located in the main menu bar. This menu establishes the compression ratio for the simulated engine. The compression ratio is a comparison of the geometric volume that exists in the cylinder when the piston is located at BDC (bottom dead center) to the "compressed" volume when the piston reaches TDC (top dead center). Changing compression ratio has a pronounced effect on engine power.

that affect compression ratio. However, each of these variables is made up of multiple elements, so the first step in exploring compression ratio must be to "dissect" these variables.

Swept cylinder volume is the most straightforward of the two. As you discovered in the previous **Bore/Stroke** section of this chapter, swept volume is calculated by Motion's Filling And Emptying simulation—and displayed in the Component Selection Box—as soon as the bore and stroke have been selected for the test engine. Swept volume is simply the three-dimensional space displaced by the piston as it "sweeps" from BDC to TDC, and is determined solely by the bore diameter and stroke length.

The other variable in the compression-ratio equation is combustion-space volume. This is the <u>total volume</u> that exists in the cylinder when the piston is located at TDC. This space includes the volume in the combustion chamber, plus any volume added by the piston not rising fully to the top of the bore, less any volume due to the piston protruding above the top of the bore. The complexity involved in combustion-space volume can be a stumbling block for some enthusiasts. You may find it helpful to refer to the accompanying drawings for illustrations of these concepts.

A good way to visualize these variables is to imagine yourself a "little man" wandering around inside the engine. Let's take a walk inside the combustion space. Picture what it would look like in the cylinder with the piston at TDC. You would see the combustion chamber above you like a ceiling. Your floor would be the top of the piston. If the piston (at TDC) didn't rise completely to the top of the cylinder, around the edges of the floor you would see a bit of the cylinderwall, with the head gasket sandwiched between the head and block, like a low molding around the room. There may be notches in the top of the piston just under your feet (don't trip!). If the piston had a dome, it might look like a small retaining wall rising from the floor, to perhaps knee high. The combustion space would be larger if the piston was positioned lower down the bore or if the notches under your feet were deeper, and it would be smaller if the retaining wall (dome) volume was larger. This entire space is "home" for the compressed charge when the piston reaches TDC. This is the volume that makes up the denominator of the compression-ratio calculation. Now let's continue our "ride" in the cylinder, but this time picture what it looks like when the piston is positioned at BDC. The very same volumes that we just described (chamber, dome, notches, gasket, etc.) are still there, but are now located well above our head. It looks like the room has been stretched, like the elevator ride in the Haunted House at Disneyland. This "stretched" volume is what is described in the numerator of the equation. It's simply the original combustion volume plus the volume added by the "sweep" of the piston as it traveled from TDC to BDC. The ratio between these two volumes is the compression ratio.

Changing Compression Ratio

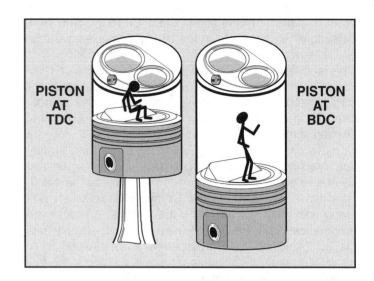

Picture yourself as a "little man" inside the cylinder. You would see the combustion chamber above you like a ceiling. Your floor would be the top of the piston. If the piston (at TDC) didn't rise completely to the top of the cylinder, around the edges of the floor you would see a bit of the cylinderwall, with the head gasket sandwiched between the head and block, like a low molding around the room. With the piston at BDC, the very same volumes are still there, but now the swept-volume of the cylinder has been added. The ratio between these two volumes is the compression ratio.

A quick look at the compression-ratio equation reveals that if engine displacement (swept volume) is increased, either by increasing the bore or stroke, the compression ratio will rise. In fact, with everything else being equal, a longer stroke will increase compression ratio much more effectively than increasing bore diameter. This is due to the fact that a longer stroke not only increases displacement, but it tends to <u>decrease</u> combustion space volume since the piston moves higher the bore (in our "little man" example, raising the floor closer to the ceiling). This "double positive" effect results in rapid increases in compression ratio for small increases in stroke length. On the other hand, increasing cylinder bore diameter also increases compression ratio but much less effectively. This is caused by the <u>increase</u> in combustion volume that accompanies a larger bore (again, using our "little man," a larger bore adds more floor space by increasing the diameter of the room), partially offsetting the compression-ratio increase that occurs from increasing cylinder displacement.

Changing combustion space, the other element in the equation, will also alter the compression ratio. Anything that reduces the combustion volume, while maintaining or increasing the swept volume of the cylinder, will increase the compression ratio. Some of the more common methods are decreasing the volume of the combustion chambers (by replacing or milling the heads), using thinner head gaskets, changing the location of the piston-pin or rod length to move the piston closer to the combustion chamber, installing pistons with larger domes, and others. All of these modifications will increase compression ratio. And that increases horsepower, right? Well, surprisingly, the answer to that question is often "Yes!". But do you know why?

Why Higher Compression Ratios Produce More Horsepower

Most automotive enthusiasts believe that a higher compression ratio directly raises horsepower output. Before you read the next few paragraphs, see if you can explain to yourself why compressing the charge before combustion is necessary. Or is it necessary? If it is, what causes a boost in power? Does it burn the fuel more completely or efficiently? What about the power that's needed to compress the charge? Is it simply "lost" energy?

The answers to these questions lie in the laws of thermodynamics. Luckily, we don't have too delve to deeply into this complex subject to gain an insight into how compression before ignition works. Let's take a simplified look at what happens inside the engine when the compression ratio is increased. Picture a spherical combustion space containing twice as much volume as the cylinder that's attached to it. This configuration produces an engine with a very low 1.5:1 compression ratio. Just

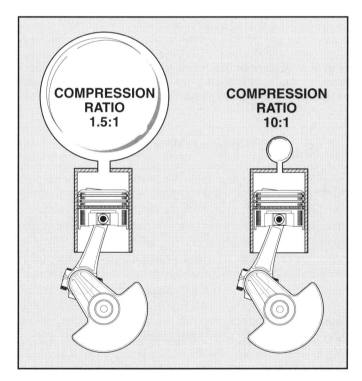

A spherical combustion space containing twice as much volume as the cylinder produces a 1.5:1 compression ratio. Peak cylinder pressures (see text) will be about 250psi. With a combustion space about 1/10th of the volume of the cylinder, the compression ratio is now 10:1. Peak pressures now reach about 1500psi. The higher compression ratio produced much higher cylinder pressures throughout the first half of the piston's travel from TDC and BDC on the power stroke. This additional pressure generates a much larger force across the surface of the piston, and that increases torque and horsepower.

before the intake valve closes, the piston is positioned at BDC, and the cylinder and the spherical volume are exposed to atmospheric pressure of about 14psi. As the piston moves up the bore, the valve closes and the charge is compressed. When the piston reaches TDC the pressure in the cylinder will rise to about 21psi. At this point the spark plug fires and drives the post-combustion pressure to about 250psi and the piston is pushed back down the bore. About 12 to 14 degrees after TDC, the cylinder pressure driving the piston down the bore will be about 230psi.

Now picture the same engine, except this time the spherical combustion space has been reduced in size to about 1/10th of the volume of the cylinder. The compression ratio is now 10:1. As the intake valve closes at BDC, the cylinder and the volume are once again at atmospheric pressure. When the piston reaches TDC on the compression stroke, the small volume has driven the compression pressure to about 400psi, or 18 times as high (the new volume is about 18 times smaller). When the piston reaches 12 to 14 degrees after TDC, the pressure on the piston is about 1500psi. The higher compression ratio produces much higher cylinder pressures throughout the first half of the piston's travel from TDC and BDC on the power stroke. This additional pressure generates a much larger force across the surface of the piston and that increases torque and horsepower.

While it may now be clear that higher post-ignition pressures result in increases in torque output, you may still be wondering how much power is *consumed* to compress the charge to higher initial pressures. This is more easily understood if you picture what happens when the spark plug doesn't fire. It certainly takes power to drive the piston up the bore to compress the charge, but without ignition nearly identical pressures drive the piston back down the bore on the "power" stroke. The net result (forgetting about friction, mechanical, and heat losses) is zero. In other words, under ideal circumstances it take no more net power to compress a charge to a lazy 21psi with a 1.5:1 compression ratio than it does to raise it to 400psi with 10:1 compression because the consumed work is returned on the power stroke. In a real engine, higher compression ratios increase losses from charge heating and, especially, from increased ring-to-cylinder-wall friction. But the power lost is usually smaller than the power gained. Testing done by GM many years ago indicated that, for gasoline as the fuel, power will continue to increase until compression ratios reach about 17:1. Considering that many racing engines are now hovering around this level, GM may have been right.

Other Effects Of Increasing Compression Ratio

As mentioned above, the greatest losses from high compression and high cylinder pressures (except when detonation is induced) occur from ring/cylinderwall friction and heat losses into the pistons and water jackets. Beyond these well-known effects, changing the compression ratio has other subtle consequences, some of which are largely unexplored.

Let's examine a potential source of "hidden" power. The combustion space volume above the piston tends to act as an absorber, slightly smoothing the pressure pulses in the cylinder. This effect can dampen the peaks of the negative pressure waves created when the piston moves down the bore on the intake stroke. When the compression ratio is increased, the combustion space decreases. With less volume to absorb pressure pulses, the pressure drop on the intake stroke may be more "directly linked" to the induction system, improving cylinder filling. You can visualize this effect by picturing a small cylinder attached to a large room (the room exaggerates the effects of the large combustion space used in low compression ratio applications). As the piston moves down the bore, any drop in pressure is dissipated in the room, so that the carburetor—attached at the adjacent wall— receives an extremely weak signal and virtually no air/fuel mixture flows into the room or cylinder. Now reduce the size of the room to a small space, more like the real-world conditions in a high-compression engine. As the piston moves down the bore, the drop in pressure is almost directly "linked" to the induction system, instantly drawing air and fuel into the cylinder. These same positive effects, though not as pronounced, should occur anytime the compression ratio is increased by decreasing the combustion space.

Compression Ratio Assumptions

Changes in compression ratio have hundreds of consequences throughout the engine. However, Motion's Filling And Emptying simulation program analyzes only some of these changes. Changes that occur because of alterations in the wave dynamics within the engine are not well predicted by the current program. Thermodynamic effects, however, are very accurately modeled in the simulation. In order to understand the variations in power and torque curves produced as the compression ratio is changed, it is helpful to understand a few "internal" program assumptions.

The simulation program assumes that ignition timing is always optimum. That is, based on the gasoline burn model used by the simulation, ignition occurs at a point that produces peak cylinder pressures between 12 to 14 degrees after top dead center. Tests have indicated that these same conditions reproduced in the real world often optimize power output.

The limitations of the combustion model prevent changing the ignition point. The simulation of varying ignition timing or performing sophisticated combustion analysis to reveal preignition, detonation, or provide emissions analysis requires advanced techniques. While these models do exist, they not only need full three-dimensional maps of the constantly-varying combustion space, but they consume, literally, days of computational time. Obviously, this is not practical approach for a quick-response "what-if" program.

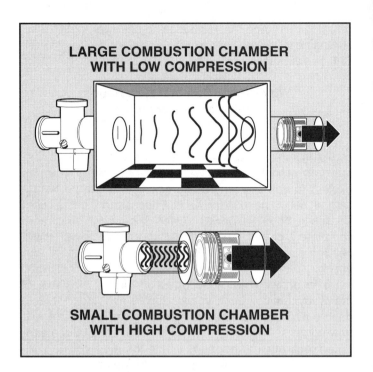

Here's a source of "hidden" power. A large combustion space that accompanies a low compression ratio (illustrated here by the large box attached to the carburetor) tends to act as an absorber, smoothing the pressure pulses in the cylinder. This can dampen the peaks of the negative pressure waves created when the piston moves down the bore on the intake stroke. When the compression ratio is increased, the combustion space decreases. With less volume to absorb pressure pulses, the pressure drop on the intake stroke can be more "directly linked" to the induction system, improving cylinder filling.

THE INDUCTION MENU

The fourth main component menu establishes an **Induction** system for the simulated test engine. An induction system, as defined in Motion's simulation, is everything upstream of the intake ports, including the intake manifold, common plenums (if used), carburetor/throttle main body, venturis (if used), and opening to the atmosphere. The Induction menu is divided into two submenus: an Airflow menu to select the maximum-rated airflow that can pass through the induction system, and the Manifold submenu to establish an intake-manifold configuration. One choice from each of these two groups fixes a specific induction system from among thousands of possible combinations.

Airflow Selection

The first Induction submenu is used to select the rated airflow for the induction system. This menu consists of two 2-barrel carburetor selections, twelve 4-barrel carburetor/fuel injection choices, and an "Other..." selection in which you can directly specify the rated airflow from 100 to 3000cfm. The first two selections "install" either a 300- or 500-cfm 2-bbl carburetor on the test engine. These are the only 2-barrel choices directly available in the menu. The remaining choices range from 300 to 1100cfm on 4- or 8-barrel carburetor and fuel injection applications.

In order to perform "apple-to-apple" comparisons among the Airflow selections, it is important to realize that the ratings for 2-barrel carburetors are measured at a pressure drop twice as high as the pressure used to rate 4-barrel carburetors and fuel-injection systems. Rated airflow for 2-barrels is typically measured at a pressure drop of 3 inches of mercury (the pressure differential maintained across the carburetor during airflow measurement at wide-open throttle). This is often written as "3-in/Hg" ("Hg" is the symbol for mercury used in the periodic table of elements). The higher pressure drop increases the measurement resolution for smaller carburetors and "shifts" the flow numbers toward the range commonly found in automotive applications (roughly, 100 to 700cfm).

Knowing the differences in rating methods, it is a simple task to convert any 2-bbl flow into it's 4-bbl equivalent. Here's the formula:

$$\text{4-bbl Flow} = \frac{\text{2-bbl Flow}}{1.414}$$

Using this conversion, it is possible to simulate virtually any 2-barrel carburetor induction system. For example, a custom 2-barrel that flows 650cfm at 3-in/Hg, would flow 460cfm if measured at 1.5-in/Hg (you can confirm this using the above formula). By manually entering 460cfm into the Component Selection Box of the simulation, the program will accurately model this custom 2-barrel.

The remaining choices in the Induction Airflow menu are labeled with "4/8-BBL Carb Or Fuel Inj." This means that the selections below the first two designate airflow ratings that were measured at 1.5-in/Hg. The "4/8-BBL" indicates that the induction system can consist of single or multiple carburetors that, combined, produce the rated airflow. For example, the menu choice "1000 CFM 4/8-

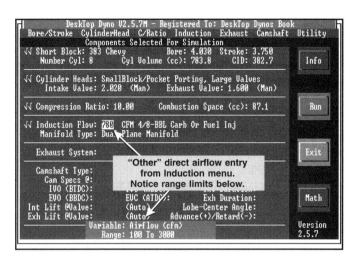

Choosing "Other" from the Induction Airflow menu allows direct entry of any airflow rating for the simulated induction system, providing it falls within the acceptable range limits. Airflow values entered using this technique are assumed to be rated at a pressure drop of 1.5-in/Hg, the standard of measurement for 4-barrel carburetors.

BBL Carb Or Fuel Inj" can indicate one 1000cfm 4-bbl carburetor or two 500cfm 4-bbls. The same 1000cfm selection could even indicate three 470cfm 2-bbls (i.e., 3 x 470 = 1410cfm; converting to 4-bbl flow: 1410/1.414 = 997cfm). The important thing to remember about airflow selection is that the program *makes no assumption about the type of restriction* that makes up the carburetor or injection system. The airflow is simply a rating of the total restriction of the induction system.

Motion's Filling-And-Emptying model uses this restriction value to calculate a critically important variable needed by the simulation to accurately determine mass flow into the cylinders: manifold vacuum. Here's how the process works:

1) The simulation runs through an entire cycle (all four Otto cycles) to initially determine the total mass flow into the cylinders. This determination—because it is based on a degree-by-degree, crank-angle analysis—takes the entire range of engine variables into consideration, including displacement, engine speed, valve size, cam timing, compression, and assumptions about the intake manifold, exhaust system, and more.

2) Since there can never be mass accumulation or loss within the engine, the same mass that flows into the cylinders must also flow through the induction (and exhaust) system.

3) Since atmospheric pressure exists on one side of the carburetor or throttle body, using the selected induction restriction (chosen from the airflow submenu), the program can calculate the vacuum generated in the manifold that will produce the predicted flow rate.

4) When the manifold vacuum has been determined, the charge density can be calculated. Knowing the charge density is the final step used by the program to "iterate," or home-in on, a precision determination of the air/fuel mass entering the cylinder.

Throughout these simulation steps, the carburetor

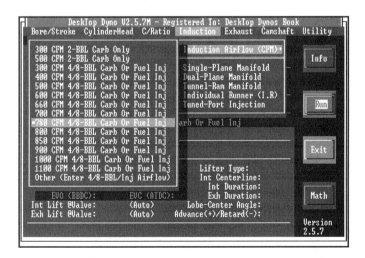

The first Induction submenu is used to select the rated *Airflow* for the induction system. This menu consists of 2-barrel and 4/8-barrel carburetor/fuel injection choices, and an "Other..." selection by which you can directly specify the rated airflow from 100 to 3000cfm.

creates a restriction that produces a vacuum in the manifold. Larger carburetors produce less restriction and decrease vacuum. As vacuum drops and manifold pressure approaches atmospheric levels, the density of the charge becomes greater. When the density of the air/fuel charge increases, a greater mass of air and fuel can be drawn into the cylinders, resulting in higher power output. Seemingly, the conclusion here is that the greater the flow capacity of the carburetor, the more power the engine can produce. While this may hearken back to the old cliché "the bigger the better," in theory, at least as it applies to the induction system, this trend is absolutely correct. The carburetor can be thought of as a density-regulating device, and any restriction generated by the carburetor (or injection system) increases manifold vacuum, decreasing charge density and power.

In the real world, however, carburetors must generate a pressure drop across the venturis in order to atomize fuel and air in the proper proportions. In fact, most carburetors must generate at least 0.5-in/Hg pressure drop at the lowest airflow levels to function properly (e.g., during part throttle transition to full throttle at low engine speeds). This same requirement does not exist for modern fuel-injection systems. Many high-performance electronic and mechanical injection systems maintain precise air/fuel mixtures throughout the rpm range while generating negligible restriction and manifold vacuum at full throttle. While there are practical limitations to "the bigger is better" rule, in theory, low restriction and high charge density clearly produce more power.

Airflow Menu Assumptions

As higher airflow levels are selected from the Induction menu, the simulation lowers the restriction within the induction system. This decrease in restriction increases charge density. Along with this concept, the simulation assumes that *the air/fuel ratio is always at the precise proportion for optimum power*. While optimum air/fuel ratios are more achievable with fuel injection systems, a carefully tuned carburetor also can come remarkably close to ideal fuel metering. Regardless of whether the simulated engine uses carburetors or fuel injection, the power levels predicted by the program can be considered optimum, achievable when the engine is in "peak" tune and the induction system is working properly.

The airflow (in Cubic Feet per Minute, or CFM) selected from the Induction Airflow menu is also assumed to be the *total rated airflow into the engine*. On dual-inlet or multiple-carburetor systems, the total airflow is the sum of all rated airflow devices. So a manifold equipped with twin 1100cfm Holley Dominator carburetors would have a rated airflow of 2200cfm. If an air cleaner has been installed, total airflow must be adjusted to compensate for the increase in restriction (contact the element manufacturer or flow test the carburetor/air-cleaner as an assembly).

Also keep in mind the unique way airflow capacities are handled on Individual Runner (I.R.) manifolds. On

Larger carburetors produce less restriction and decrease manifold vacuum. Seemingly, the greater the flow capacity, the more power the engine will produce. In theory this trend is correct. The carburetor can be thought of as a density-regulating device, and any restriction generated by the carburetor increases manifold vacuum and decreases charge density and power. In the real world, carburetors must generate a pressure drop of about 0.5-in/Hg to function properly.

these induction systems, each cylinder is connected to a single "barrel" or injector stack with no connecting passages that allow the cylinders to "share" barrels. The total rated flow for these induction systems is divided among the number of cylinders. For example, a small-block V8 equipped with 4 Weber carburetors (having 8 barrels) may have a total rated flow of 2000cfm. To properly model this system, 2000cfm is directly entered into the simulation by choosing "Other..." from the Airflow menu. When an "I.R." manifold is selected from the second part of the Induction menu (more on manifolds next) the airflow is divided into all 8 cylinders, allotting 250cfm to each cylinder. For more information on modeling Weber carburetors or "injector stack" induction systems, refer to *Manifold Selection Advice* on page 66.

Induction Manifold Basics

The lower half of the Induction menu consists of five manifold choices. Each of these manifolds applies a unique tuning model to the induction system, but before we cover the particulars of each selection, it is helpful to review induction tuning and how wave-dynamic models are used to reveal manifold function. For a more in-depth look at induction tuning and wave dynamics, refer to Chapter 6 on the *Dynomation* program.

As we have discussed many times in this book, the flow of air and fuel within engine passages is influenced by waves generated by rapidly changing pressures within the induction and exhaust systems. These pressure "pulses" arise from the release of high pressure exhaust

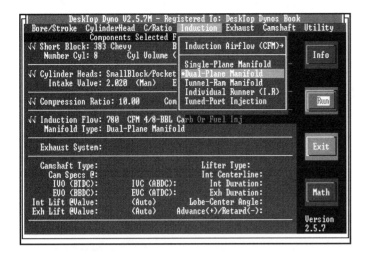

DeskTop Dyno V2.5.7M - Registered To: DeskTop Dynos Book
Bore/Stroke CylinderHead C/Ratio Induction Exhaust Camshaft Utility
                    Components Selected F
√√ Short Block: 383 Chevy   B   Induction Airflow (CFM)→
    Number Cyl: 8   Cyl Volume (
                                              Single-Plane Manifold   Info
√√ Cylinder Heads: SmallBlock/Pocket   •Dual-Plane Manifold
    Intake Valve: 2.020 (Man)   E   Tunnel-Ram Manifold
                                              Individual Runner (I.R)
√√ Compression Ratio: 10.00   Com   Tuned-Port Injection   Run

√√ Induction Flow: 780 CFM 4/8-BBL Carb Or Fuel Inj
    Manifold Type: Dual-Plane Manifold
                                                                          Exit
    Exhaust System:

    Camshaft Type: Lifter Type:
    Cam Specs @:   Int Centerline: Math
    IVO (BTDC):   IVC (ABDC):   Int Duration:
    EVO (BBDC):   EVC (ATDC):   Exh Duration:
Int Lift @Valve: (Auto)   Lobe-Center Angle:
Exh Lift @Valve: (Auto)   Advance(+)/Retard(-):
                                                                       Version
                                                                       2.5.7

The lower half of the Induction menu consists of five *Manifold* choices. Each of these manifolds applies a unique tuning model to the induction system. Refer to the text for information on the design of each manifold, an overview of how the manifold boosts power or torque, and finally, a description of the assumptions and recommendations associated with that individual design.

gasses into the ports and headers during the exhaust cycle and by the "pumping action" of the piston during the intake cycle. These pressure waves are thousands of times stronger than waves we are familiar with in everyday life: common acoustic or sound waves. At these high energy levels, IC engine pressure waves, now referred to as *finite-amplitude waves*, alter their shape as they travel through passages, and they interact with each other in ways considerably more complex than simple acoustic waves. The combination of these phenomena make the "solutions" to finite-amplitude wave analysis

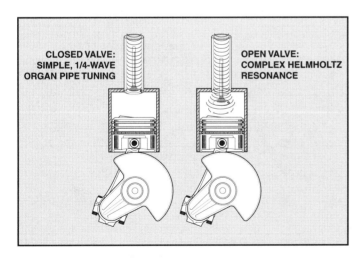

CLOSED VALVE: SIMPLE, 1/4-WAVE ORGAN PIPE TUNING

OPEN VALVE: COMPLEX HELMHOLTZ RESONANCE

When the intake valve is closed, the port/runner system forces pressure waves through a basic oscillation cycle called *1/4-wave* or *organ-pipe tuning*. This delivers a series of decaying-amplitude pressure pulses to the closed intake valve. When the intake valve is open, the system switches from organ-pipe tuning to a much more complex Helmholtz resonator with <u>changing volume</u> as the piston moves in the cylinder and <u>varying restriction</u> as the valve moves through its lift curve.

extremely difficult.

This complexity is multiplied by the configuration of the ports, valves, manifold runners and plenum shapes. The levels of complexity continue to grow as the intake and exhaust valves open and close. Initially, with the intake valve closed, the port/runner system forces pressure waves through a basic oscillation cycle, bouncing back and forth off of the closed valve at one end of the runner and the open manifold plenum at the other. This "reasonably simple" process, called *1/4-wave* or *organ-pipe tuning*, delivers a series of decaying-amplitude pressure pulses to the closed intake valves. When the intake valves are open, however, the system switches from organ-pipe tuning to a much more complex Helmholtz resonator. This is the same resonance that you can duplicate by blowing into the neck of a jug, creating a deep "whirring" sound. Not only does pressure-wave analysis have to deal with this more complex resonance, but the Helmholtz resonator is <u>changing its volume</u> as the piston moves in the cylinder, and the <u>restriction at the "neck" is also varying</u>, as the valve moves through its lift curve. Combining all these factors with the already complex interaction of finite-amplitude waves gives a glimpse of the mathematical sophistication needed to analyze pressure waves inside the IC engine.

After all this, you may be wondering how much of an influence this morass of complex pressure waves has on engine performance. The answer is a lot! They can either aid or restrict cylinder filling depending on the design of inlet ducting. A carefully constructed Pro-Stock induction system will use these invisible pressure waves to gain hundreds of horsepower. Even street engines can use induction tuning to improve throttle response, fuel economy, and add considerable "seat-of-the-pants" power.

Induction-tuning power benefits come from several techniques, but the most direct is to harness the suction wave created during the intake stroke. Optimum runner lengths will return a reflection of this negative pressure wave to the intake valve on the next intake cycle—when the piston reaches maximum velocity on the intake stroke—at about 70 degrees after TDC. The returning suction wave combines with the low pressure created by the piston rapidly moving down the bore to produce a powerful draw of air and fuel into the cylinder. Then, again, just before the intake valve closes as the piston is beginning to move up the cylinder, the induction system returns a positive pressure pulse to minimize or prevent "reversion" or flow of charge back out of cylinder.

These tuning effects can be adjusted for specific applications by changing runner length, volume, passage interconnections, and plenum configuration. In other words, installing intake manifolds of different design can have dramatic effects on how the pressure waves are used to assist cylinder filling and control engine power. The following section details each of the manifold choices provided in the Induction menu and explains the assumptions and limitations associated with each of these designs.

Manifold Selection Advice
And Design Assumptions

The complex interaction of pressure waves within the induction system require a rigorous mathematical analysis, involving the Method Of Characteristics described in Chapter 6 and elsewhere in this book. This advanced technique uses considerable computational time and does not lend itself to simulations designed for a rapid "what-if" interaction with the user. Furthermore, extensive analysis of intake manifold configurations would require the input of many detailed variables, such as runner lengths, volumes, taper angles, plenum configuration and dimensions, and much more. These technical inputs would further shift the emphasis away from ease of use toward a dedicated research tool. However, in order to evaluate manifold differences, any program—including Motion's Filling-And-Emptying simulation—must incorporate some pressure-wave analysis to make accurate estimations of power and torque differences. Motion's program uses a "mini-wave action" model that offers three advantages for most users: 1) rapid calculation times allowing fast back-to-back testing, and 2) the mini-model does not require dimensional data entry for the ports and runners, making component selection extremely simple, and 3) overall accuracy is quite good (within 10%) and trends in power differences between the five manifold types are reliable. For those individuals involved in engine development programs or intake manifold research, the mini-model will not provide sufficient data resolution to make subtle design changes (refer to Chapter 6 on the Dynomation program—it is used to perform this type design analysis). However, for nearly everyone else, the mini-model should provide a good compromise between speed, ease of use, and predictive accuracy.

The five manifolds included in Motion's simulation are, by no means, a comprehensive list of all the intake manifolds available for IC engines. The list of five should, instead, be interpreted as five discrete designs that approach the limits of resolution of the mini-model within the program. If you are interested in a manifold with a design that falls in between two menu selections, you can often use the "trend" method to estimate power for a hybrid design. For example, run a test simulation using manifold Type A, then study the differences in power attributed to manifold Type B. The changes will indicate trends that should give you insight into how a hybrid manifold Type A/B *might* perform. Because a rigorous analysis of pressure waves is not performed by the current program, always keep in mind that the data you obtain might not match real-world dyno data with some cylinderhead, camshaft, exhaust-header, and intake-manifold combinations. In general, however, the trends and overall accuracy obtained with any of the menu selections should be within 10%.

For each manifold described below, you will find information about its basic design, an overview of how the manifold boosts power or torque, and finally, a description of the assumptions and recommendations associated with that individual design.

Dual-Plane Manifold—Remarkably, the well-known and apparently straightforward design of the dual-plane manifold is, arguably, the most complex manifold on the list. An intake manifold is considered to have a dual-plane configuration when 1) the intake runners can be divided into two groups, so that 2) each group alternately receives induction pulses and 3) the pulses are spaced at even intervals. If all of these criteria are met, the manifold is said to have a 2nd degree of freedom, allowing it to reach a unique resonance causing the entire manifold and all the runners oscillate in unison. During this period, pressure readings taken throughout the manifold will be in "sync" with one another. This powerful resonance multiplies the force of the pressures waves, simulating the effects of long runners. Since longer runners typically tune at lower engine speeds, not surprisingly, the dual-plane manifold is most known for its ability to boost low-end power.

The divided plenum is another common feature of dual-plane manifolds that further boosts low-end power. Since each side of the plenum is connected to only one-half of the cylinders (4-cylinders in a V8), each cylinder in the engine is "exposed" to only half of the carburetor. This maximizes wave strength and improves low-speed fuel metering (these effects are much less pronounced with throttle-body fuel-injection systems). However, the divided plenum can become a significant restriction at higher engine speeds and limit peak horsepower.

The main benefits of the dual-plane are its low-speed torque boosting capability, compact design, and wide

The Edelbrock Performer Q-Jet represents the current state-of-the-art in dual-plane manifold designs. This manifold is said to have a 2nd degree of freedom. During this period, pressure readings taken throughout the manifold will be in "sync" with one another. This powerful resonance multiplies the force of the pressures waves, simulating the effects of long runners. Since longer runners usually tune at lower engine speeds, not surprisingly, the dual-plane is most known for its ability to boost low- and mid-range power.

The basic difference between single- and dual-plane manifolds are clearly illustrated here. The dual-plane (left) divides the plenum in half, with the runners grouped alternately by firing order. Each cylinder "sees" only one-half of the carburetor, transferring a strong signal to the venturis. This manifold design is said to have a 2nd degree of freedom, allowing it to reach a unique resonance that make its short runners boost low-speed power. The single-plane manifold (right) has short, nearly equal-length runners with an open plenum, much like a tunnel ram but "laid" flat across the top of the engine. The manifold has excellent high-speed performance, but a loss of 2nd degree of freedom prevents full-manifold resonance. That reduces low-speed torque and can degrade driveability and fuel economy.

availability for use with both carburetors and injection systems. However, not all engines are capable of utilizing a dual plane. Typically, engines that do not have an even firing order or have too many cylinders to generate a resonance effect will not benefit from a dual-plane manifold. While there are some exceptions, engines having 2 or 4 cylinders work best with this manifold. Since most V8 engines are basically two 4-cylinder engines on a

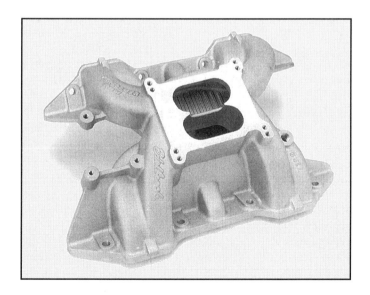

Many dual-plane manifolds are hybrids incorporating facets of other manifolds. This Edelbrock dual-plane manifold is designed for the 440 Chyrsler engine and has a partially open plenum. In this case, the opening adds mid-range and high-speed performance with little sacrifice in low-speed driveability. Not all hybrid designs are as successful as this one. In situations where you are not familiar with engine or manifold characteristics, it may be worthwhile to stick with "plane-vanilla" designs.

common crankshaft, even-firing V8s also benefit from the resonance effects of the dual-plane manifold. Motion's simulation does not prevent choosing a dual-plane manifold on engines that will not develop a full resonance effect. For example, you <u>can</u> install a dual-plane manifold on a 5-cylinder engine, but the results—a low-end power boost—are not reproducible in the real world, since an effective dual-plane manifold cannot be built for this engine. The simulation is best utilized by modeling dual-plane manifolds combinations that <u>already exist</u> rather than testing theoretical fabrications.

Many dual-plane manifolds are hybrids incorporating facets of other manifold designs. Especially common is the use of an undivided or open plenum typically associated with single-plane manifolds. These hodgepodge designs are attempts at harnessing the best features while eliminating the worst drawbacks of various designs. Sometimes, the combinations are successful, adding more performance without much of a sacrifice in low-speed driveability. With these designs, you can successfully use the "trend" method described earlier to estimate engine torque and power. However, there is no shortage of manifolds that can reduce power without giving anything back in driveability or fuel economy. In fact, some of the worst designs are remarkably bad. It is impossible to determine which of these combo designs is better than others using the Filling And Emptying simulation. Only a simulation that model intake passages, including the complex effects of multicylinder interference, can perform this analysis. Unless you can perform actual dyno testing on these manifolds to find what works and what doesn't, it may be worthwhile to stick with more "plain-vanilla" designs that produce predictable results. (Note: A version of the *Dynomation* program will be released in the future that will perform manifold modeling on multicylinder engines; more on this in the next chapter.)

Single-Plane Manifold—In a very real sense, a single-plane manifold as used on most V8 engines is simply a low-profile tunnel ram. The tunnel-ram manifold (discussed next) is a short-runner system combined with a large common plenum; a design that optimizes power on all-out racing engines where hood clearance is not an issue. The single-plane manifold combines short, nearly equal-length runners with an open plenum, but "lays" the entire configuration flat across the top of the engine. The results are quite predictable. A loss of 2nd degree of freedom prevents full-manifold resonance. That produces a loss of low-speed torque, and depending on the size of the plenum and runners, single-plane manifolds can also degrade driveability and fuel economy. Furthermore, a large-volume, undivided plenum contributes to low-speed problems by presenting every cylinder to all barrels of the carburetor, lowering venturi signal and low-speed fuel metering accuracy (again, this drawback is minimized with a fuel-injection system). On the other hand, the single-plane manifold (like the tunnel ram) combines improved flow capacity, potentially higher charge density, and short runner lengths to build substantially more horse-

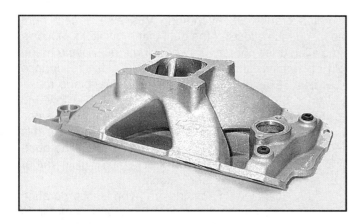

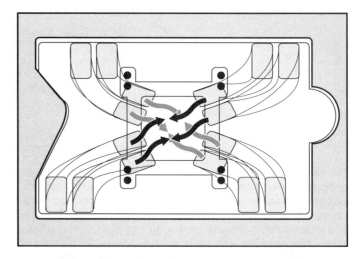

A single-plane manifold is simply a low-profile tunnel ram. The design combines short, nearly equal-length runners with an open plenum, but "lays" the entire configuration flat across the top of the engine. A loss of 2nd degree of freedom prevents full-manifold resonance and reduces low-speed torque. However, the single-plane manifold combines improved flow capacity, higher charge density, and short runner lengths to build substantial horsepower at higher engine speeds.

The typically compact, low-profile design of the single-plane manifold has drawbacks. The runners are connected to a common plenum like spokes to the hub of a wheel. This arrangement tends to create unpredictable interference effects as pressure pulses moving through the runners meet in the plenum and stir up a complex soup, sometimes creating irregular fuel-distribution.

power at higher engine speeds.

As a high-performance, high-speed manifold, the single-plane design has many advantages, but it's compact, low-profile design has drawbacks too. The runners are connected to a common plenum like spokes to the hub of a wheel. This arrangement tends to create unpredictable interference effects as pressure pulses moving through the runners meet in the plenum and stir up a complex soup. Large plenum volumes help cancel some these effects, but open-plenum, single-plane manifolds may produce unexpected changes in fuel distribution and pressure-wave tuning with specific camshafts, headers, or cylinder heads (to some degree, these effects are present in all manifold designs). Predicting these will-o'-the-wisp anomalies requires rigorous modeling, well beyond the capabilities of the Filling-And-Emptying simulation. Currently, pinning down these problems requires dyno testing with exhaust temperature probes to measure fuel distribution accuracy.

Designers and engine testers have experimented with hybrid single-plane manifold designs that incorporate various dual-plane features. One common modification is to divide the plenum into a pseudo dual-plane configuration. While this does increase signal strength at the carburetor, uneven firing does not allow 2nd degree of freedom resonance. This modification can cause sporadic resonances to occur throughout the rpm range with unpredictable results. Spacers between the carburetor and plenum are also commonly used with single-plane manifolds often with positive results, particularly in racing applications. Spacers probably increase power for two reasons: 1) By increasing plenum volume they tend to reduce unwanted pressure-wave interactions, and 2) A larger plenum improves airflow by reducing the angle the air/fuel must negotiate as it transitions from "down" flow from the carburetor to "side" flow into the ports. While

there is no way to use trend testing to evaluate the effects of a divided plenum, spacers can be partially simulated. The increase in plenum volume tends to mutate the single-plane manifold into a "mini" tunnel ram, so horsepower gains tend to mimic those obtained by switching to a tunnel ram design (i.e., small performance improvements, when found, usually occur at high rpm).

Since the single-plane manifold typically reduces low-speed torque and improves high-speed horsepower, it is often the best compact manifold design for applications where engine speed is typically 4000rpm or higher. If the engine commonly runs through lower speeds, a dual-plane, individual runner, or tuned-port injection system will usually provide better performance, driveability, and fuel economy.

Tunnel-Ram Manifold—This intake manifold is a single-plane induction system designed to produce optimum power on all-out racing engines. The advantages of the tunnel ram come from its combination of a large common plenum and short, straight, large-volume runners. The large plenum has plenty of space to bolt on two carburetors, potentially flowing up to 3000+cfm to optimize charge density. The large plenum also minimizes pressure-wave interaction and fuel distribution issues. The short runners can be kept cooler than their lay-flat, single- and dual-plane counterparts, and they offer a straight path into the ports, optimizing ram-tuning effects.

Applications for the tunnel ram are quite limited because of its large size; vehicles using tunnel-ram manifolds often require a hole in the hood and/or a hood scoop for manifold and carburetor clearance. While a protruding induction system may be a "sexy" addition to a street rod, in single-carburetor configurations the tunnel ram offers very little potential power over a well-designed, single-plane manifold. Only at very high engine speeds, with multiple carburetors, will the advantages in the tunnel ram contribute substantially to power.

This tunnel-ram selection can also accurately model fuel-injection systems with large, individual stacks. Strictly speaking, while the simulation combines short runners and a large-volume plenum, this design mimics short injector stacks that open to the atmosphere quite well. For one-barrel-per-cylinder Weber carburetion or small-diameter, individual-injector systems, use the Individual Runner manifold described next. However, for large-diameter injectors, like Hillborn or Crower systems, the tunnel-ram manifold—along with the appropriate airflow selection (for all cylinders combined)—is a good induction model.

The tunnel ram manifold selection has the potential to produce the highest peak horsepower of all the manifolds listed in the Induction menu. The large cross-sectional areas, straight runners, and short tuned lengths make this manifold a "no compromise" racing design.

Individual Runner—A manifold that connects each cylinder to one "barrel" of single or multiple carburetors *with no interconnecting passages for shared flow* is considered an individual (or isolated) runner system (I.R. for short). A multiple Weber or Mikuni carburetor setup is a well-known example of this type of induction system.

On a V8 engine, four twin-barrel Webers make a very impressive sight, and at first glance they may appear to offer more airflow potential that any engine needs, particularly any street engine. While it may look like overkill, the one-barrel-per-cylinder arrangement often has substantial horsepower limitations due to <u>airflow restriction</u>! A typical Weber 48IDA carburetor flows about 330cfm per barrel. While the sum total of all eight barrels is over

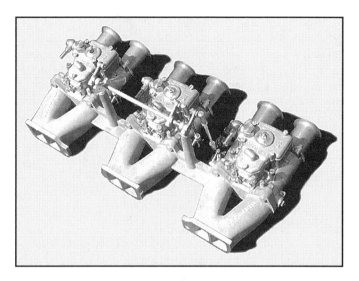

A manifold that connects each cylinder to a single carburetor barrel *with no interconnecting passages for shared flow* is considered an individual (or isolated) runner system (I.R. for short). Multiple Weber or Mikuni carburetor systems are well-known examples of this type of induction system. This I.R. manifold was designed for early OHC Pontiacs.

2600cfm (a flow rating equivalent to two Holley Dominators), the important difference here is that each cylinder can draw from only one 330cfm barrel. In a single- or even a dual-plane manifold, each cylinder has access to more than one carburetor barrel, reducing restriction during peak flow and increasing high-speed horsepower. While an I.R. system offers substantial low-end performance benefits (more on that next), at 5000rpm and higher on typical smallblock installations, power can fall below the levels of an average single four-barrel, 780cfm induction system.

This Weiand BB Chevy tunnel ram manifold is a single-plane induction system designed to produce optimum power on all-out racing engines. It has a large common plenum and short, straight, large-volume runners. The tunnel ram manifold menu selection has the potential to produce the highest peak horsepower of all the manifolds listed in the *Induction* menu.

A multiple-carburetor I.R. induction may seem to offer way too much flow capacity. Surprisingly, the one-barrel-per-cylinder transmits strong pressure waves to each carburetor barrel, producing excellent throttle response. Individual-runner manifolds are an outstanding induction choice for high-performance street engines.

Again, on first impression, a multiple-carburetor I.R. induction may seem to offer way too much flow capacity, making it easy to believe that it's plagued with low-speed carburetion problems. Surprisingly, the same one-barrel-per-cylinder arrangement that produces a restriction at high engine speeds, transmits strong pressure waves to each carburetor barrel at low speeds, producing ideal conditions for accurate fuel metering. Furthermore, the pressure waves moving in the runners are not dissipated within a plenum and don't interact with other cylinders. This ensures that the reflected waves strongly assist cylinder filling and reduce reversion. The combination of these effects makes individual-runner manifolds an outstanding induction choice for low-speed to medium/high-speed engine applications, such as high-performance street engines. Unfortunately, the high cost of these systems—and current smog regulations—prevents their wider acceptance.

The simulation model for the Individual Runner choice in the Induction menu assumes that the runner sizes and the carburetor venturi diameters are of "medium" dimensions. Runner length, that is, the distance from the valve head to the top of the carburetors, is also assumed to be "mid-length," and so the simulation uses a mid-range rpm power bias. These assumptions work well with most I.R. applications, since this induction system is commonly used on street engines or in road racing applications that require good throttle response and a wide power band.

The I.R. menu selection can also model fuel-injection systems with small-diameter, medium-to-long length individual stacks. For large-diameter, short-length injectors, like drag-racing Hillborn or Crower systems, the tunnel-ram manifold selection provides a better induction model (see the above tunnel-ram description).

Tuned-Port Injection—This manifold was introduced by automakers in the mid 1980's and millions of them remain on the road today. It represents the first mass-produced induction system that clearly incorporated modern wave-dynamic principals. To optimize low-speed torque and fuel efficiency, the TPI manifold has very long runners (many configurations measure up to 24-inches from valve head to airbox). The runners on most TPI systems are also quite small in diameter—again, to optimize low-speed power—and, unfortunately, create considerable restriction at higher engine speeds. Characteristic power curves from this type of manifold fall slightly to significantly above a dual-plane up to about 5000rpm, then runner restriction and an out-of-tune condition substantially lowers peak power.

The TPI is a single-plane design that functions like a long-runner tunnel ram. Each runner is completely isolated until it reaches the central plenum. This design tends to maximize pressure-wave tuning and minimize wave interactions. Since fuel is injected near the valve, the TPI system delivers precise air/fuel ratios with no fuel distribution or puddling problems.

There is a wide range of aftermarket parts available for the TPI, including enlarged and/or Siamesed runners,

The I.R. menu selection can also model fuel-injection systems with <u>small-diameter, long-length</u> individual stacks. For larger-diameter, shorter-length injectors, like Hillborn or Crower systems, the "tunnel-ram manifold" provides a better induction model.

improved manifold bases, high-flow throttle bodies, and sensor and electronic modifications. The Tuned-Port Injection selection in the Induction menu models a stock TPI. However, increasing the airflow (from the Induction Airflow menu) makes it possible to model some of the benefits of larger runners and high-flow throttle bodies.

There are now many "TPI-like" and EFI (electronic fuel injection) systems available for small- and big-block engines. Some of these custom packages are based on a short-runner tunnel ram model. Do not use the TPI manifold model to simulate these manifolds, instead, select a single-plane (for small-runner systems) or tunnel ram (for large-runner packages) to obtain more realistic

The TPI manifold was introduced by automakers in the mid 1980's and millions of them remain on the road today. It represents the first mass-produced induction system that clearly incorporated modern wave-dynamic principals.

Some custom high-performance TPI and EFI (electronic fuel injection) packages are based on short-runner, high-flow tunnel ram bases. Even some long-runner systems, like this manifold from Induction Technology, allow much greater airflow than the original factory TPI. Do not use the TPI manifold menu selection to model these manifolds, instead, select a dual-plane (for small-runner systems) or tunnel ram (for large-runner packages) to obtain more realistic power curves.

power curves. Only choose a TPI manifold when the induction system uses a typical long-runner TPI configuration.

THE EXHAUST MENU

The **Exhaust** menu, the fifth component menu in the main menu bar, establishes an exhaust manifold or header configuration for the simulated test engine. The

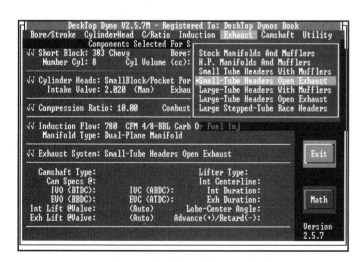

The Exhaust menu selection establishes an exhaust manifold or header configuration for the simulated test engine. The menu includes seven choices, four of which include mufflers. Since the program simulates an engine mounted on a dyno, the exhaust system for muffled engines ends at the outlet of the muffler.

menu includes seven selections, four of which include mufflers. Since the program is designed to simulate the power levels for an engine mounted on a dyno testing fixture, the exhaust system for muffled engines ends at the outlet of the muffler and does not include any additional tubing used to route exhaust gasses to the rear of a vehicle.

Each of these exhaust system selections apply a unique tuning model within the simulation. However, before we uncover the particulars of each choice, a short review of the wave dynamics acting within the exhaust system will help explain how "simple tubing" can boost power and engine efficiency. (Refer to Chapter 6 for a more rigorous look at the theory of exhaust-system tuning.)

Wave Dynamics In The Exhaust System

First of all, let's begin our discussion of exhaust wave-dynamic theory by recalling its antithesis: the "Kadenacy" hypothesis described in the previous chapter. It claimed that a high pressure "slug" of gas blasted out of the port and down the header pipe when the exhaust valve opened. This moving mass was said to create a low pressure behind it, drawing additional gasses from the cylinder. This theory is analogous to compression waves traveling through a Slinky™ coil-spring toy (refer to illustration on page 37); a tight group of coils representing high pressure waves moves along the spring followed by a more open group of coils that represent low-pressure waves. Despite the fact that this theory was conclusively proven to be incorrect in 1940, it is still believed by some engine "experts" to this day!

Earlier in this chapter we described the high-pressure waves that move inside the induction system. These *finite-amplitude waves* contain so much energy that they no longer obey the simple laws of acoustic theory. Instead they follow an entirely different set of rules that describe interactions and wave transitions that do not occur with low-power sound waves. Induction system energies are just high enough to create finite-amplitude waves. However, exhaust system pressures are much higher and generate finite-amplitude waves even at lower engine speeds.

The same laws that describe the movement of finite-amplitude waves and gas particles in the induction system apply to exhaust flow. Without exploring the "depths" of finite-amplitude theory, the following principles should be considered essential knowledge to understanding wave action in IC engine passages, particularly the exhaust system: 1) Pressure waves and gas particles do not necessarily move at the same speeds. This phenomenon is visible as the waves on the surface of a lake wash through floating logs, pushing them nearer the shore. The waves move fairly quickly and the logs (an analogy for the gas particles) move more much slowly. 2) When a positive pressure wave reaches an area of transition, such as the end of an open pipe, a negative suction wave is created

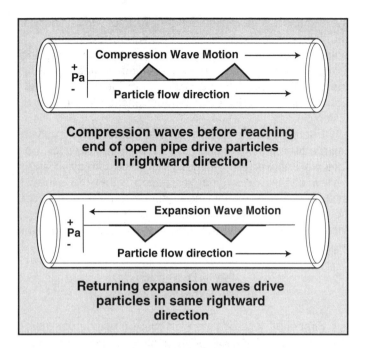

Compression waves before reaching end of open pipe drive particles in rightward direction

Returning expansion waves drive particles in same rightward direction

In order to understand how pressure waves move within the exhaust system, these are the two most important things to remember: 1) When a positive pressure wave reaches the end of an open pipe, a negative suction wave is created that moves back up the pipe and vice versa, and 2) positive pressure waves move gas particles in the same direction as the waves, and negative pressure waves move gas particles in the opposite direction of the waves.

that moves back up the pipe. 3) Positive pressure waves move gas particles in the same direction as the waves; negative pressure waves move gas particles in the opposite direction of the waves.

Now let's apply this tuning theory to the exhaust system. When the exhaust valve opens, a high pressure blast (in other words, a finite-pressure wave) moves down the port and into the exhaust header pipe. This high intensity pressure wave drives gas particles in the same direction as wave motion and therefore assists the outflow of exhaust gasses. When the pressure wave reaches the end of the header pipe that's open to the atmosphere, a negative pressure wave of almost the same intensity is created and begins to travel back up the pipe toward the cylinder. Negative pressure waves move gas particles in the opposite direction as the wave, so this returning wave also assists exhaust gas outflow. When the negative pressure wave (or suction wave) reaches the cylinder, it delivers a substantial drop in pressure. If this wave arrives during the valve overlap period (when both the exhaust and intake valves are open) the pressure drop will help draw in fresh charge, a phenomenon called scavenging. The overall effects substantially boost power by 1) assisting exhaust gas outflow, 2) beginning air/fuel charge flow into the cylinder, and 3) helping to purge the cylinder of residual exhaust gasses.

Many factors contribute to optimizing these tuning effects. Two of the most important are header tubing size and length. Tubing size is really a measure of system volume and, on open headers at least, determines

the restriction of internal passages. Large, free-flowing tubes produce lower pressures. Lower positive wave pressures generate lower amplitude suction waves, reducing scavenging and cylinder filling. On the other hand, smaller diameter tubing creates higher pressures that, while generating strong scavenging waves, increase restriction and pumping work. As is the case with every component category in the IC engine, the best power is produced by finding a balance between two or more counterbalancing factors. Here an optimum balance lies between the excellent scavenging effects of small tube headers vs. the reduction in restriction and pumping work produced by large tubes. The balance tilts one way or the other depending on cam timing, engine displacement, rpm, and several other factors!

Tubing length affects when the negative suction wave arrives at the cylinder. Longer tubes delay the arrival of the scavenging wave, appropriate for lower-speed applications when more time elapses between the opening of the exhaust valve and the overlap period. Shorter tubes return a scavenging wave more quickly and "tune" at higher rpm. Once again, several counterbalancing factors must be included in the analysis. The first is cam timing. As engine speed increases, there is less time for exhaust gasses to "blowdown" from the cylinder after the exhaust valve opens. The higher residual cylinder pressures increase pumping work on the exhaust stroke. To counteract this, earlier EVO timing will assist blowdown, but it also tends to "waste" cylinder pressures that would otherwise drive the piston and generate power. At higher engine speeds, the net results show benefits from a shift

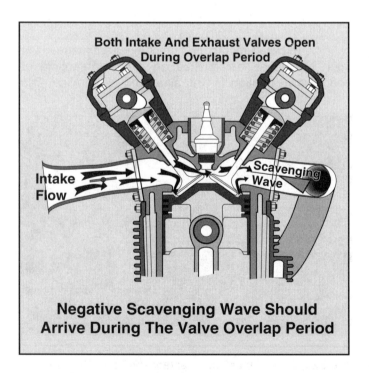

Negative Scavenging Wave Should Arrive During The Valve Overlap Period

Exhaust tubing **length** affects **when** the negative suction wave arrives at the cylinder. Longer tubes delay the arrival of the scavenging wave, appropriate for lower-speed applications. Shorter tubes return a scavenging wave more quickly and "tune" at higher rpm.

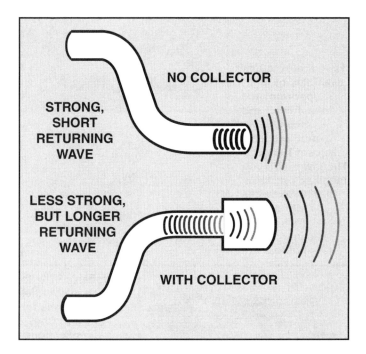

When primary header tubes terminate directly into the atmosphere, they generate a strong but narrow suction wave. The returning wave is "peaky" and only assists cylinder filling through a very narrow rpm range. Primary tubes terminating in a larger "collector" produce a wider suction wave, broadening the effective tuning range.

toward earlier EVO timing. To adjust for this, exhaust tubing length must be increased to maintain the same scavenging wave arrival time. So again, another pair of counterbalancing factors are at work: Higher engine speeds require shorter tubing lengths, but higher speeds also require earlier EVO timing and that needs longer header tubes to maintain optimum scavenging. Peak engine power at any particular rpm is produced by a balance between these factors.

There are still more factors that affect optimum header lengths. If the primary header tubes terminate directly into the atmosphere, they generate a strong but narrow suction wave. The returning wave is so "peaky" that it only assists cylinder filling through a very narrow rpm range. To broaden the suction wave and extend the effective tuning range of the exhaust system, most headers group the primary tubes together in a larger "collector" before they open to the atmosphere. The collector produces a transition to a larger volume before the final transition to the atmosphere. This splits up or extends the width of the returning suction wave, broadening the effective rpm range during which the header system can deliver an effective scavenging wave. The <u>diameter</u> of the collector dictates which end of the suction wave has "emphasis." Larger collectors mimic a more direct opening to the atmosphere, so they emphasize the initial portion of returning suction wave. Smaller collectors provide less of a transition from the individual primary tubes and tend to emphasize the trailing edge of the suction wave. The length of the collector changes the time between the leading and trailing edges of the suction wave and can

also affect the optimum primary tube length.

Most header systems are designed so that the lengths of the primary tubes are nearly equal. This, too, leads to another balancing act between the higher number of bends needed to obtain equal-length primary tubes vs. the use of low-restriction straight tubes. While increased restriction almost always hurts performance, unequal primary lengths can broaden the power range and provide more usable power in racing situations. As a result, the most effective header designs use as few bends as possible to minimize restriction and relinquish equal primary lengths to a role of lesser importance.

Exhaust Menu Selections

Now that we have peeked into the wave dynamics at work inside the exhaust system, we can turn our attention to how these effects are simulated by the various choices in the Exhaust component menu. As you have discovered, the exhaust system—perhaps more than any other single part of the IC engine—is a virtual "playground" for finite-amplitude waves. You are also well aware that these interactions can be solved only by sophisticated, computationally-intensive methods (as described in Chapter 6), that are not part of the Motion Filling And Emptying program. While flow restriction (back pressure) is accurately modeled using "pressure-drop" techniques, the effects of changes in tubing lengths and diameters that influence the flow of exhaust and induction gasses are closely tied to high-pressure wave dynamics. However, the program does use a powerful "mini-wave model" that *accurately simulates scavenging effects for three classes of headers with optimum tubing lengths and diameters.* So while the program does not resolve specific header dimensions, the model can predict engine power changes from various exhaust manifolds and headers of large and small tubing diameters (relative to the engine under test).

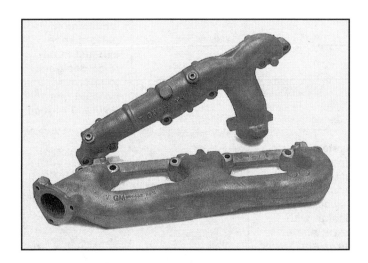

The *Stock Manifolds And Mufflers* selection assumes that the exhaust manifolds are a typical, production, cast-iron "log-type" design, where all ports connect at nearly right angles to a common "log" passage.

Stock Manifolds And Mufflers—The first choice in the Exhaust menu simulates the most restrictive exhaust system. It assumes that the exhaust manifolds are a typical, production, cast-iron, "log-type" design, where all ports connect at nearly right angles to a common "log" passage. These manifolds are designed more to provide clearance for various chassis and engine components than to optimize exhaust flow. Exhaust manifolds of this type have widespread application on low-performance production engines.

The *Stock Manifolds And Mufflers* selection assumes that the exhaust manifolds are connected to twin mufflers with short sections of pipe. Because the engine environment is a simulated dyno cell, the exhaust system terminates at the muffler outlets.

The exhaust manifolds and mufflers cancel all scavenging effects, and the system is a completely "non-tuned" design. Any suction waves that might be generated are fully damped or never reach the cylinders during valve overlap. The restriction created by this system mimics most factory muffler and/or catalytic converter with muffler combinations. Back pressure levels in the exhaust system nearly cancel the blowdown effects of early EVO timing and increase the pumping work losses during the exhaust cycle.

H.P. Manifolds And Mufflers—This choice offers a measurable improvement over the stock exhaust system modeled in the previous selection. The high-performance exhaust manifolds simulated here are designed to improve exhaust gas flow and reduce system restriction. They are usually a "ram-horn" or other "sweeping" design with fewer sharp turns and larger internal passages. The connecting pipes to the mufflers are large diameter and the mufflers generate less back pressure and, typi-

The *H.P. Manifolds And Mufflers* choice simulates high-performance exhaust manifolds designed to improve exhaust gas flow and reduce

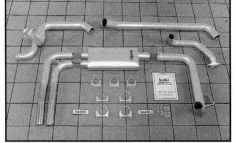

system restriction. They are usually a "ram-horn" or other "sweeping" design with fewer sharp turns and larger internal passages. The connecting pipes to the mufflers are large diameter and the mufflers generate less back pressure, like this PowerPack system from Banks Engineering.

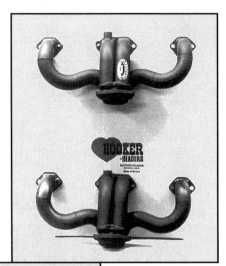

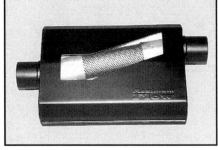

Here are excellent examples of high-performance "manifolds" and free-flowing mufflers from Hooker Headers. The low-restriction manifolds fit 1992-1995 Corvettes with an LT1 engine. The Maximum-Flow mufflers are available in 2- to 3-inch inlet/outlet configurations for Ford and Chevy applications. Model these components using the *H.P. Manifolds And Mufflers* menu choice.

cally, produce more noise.

While this system is a "high-performance" design, it offers no tuning effects and all suction waves are fully damped or never reach the cylinders during valve overlap. All performance benefits from this selection are due to a decrease in passage restrictions and lower system back pressure. System pressure levels mimic factory high-performance mufflers and/or catalytic-converter with muffler combinations. This exhaust system may allow some benefits from early-EVO timing blowdown effects (depending on the engine component combination) and overall pumping work losses are slightly reduced by lower back pressures.

IMPORTANT NOTE FOR ALL HEADER CHOICES: Some engines, in particular, 4- or 2-cylinder applications, can develop a "full resonance" in the exhaust system—refer to the previous discussion of dual-plane manifolds for information about "full" induction system resonance. This phenomenon can derive scavenging benefits (although some studies have revealed that the benefits are relatively small) from suction waves created in the collector by adjacent cylinders. These "one-cylinder-scavenges-another" tuning techniques are not modeled in the simulation. Instead, the headers are assumed to deliver a scavenging wave only to the cylinder that generated the initial pressure wave.

Small Tube Headers With Mufflers—This is the first component selection that begins to harness the tuning potential of wave dynamics in the exhaust system. These simulated headers have primary tubes that individually connect each exhaust port to a common collector. The

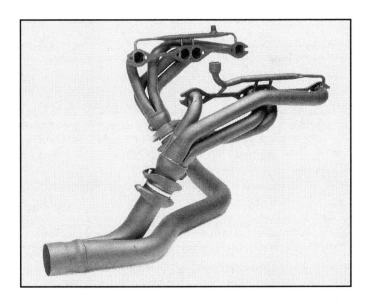

While not a "true" header, this tubular exhaust system from Edelbrock for late model cars and trucks is CARB certified and offers some controlled wave dynamics for improved scavenging. The Filling-And-Emptying simulation will model these headers more accurately with mufflers than without.

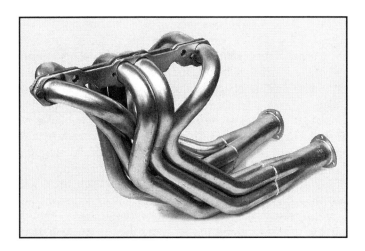

Typical small-tube headers are usually designed with high-performance street applications in mind. The better pieces have 2-1/2-inch collectors and 1-1/2- or 1-5/8-inch primary tubes. They are made from heavy-gauge tubing that will withstand years of use, and do not necessarily have equal-length tubes.

collector—or collectors, depending on the number of cylinders—terminates into a high-performance muffler(s). Suction waves are created in the collector, but are somewhat damped by the attached muffler. Since exact tubing lengths are not simulated, the program assumes that the primary tube will deliver the scavenging wave to the cylinder during the valve overlap period.

The primary tubes modeled by this menu selection are considered "small," and should be interpreted to fall within a range of dimensions that are commonly associated with applications requiring optimum power levels at or below peak-torque engine speeds. These headers typically show benefits on smaller displacement engines (such as "smallblocks"), but may produce less than optimum power on large displacement engines. The following rules of thumb should give a reasonable approximation of tubing diameters used by the simulation: Headers with tubes that measure 95% to 105% of the exhaust-valve diameter are considered "small" for any particular engine; tubes that measure 120% to 140% of the exhaust-valve diameter are "large" tube headers.

Small-Tube Headers Open Exhaust—This menu selection simulates headers with "small" primary tubes individually connecting each exhaust port to a common collector. The collector—or collectors, depending on the number of cylinders—terminates into the atmosphere. Strong suction waves are created in the collector that provide a substantial boost to cylinder filling and exhaust gas outflow. Since exact tubing lengths are not simulated, the program assumes that the primary tube will deliver the scavenging wave to the cylinder during the valve overlap period.

The primary tubes modeled by this menu selection are considered "small," and should be interpreted to fall

within a range of dimensions that are commonly associated with applications requiring optimum power levels at or slightly above peak-torque engine speeds. These headers typically show benefits on smaller displacement engines but may produce less than optimum power on large-displacement "big-block" engines. The following rules of thumb should give a reasonable approximation of tubing diameters used by the simulation: Headers with tubes that measure 95% to 105% of the exhaust-valve diameter are considered "small" for any particular engine; tubes that measure 120% to 140% of the exhaust-valve diameter are "large" tube headers.

Large-Tube Headers With Mufflers—This menu selection simulates headers with "large" primary tubes individually connecting each exhaust port to a common collector. The collector—or collectors, depending on the number of cylinders—terminates into a high-performance muffler(s). Suction waves are created in the collector, but are somewhat damped by the attached muffler. Since exact tubing lengths are not simulated, the program assumes that the primary tube will deliver the scavenging wave to the cylinder during the valve overlap period.

The primary tubes modeled by this menu selection are considered "large," and should be interpreted to fall within a range of dimensions that are commonly associated with applications requiring optimum power at peak engine speeds. These headers typically show benefits on high-rpm racing smallblocks or large displacement big-block engines. These headers may produce less than optimum power on small-displacement engines operating in the lower rpm ranges. The following rules of thumb should give a reasonable approximation of tubing diameters used by the simulation: Headers with tubes that measure 95% to 105% of the exhaust-valve diameter are considered "small" for any particular engine; tubes that measure 120% to 140% of the exhaust-valve diameter are "large" tube headers.

Large-Tube Headers Open Exhaust—This menu selection simulates headers with "large" primary tubes individually connecting each exhaust port to a common collector. The collector—or collectors, depending on the number of cylinders—terminates into the atmosphere. Strong suction waves are created in the collector that provide a substantial boost to cylinder filling and exhaust gas outflow. Since exact tubing lengths are not simulated, the program assumes that the primary tube will deliver the scavenging wave to the cylinder during the valve overlap period.

The primary tubes modeled by this menu selection are considered "large," and should be interpreted to fall within a range of dimensions that are commonly associated with applications requiring optimum power at peak engine speeds. These headers typically show benefits on high-rpm racing smallblocks or large displacement big-block engines. These headers may produce less than optimum power on small-displacement engines, particularly those operating in the lower rpm ranges. The following rules of thumb should give a reasonable approximation of tubing diameters used by the simulation: Headers with tubes that measure 95% to 105% of the exhaust-valve diameter are considered "small" for any particular engine; tubes that measure 120% to 140% of the exhaust-valve diameter are "large" tube headers.

Large Stepped-Tube Race Headers—This menu selection simulates headers with "large" primary tubes individually connecting each exhaust port to a common col-

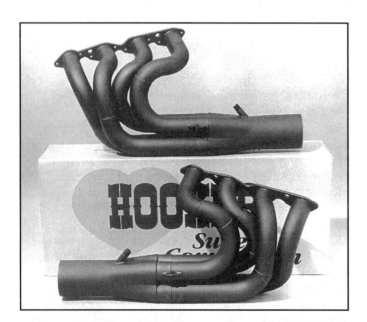

Large-tube stepped headers have large-diameter primary tubes with several transitions to slightly larger tubing diameters. These "steps" can reduce pumping work and improve horsepower on large displacement and/or high-rpm applications. These Hooker Pro-Stock BB Chevy headers have 2-3/8-inch primary tubes that step to 2-1/2-inch by the time they reach the 4-1/2-inch collectors.

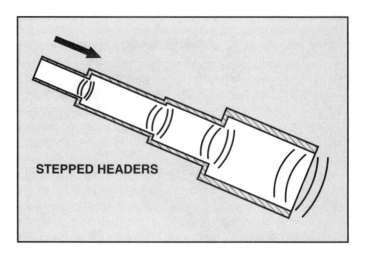

STEPPED HEADERS

"Stepped" headers can reduce pumping work in some engines. As the high-pressure compression wave leaves the port and encounters a step, it returns a short duration expansion wave. These low-pressure "pulses" move back up the header and assists the outflow of exhaust gasses. This can generate a measurable increase in horsepower on engines that are suffering from substantial pumping-work losses, such as large-displacement, high-rpm, drag-racing engines.

lector. Each primary tube has several transitions to slightly larger tubing diameters as it progresses towards the collector. These "steps" can reduce pumping work and improve horsepower as described below. The collector—or collectors, depending on the number of cylinders—terminates into the atmosphere. Strong suction waves are created in the collector that provide a substantial boost to cylinder filling and exhaust gas outflow. Since exact tubing lengths are not simulated, the program assumes that the primary tube will deliver the scavenging wave to the cylinder during the valve overlap period.

The "stepped" design of the primary tubes can reduce pumping work on some engines. As the high-pressure compression wave leaves the port and encounters a step in the primary tube, it returns a short-duration rarefaction wave. This low-pressure "pulse" moves back up the header and assists the outflow of exhaust gasses. When the rarefaction wave reaches the open exhaust valve, it helps depressurize the cylinder and lower pumping work. This can generate a measurable increase in horsepower on engines that are suffering from substantial pumping-work losses. Very large displacement and/or high-rpm applications are good candidates for stepped headers.

The primary tubes modeled by this menu selection are considered "large," and should be interpreted to fall within a range of dimensions that are commonly associated with applications requiring optimum power at peak engine speeds. The following rules of thumb should give a reasonable approximation of tubing diameters used by the simulation: Headers with tubes that measure 95% to 105% of the exhaust-valve diameter are considered "small" for any particular engine; tubes that measure 120% to 140% of the exhaust-valve diameter are "large" tube

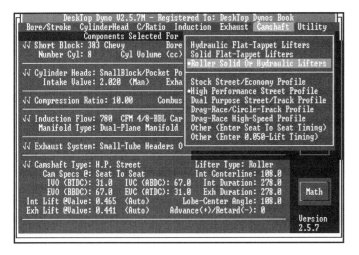

The *Camshaft* menu is the final component menu. With it you select cam profiles for the simulated engine. The following pages in this chapter provide essential information about cam design and program assumptions that will help you use this powerful feature of Motion's Filling-And-Emptying simulation software.

headers.

The Camshaft Menu

The final component menu allows the selection of the single most important part in the IC engine: the camshaft. For many enthusiasts and even professional engine builders, the subtleties of cam timing defy explanation. The reason for this confusion is understandable. The camshaft is the "brains" of the IC engine, directing the beginning and ending of all four engine cycles. Even with a good understanding of all engine systems, the interrelatedness of the IC engine can make the results of cam timing changes read like a mystery story. In many cases there are only two ways to determine the outcome of a modification: 1) run a real dyno test or 2) run a

simulation. Since the camshaft directly affects several functions at once, e.g., exhaust and intake scavenging, induction signal, flow efficiency, cylinder pressures, etc., using a computer-based engine simulation program is often the only way to *predict* the outcome.

Motion Software's Filling-And-Emptying simulation makes it possible to test the effects of cam timing in seconds. The ability of the program to take multiple elements into consideration and "add up the effects over time" is key to analyzing the effects of camshaft timing. Unfortunately, even with such a powerful tool at hand, the subject of cam timing cannot be made simple. The camshaft is a component that will thoroughly test your knowledge and comprehension of the IC engine. Review this section in light of what has been discussed throughout this book, and we hope you'll find a deeper understanding of camshaft operation and new insight into IC engine function.

Cam Basics

In the simplest terms, the camshaft is a straight steel or iron shaft with eccentric lobes. It is connected to the crankshaft with a chain or gear train and is usually rotated at one-half crank speed. Lifters (or cam followers)—and in the case of in-block cam locations, pushrods, and rockerarms—translate the rotary motion of the cam into an up-and-down motion that opens and closes the intake and exhaust valves. This entire assembly must function with high precision and high reliability. Street engines driven hundreds-of-thousands of miles operate their valvetrain components *billions of cycles*. If the overall camshaft and valvetrain design is good, a precision micrometer will detect only negligible wear.

The camshaft controls the valve opening and closing points by the shape and rotational location of the lobes. Most cams are ground to a precision well within one crankshaft degree, ensuring that the valves actuate ex-

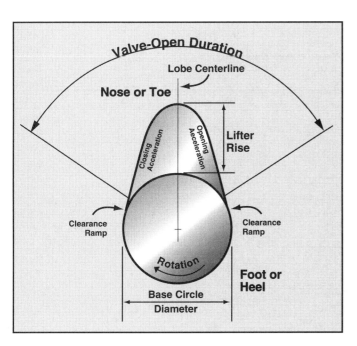

Camshaft terminology can be confusing, so here's the lowdown. To start off, the camshaft is a round shaft incorporating cam *lobes*. The *base circle diameter* is the smallest diameter of the cam lobe and is shaped perfectly round. *Clearance ramps* form the transition from the round base circle to the *acceleration ramps*. As the cam turns, the lifter smoothly accelerates up the *clearance ramp* and continues to rise as it approaches the *nose*, then begins to slow to a stop as it reaches maximum *lift* at the *lobe centerline*. Maximum *lifter rise* is determined by the height of the *toe* of the cam lobe over the base circle diameter. The lifter then accelerates in the closing direction and when the valve approaches its seat, the lifter is slowed down by closing clearance ramp. *Valve-open duration* is the number of crankshaft degrees that the valve or lifter is held above a specified height by the cam lobe (usually 0.006-, 0.020-, or 0.050-inch). A symmetric lobe has the same lift curve on both the opening and closing sides; an asymmetric lobe is shaped differently on each side of the lobe. A single-pattern cam has the same profile on both the intake and exhaust lobes; a dual-pattern cam has different profiles for the intake and exhaust lobes.

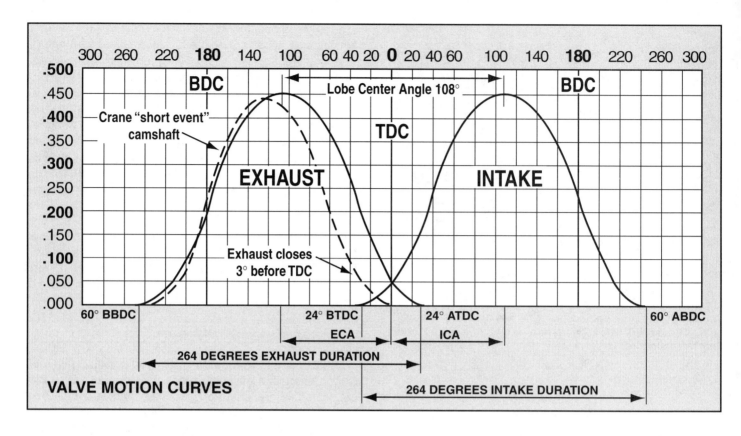

The scale at top reads: 300 260 220 **180** 140 100 60 40 20 **0** 20 40 60 100 140 **180** 220 260 300

Left vertical scale: .500 .450 .400 .350 .300 .250 .200 .150 .100 .050 .000

BDC · **BDC**

Crane "short event" camshaft

Lobe Center Angle 108°

TDC

EXHAUST · **INTAKE**

Exhaust closes 3° before TDC

60° BBDC · 24° BTDC · 24° ATDC · 60° ABDC

ECA · ICA

264 DEGREES EXHAUST DURATION

VALVE MOTION CURVES

264 DEGREES INTAKE DURATION

actly when intended. Timing variations of a few degrees can develop in the cam drive, especially in chain-drive systems, but racing gear drives reduce variations to within one or two crank degrees of indicated timing. Camshaft lobes also determine how far the valves will lift off of the valve seats by the height of the lobes (heal to toe height) and the multiplying ratio of the rockerarms (if used). The rates at which the valves are accelerated open and then returned to the seats are also "ground into" cam lobe profiles. Only a limited range of contours will maintain stable valve motion, particularly with high-lift, racing profiles. Unstable profiles or excessive engine speed will force the valvetrain into "valve float," leading to rapid component failure.

Visualizing And Calculating Valve Events

There are six basic cam timing events ground into the lobes of every camshaft. These timing points are:

1—Intake Valve Opening (IVO)
2—Intake Valve Closing (IVC)
3—Exhaust Valve Opening (EVO)
4—Exhaust Valve Closing (EVC)
5—Intake Valve Lift
6—Exhaust Valve Lift

These six points can be "adjusted" somewhat (we'll discuss which and how cam timing events can be altered in the next section), but for the most part they are fixed by the design of the cam. Other timing numbers are often discussed, but they are always derived from these basic six events. These derivative events are:

7—Intake Duration

8—Exhaust Duration
9—Lobe Center Angle (LCA)
10—Valve Overlap
11—Intake Center Angle or Centerline (ICA)
12—Exhaust Center Angle or Centerline (ECA)

The first four basic timing points (1 thorough 4) pinpoint the "true" beginning and end of the four engine cycles. These valve opening and closing points indicate when the function of the piston/cylinder mechanism changes from intake to compression, compression to power, power to exhaust, and exhaust back to intake. What could be more important from the standpoint of understanding engine function and performing engine simulations?

Compared to the basic timing events, many simulation experts believe that most of the second six timing values are not only unimportant, they actually "blow smoke" over the whole issue of cam timing analysis. Naturally, four of the <u>second</u> six events are the most publicized by the cam manufacturers and enthusiast magazines. This unfortunate situation evolved over many years of selling and marketing camshafts in the automotive aftermarket. Long before engine simulations were widely used and a good understanding of the relationship between the individual valve events and engine power ever existed, the descriptions of the *distance <u>between</u> valve events rather than the valve events themselves* became a standard measure of a camshaft.

Since this assortment of cam specifications is used almost interchangeably, it is almost impossible to "talk camshaft" without a good understanding of all these terms. Probably the best way to organize and visualize this nomenclature is to picture the common "twin-hump" event drawing. This illustration depicts valve-motion curves (sometimes called valve displacement curves) for the exhaust lobe on the left and the intake lobe on the right, locating the valve overlap period and TDC (top dead center) at the center of the graph. If you become sufficiently familiar with this drawing so that you can easily picture it in your mind, you should be able to figure out any of the cam timing specs and how they relate to one another.

The graph plots crank degrees on the X-axis (left to right) and valve lift on the Y-axis (up and down). The width of the graph is slightly shortened. Since no valve motion occurs during about 200 degrees of crank rotation when the "true" compression and power strokes take place, the graph chops off 60-degrees on each end, running from 300-degrees before to 300-degress after TDC (total four-cycle sweep is actually 720 degrees).

Picture events on the graph taking place from left to right, passing through TDC at the center. The left "hump" is the exhaust valve motion curve. Focus your attention at the 240-degree point before TDC. Note that the 180-degree vertical line is actually a BDC (bottom dead center) marker, so 240-degrees before TDC lies 60-degrees before BDC. This is the EVO (exhaust valve opening) timing point, the beginning of exhaust blowdown and rapid cylinder decompression. Follow the exhaust valve curve through its maximum lift—about 0.450-inch—that occurs at 108-degrees before TDC to its closing point at 24-degrees after TDC. Now notice the intake valve motion

curve. At 24-degrees before TDC, when the exhaust valve is still open, the intake valve leaves its seat and begins to follow its motion curve. During the space between 24-degrees before TDC and 24-degrees after TDC, both valves are open, defining the overlap period when exhaust scavenging can take place. Now continue to follow the intake motion curve to its maximum lift—also about 0.450-inch—at 108-degrees after TDC. The intake closing point occurs at 240-degrees after TDC or 60-degrees after BDC (the 180-degree line). You have now traced out the six basic cam timing points. Let's see how these relate to the six derivative events.

First consider duration—the number of crank degrees that the valves are off their seats. This "length of time," expressed in crank degrees, is a measure of the true intake and exhaust cycles. The exhaust valve opens 60-degrees before BDC and closes 24-degrees after TDC, and since 180 degrees of crank rotation exists between BDC and TDC, the exhaust duration is: 60 + 180 + 24 = 264 degrees off-seat duration. In the case of the intake valve, valve opening occurs 24-degrees before TDC and closing 60-degrees after BDC, so the intake duration is: 24 + 180 + 60 = 264 degrees. Duration is easy to calculate from the opening and closing points; however, watch out for the one "tricky" element: *short events*. For cams that open the intake valve *after TDC* instead of before TDC or close the exhaust valve *before TDC* instead of after TDC (common with 0.050-timing specs), make sure to subtract the timing point instead of adding it to calculate the duration. For example, a Crane Cams, Inc. profile HMV-272-2-NC opens the exhaust valve 51-degrees before BDC and closes it 3-degrees *before TDC*. To calculate the duration subtract the "short" closing point: 51 + 180 −3 = 228 degrees. While these "short" timing events are much more common when working with 0.050-inch timing specs, you may also come across seat-to-seat timing specs for emissions-restricted camshafts with "short" events, designed to minimize or eliminate valve overlap. In a nutshell, the duration is simply the number of crank degrees swept out by the lift curve.

Next, let's look at the three centerline angles: Intake Centerline, Exhaust Centerline, and Lobe Center Angle (sometimes called Lobe Centerline). The terms "Centerline" and "Center Angle" are methods of describing the distance to or from the exact center of a lobe. The Intake and Exhaust Centerlines describe the distance from the center of the Intake and Exhaust lobes to TDC. Both of

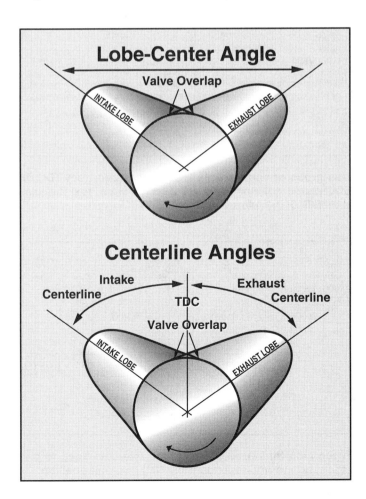

Lobe Center Angle is the angle measured in camshaft degrees (multiply by two for equivalent crankshaft degrees) between the maximum-lift points on the intake and exhaust lobes for the same cylinder. The lobe center angle is "ground" into the cam when it is manufactured and cannot be changed (unless the cam is reground). As the lobe-center angle is decreased, the valve overlap period (when both intake and exhaust valves are open) is increased. The *lobe centerline angles* are the angles measured in crankshaft degrees between the points of maximum lift on the intake and exhaust lobes and Top Dead Center. These values are determined by the "indexing" of the cam to the crankshaft.

these timing specs are measured in crank degrees. That means that the number of degrees the crank rotates from the point at which the piston rests at TDC until the lifter contacts the exact center of the intake lobe is the Intake Centerline. When the lobes are symmetric, that is they have the same shape and valve motion rates on the opening and closing sides, the Intake Centerline and Exhaust Centerlines will occur at the point of maximum valve lift. Asymmetric profiles are quite common, although, the amount of asymmetry typically is very small, so the centerlines should still fall within two or three of degrees of maximum lift point.

All but one of the basic and derivative cam-timing specs are measured in crank degrees. This makes sense since the timing specs fundamentally describe valve positions (and durations) as they relate to piston positions (and piston movement). This applies to every timing spec but Lobe Center Angle (LCA). The LCA is meant to describe *the angular distance between the centers of the intake and exhaust lobes as viewed on the cam itself.* This distance is a cam-specific measurement, not relative to TDC, and is the only cam spec that cannot be altered regardless of how the cam is "degreed" with crankshaft. It is said to be "ground into" the cam. Because this spec relates one lobe position to the other, independent of the engine or crankshaft, it is measured in <u>cam degrees</u>. The number of <u>crank degrees</u> between the center of the lobes is twice the LCA.

All of the camshaft specifications described thus far tell something about how the cam is manufactured and how it should be installed in the engine. To help keep them straight in your mind, let's reorganize them in two new groups. The first group contains all the timing specs that are measured from TDC or BDC piston positions and are dependent on how the cam is installed, or indexed, in the engine:

1—Intake Valve Opening (IVO)
2—Intake Valve Closing (IVC)
3—Exhaust Valve Opening (EVO)
4—Exhaust Valve Closing (EVC)
5—Intake Center Angle or Centerline (ICA)
6—Exhaust Center Angle or Centerline (ECA)

Each of these timing specs indicate a opening, closing, or lobe centerline point measured from a TDC or BDC piston position. If the cam is installed in an advanced or retarded position relative to TDC, the value of these timing specs will change. In fact, advancing and retarding the cam is one way to change cam timing that we'll discuss in detail later in this chapter.

The following group of cam timing events and specs are not dependant on TDC or crankshaft position:

7—Intake Duration
8—Exhaust Duration
9—Lobe Center Angle (LCA)
10—Valve Overlap
11—Intake Valve Lift
12—Exhaust Valve Lift

Each of these six terms <u>compare one cam spec to an-other</u>; they are not measured relative to any fixed crank

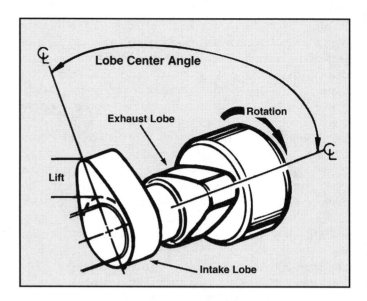

The Lobe Center Angle describes *the angular distance between the centers of the intake and exhaust lobes as viewed on the cam itself.* This distance is a measurement of the cam—not relative to TDC—and is the only cam spec that cannot be altered regardless of how the cam is "degreed" with crankshaft. Because of this, the LCA is measured in <u>cam degrees</u>. The number of <u>crank degrees</u> between the center of the lobes is twice the LCA.

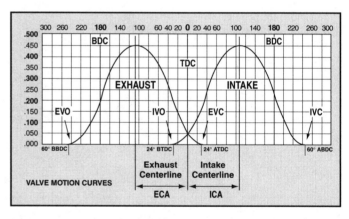

This group of valve events are all measured from TDC or BDC piston positions and are dependent on how the cam is installed, or indexed, in the engine.

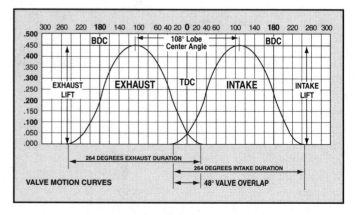

These cam timing events <u>compare one cam spec to an-other</u> and are not dependant on TDC or crank position.

position. Refer again to the valve-motion plot to confirm this. Remember that the duration of each lobe is the distance in crank degrees between the valve opening and closing points. Sliding these curves left or right (analogous to advancing or retarding the cam) does not change the distance between the opening and closing points and does not change duration. Duration is, therefore, another "ground in" cam spec. The same limitation applies to valve overlap. The lobes are spaced by a fixed LCA (discussed above), and they can't move with respect to each other, so the length of the overlap period—the distance between EVC and IVO at a specific lifter rise—never changes for a particular camshaft. Finally, valve lift is another comparison of cam specs. In this case, it's the distance between the lobe heal height and toe height multiplied by the rocker ratio. Valve lift is measured in inches (or millimeters) and is never related to crank angle or TDC.

Take some time to review the relationships between all of the cam specs and the valve motion drawings. Trace the action of the valves from left to right through the exhaust cycle and, as TDC approaches, through overlap, then continue to the right through the intake cycle. These drawings give an excellent mental "picture" of the relationships between LCA and the individual ICA and ECA values. In fact, assuming a symmetric profile, it is possible to calculate all of the center angles, durations, and the overlap from the four basic valve events (EVO, EVC, IVO, IVC). It is also possible to calculate the four valve events from the duration, the LCA, and either the ICA or the ECA. We'll discuss the details of converting timing specifications using information from cam manufacturer's catalogs later in this chapter.

How Valve-Event Timing Affects Power

As we mentioned earlier, years of marketing efforts by cam manufacturers have established an accepted methodology for identifying and classifying camshafts. The specifications most commonly listed by manufacturers are:

1—Intake Duration
2—Intake Valve Lift
3—Exhaust Duration
4—Exhaust Valve Lift
5—Lobe Center Angle (LCA)
6—Intake Center Angle or Centerline (ICA)

Long before engine simulations were widely used and designers gained an understanding of how the changes in valve-event timing affect power, "manufacturer's catalog" specs became a standard measure of cam profiles. Unfortunately, these terms place the emphasis on the span between the valve events rather than on the events themselves. For example, it is common to compare two cams by comparing their intake and/or exhaust valve-open duration. While duration does point to the intended use for the cam, it doesn't indicate the valve events, making it difficult to predict engine performance. If **Cam A** has 264 degrees of exhaust dura-

tion and **Cam B** has 300 degrees, the longer duration spec doesn't give a clue about how the additional valve-open timing will be allocated to the opening and closing events. Are the entire forty degrees added to **Cam B**'s valve opening point; are they added to the closing point; or are they split between the two in some proportion? Without knowing the exact valve events, one can only guess at the outcome. A more critical situation exists for engine simulation programs: Without knowing the exact valve events, a simulation isn't even possible! Not using exact valve timing events during a simulation is like building and testing an engine without defining when the valves open and close; the whole concept doesn't make any sense.

The emphasis on event timing in engine simulation programs has driven many leading-edge designers to discount what they now term as ambiguous or less-useful cam timing specifications, in particular, advance and

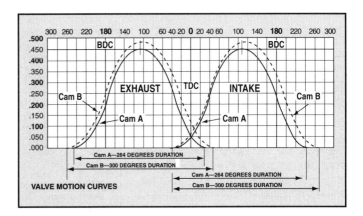

Long before engine simulations were widely used, cam manufacturers established a methodology for identifying and classifying camshafts. Unfortunately, these "catalog" specs place the emphasis on the span between the valve events rather than on the events themselves. Information presented later in this chapter will help you convert manufacturer's specs to the essential "language" of engine simulations: valve events.

A manufacturer's catalog lists *Cam A* as having 264 degrees of duration while *Cam B* has 300 degrees. But just the duration spec doesn't give a clue about how the additional valve-open timing will be allocated to the opening and closing events. These valve motion curves indicate just one of an infinite number of possibilities. Without knowing the exact valve events, running an engine simulation isn't possible.

retard figures, centerlines, and durations. For some, this may be a difficult paradigm shift, but the rewards are substantial: you may find a new understanding of the IC engine at the end of your efforts. The next few paragraphs delve into the effects of individual valve events learned from both real-world and simulated testing. We'll also relate these basic timing events to other popular cam specifications, since it will be many years—if ever—before some of the less-relevant specs disappear from cam manufacturer's catalogs.

The four basic valve-event timing points (EVO, EVC, IVO, IVC) can be grouped into three categories based on their influence on engine performance: 1) EVC and IVO are the least important individually, but together comprise the overlap period that has a significant effect on power, and 2) the EVO is the next most important timing point since is determines the beginning of the exhaust cycle and cylinder blowdown, and 3) IVC is the most critical since it fixes the balance between cylinder filling and intake reversion, each having a potent effect on engine output.

EVC/IVO, The Valve Overlap Period—The valve overlap period occurs as the piston passes through TDC after the main portion of the exhaust stroke. The intake valve opens before TDC (usually) and signals the beginning of period of time during which both intake and exhaust valves are off their seats. As we found in our discussion of exhaust systems, a high pressure wave produced when the exhaust valve opens (EVO) travels to the end of the header and returns a strong negative pressure wave that delivers a pressure drop at the exhaust valve. If this pressure drop arrives during the overlap period, it will help purge the cylinder of exhaust gasses and, despite the upward movement of the piston, begin the inflow of fresh charge from the induction system. This phenomenon is called scavenging, and an engine that delivers its scavenging wave during the overlap period is said to be "in tune." If the pressure wave is

early or late, or not even created by exhaust system, the piston rising in the bore during the first part of overlap will force exhaust gasses into the induction system, producing a phenomenon called "reversion." When this occurs, cam timing and the exhaust system are "out of tune."

Reversion is a power killer. When exhaust gasses are driven into the induction system, they force air/fuel mixtures back upstream. Severe reversion can drive the air/fuel charge out of the air inlet, creating a "standoff" of vapors above the carburetor. When the charge is drawn back into the engine, it is re-atomized with fuel creating "double-rich" mixtures. Additional, less severe, symptoms of reversion include a drop in manifold vacuum, rough idle and/or high idle speeds, and a substantial increase in emissions from over-rich mixtures.

An engine that develops reversion and runs poorly at lower engine speeds may run fine at higher speeds. In fact, most race engines exhibit these symptoms; the common side effects of a high-speed race tune. The scavenging wave that missed the overlap period at low speeds may return on time at higher engine speeds, optimizing tuning, cylinder filling, and power output. The nature of the exhaust system is to create in-and-out-of-tune conditions as the engine moves through its rpm range. The goal of the engine designer is to broaden the arrival of the scavenging wave as much as possible (remember our discussion of header-pipe collectors) "covering" the overlap period through as much of the max-power rpm range as possible. *If any part of overlap does not coincide with the presence of a low-pressure scavenging wave, reversion or reduced cylinder filling will drive the engine partially out of tune.*

Valve overlap periods vary from zero to about 40-degrees on street and basic performance engines. All-out racing engines use overlap periods as long as 120 degrees. Engines with long overlap tend to have very "peaky" power bands, since a returning scavenging wave

The goal of the engine designer is to "cover" the overlap period with the arriving scavenging wave during as wide an rpm range as possible. When this is done, the exhaust system and the engine are said to be "in tune" during that range of engine speeds. *If any part of overlap does not coincide with the presence of a low-pressure scavenging wave, reversion or reduced cylinder filling will drive the engine partially out of tune.*

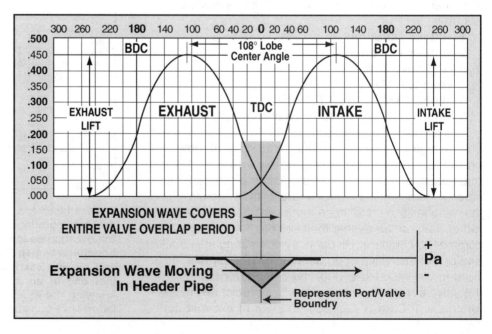

Decreasing the LCA will directly increase valve overlap by moving IVO earlier and EVC later. However, if the goal is to boost high-speed horsepower (the reason for additional overlap), narrowing the LCA also moves the IVC earlier. This <u>reduces</u> "ram effects" in the induction system at higher engine speeds, clearly the wrong approach for performance. In addition, a narrower LCA opens the exhaust valve (EVO) later and that <u>delays cylinder blowdown</u>, an effect that tends to boost low-speed—not high-speed—power. The correct method of adjusting overlap, and every other cam timing, should be to apply the appropriate changes to the individual valve opening and closing events.

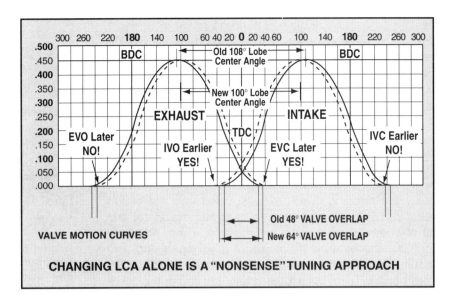

CHANGING LCA ALONE IS A "NONSENSE" TUNING APPROACH

"covers" the valve overlap period through only a relatively narrow rpm range. However, wide overlap periods are needed to effectively scavenge large-displacement engines at high engine speeds. Shorter overlap periods, on the other hand, stay in-tune through a wider rpm range, but tend to reduce peak horsepower because they limit scavenging. The number of overlap degrees is a good indicator of the intended use of the cam: short overlap for broad torque and good low-speed power, long overlap for high power at high engine speeds.

Lobe Center Angle and Overlap—Since valve overlap is directly related to the Lobe Center Angle (LCA)—refer again to the valve motion diagram—is has become commonplace to discuss changes in valve overlap as being synonymous with changes in LCA. In fact, some believe that changing LCA (requires regrinding cam) is the correct method of adjusting overlap. This is not true. This common misconception comes from an inadequate understanding of the function and effects of the individual valve-event timing points. For example, suppose that you wish to increase the valve overlap period for a particular camshaft. Decreasing the LCA will, in fact, directly increase the overlap, but let's look at the consequences. If the goal is to increase overlap, the need must be to boost high-speed horsepower. With a smaller LCA, the EVC occurs later and IVO is earlier, both of these changes directly increase overlap and tend to boost high speed power. So far, so good. However, changing the LCA has the effect of "rotating" the lobes on the camshaft and moving the IVC earlier. Since <u>later</u> IVC timing tends to take advantage of the "ram effects" in the induction system at higher engine speeds, closing the intake valve earlier is clearly the wrong approach. In addition, with a narrower LCA, the EVO occurs later and that delays cylinder blowdown, another effect that tends to boost low-speed power. Again, the wrong approach. This "schizophrenic" or nonsensical tuning approach applies the correct EVC and IVO timing, but counteracts these effects with earlier IVC and later EVO timing; the net results are often a modest shift in tuning toward higher

engine speeds. The correct method of adjusting overlap, and every other cam timing alteration, should be to apply the appropriate changes to the individual valve opening and closing events. In this case, a longer overlap should be produced by applying an earlier IVO and EVO and a later IVC and EVC. Yes, this also increases duration, but applying individual valve-event changes that <u>complement</u>—rather that counteract—each other, produce a much more effective camshaft for the intended purpose.

EVO, The Exhaust Valve Opening Point—EVO timing is the next most important of the basic valve events. Changes in this timing point can have a substantial impact on engine efficiency and performance. The opening of the exhaust valve creates a high-pressure wave that travels through the exhaust system that, with properly

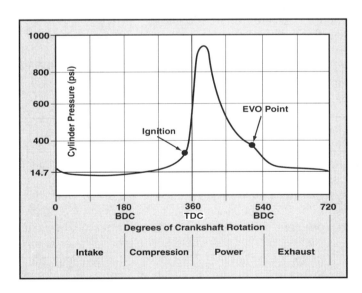

EVO signals the beginning of the blowdown phase by starting the rapid decompression of the cylinder near the end of the power stroke. The opening of the exhaust valve also creates a high-pressure wave that travels through the exhaust system that, with properly designed headers, returns as a strong scavenging wave during the overlap period.

designed headers, returns as a strong scavenging wave during the overlap period. EVO timing must be coordinated with header tubing length, engine speed, and valve overlap to obtain full benefit from scavenging. The EVO point also signals the beginning of the blowdown phase of the exhaust cycle by starting the rapid decompression of the cylinder at the end of the power stroke.

The optimum EVO timing point is another "moving target" for the engine designer. It should be no surprise that a perfectly timed EVO simply doesn't exist. However, if perfection were possible, an ideal EVO would delay the opening of the exhaust valve until the piston reached BDC, allowing the engine to harness every last bit of energy generated by combustion. Then, precisely at BDC, the exhaust valve would "pop" open and, miraculously, all of the residual gas pressure would vanish (even better, a slight vacuum would develop in the cylinder). Then as the piston moves from BDC to TDC, no horsepower would be wasted on "pumping" spent gasses from the engine. Unfortunately, the real world of engine gas dynamics is far from perfection. Substantial power is consumed by driving the piston up the bore on the exhaust stroke, especially at high engine speeds with large-displacement engines that generate prodigious amounts of exhaust gas. To offset these losses, early EVO timing starts the blowdown of high-pressure gasses before the exhaust stroke even begins. But the reduction in pumping work doesn't come without a drawback; earlier EVO timing "wastes" some of the power-producing gas pressure from combustion. The balance between these two factors optimizes power, but the balance changes as engine speed changes (and, of course, it also changes as displacement, flow restriction, and the timing of other valve events change).

To complicate matters even further, once an optimum EVO timing has been found, we need to consider how this timing affects the arrival of the scavenging wave. Remember, that the chain of events that leads to the arrival of the scavenging wave begins at the opening of the exhaust valve. When the pumping-loss/blowdown balance has been found, header lengths (and overlap timing) may need to be adjusted to harness scavenging effects to full benefit. Then when you consider that header tubing <u>diameter</u> plays a part in determining exhaust system restriction and can change blowdown and pumping-loss characteristics, the jumble of tunable elements grows even larger. Finally, if the induction system is improved, higher post-combustion pressures can worsen the pumping problem and that may require further changes to EVO timing, starting the whole tuning process over again.

Despite the fact that EVO is an extremely important factor in engine output, this web of interrelated effects make it very difficult (probably impossible) for engine experts to determine the outcome of specific changes to EVO timing. Here is another example of how engine simulations are useful. A series of simulations can "home-in" on the optimum combination from a large number of interdependent conditions.

IVC, The Intake Valve Closing Point—IVC is the

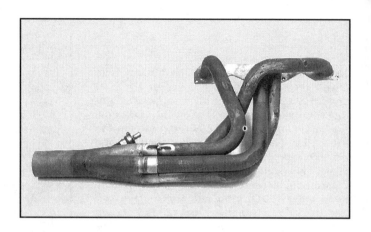

Header lengths need to be adjusted to harness scavenging effects to full benefit. However, header tubing <u>diameter</u> also plays an important part in determining exhaust system restriction and can change blowdown and pumping-loss characteristics. Despite the fact that EVO is an extremely important timing event, a combination of many tuning factors make it very difficult to determine the outcome of specific changes to EVO timing. Motion's Filling-And-Emptying simulation (and to a greater extent more advanced engine simulations like *Dynomation,* discussed in the next chapter) can "home-in" on the optimum combination from a large number of interdependent conditions.

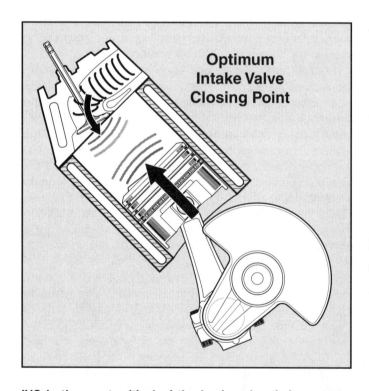

Optimum
Intake Valve
Closing Point

IVC is the most critical of the basic valve timing events. The intake valve closing point establishes a balance between cylinder filling and intake reversion, each having a potent effect on engine performance. When the pressure produced in the cylinder as the piston begins to move up the bore on the compression stroke exceeds the pressure of the incoming charge, the induced charge starts to "revert" or flow back into the induction system. This is the ideal point for IVC, because the cylinder has received the greatest volume of air and fuel and will generate the highest pressures on the power stroke.

most critical of the basic valve timing events. The intake valve closing point establishes a balance between cylinder filling and intake reversion, each having a potent effect on engine performance.

After the intake stroke is completed and the piston reaches BDC, the column of air/fuel mixture moving through the induction system has built up considerable momentum (the "ram tuning" effect). This internal energy forces additional air and fuel to flow into the cylinder even as the piston begins to move up the bore on the early part of the compression stroke. At some point, however, the pressure in the cylinder begins to exceed the pressure of the incoming charge, and the induced charge starts to "revert" or flow back into the induction system. This is the ideal point for IVC, because the cylinder has received the greatest volume of air and fuel and will generate the highest pressures on the power stroke.

Unfortunately, optimum IVC occurs only at one engine speed and is dictated by cylinder head flow, induction ram-tuning effects, intake valve opening timing, and of course by engine rpm. The longer the intake valve is held open the more "peaky" engine performance becomes. Late IVC can create induction flow reversion with an accompanying drop in manifold vacuum, rough idle and/or poor idle quality, and an increase in emissions from over-rich mixtures (rich mixtures are created when the charge is forced back up the manifold and passes through the carburetor—or by the fuel injector—a second time). When the induction system on a racing engine is properly designed, the pressure wave created when the intake valve opens is returned to the cylinder as a strong suction wave just about the time cylinder pressures begin to overcome the ram tuning effects. This momentary drop in pressure allows a bit more cylinder

filling and a slightly later IVC. This critical tuning can add the winning edge to Pro Stock engines or other max-power applications, however, induction system design, IVO, and IVC timing must all be synchronized to produce these effects. Since induction components are typically hand built "one offs" on engines of this type, custom cams are ground for individual engines to optimize power in these competitive classes.

On the other end of the spectrum, if the goal is to build an engine that performs well throughout a wide rpm range and offers good idle characteristics, late IVC is definitely the wrong approach. The intake valve must close early enough to prevent reversion at lower engine speeds, an essential step in producing low-speed torque. However, early IVC limits cylinder filling at higher engine speeds and reduces peak power. IVC timing in the high 50-degree range is typical for a mild street cam, the high 60-degree to the mid 70-degree range is common on high-performance and mild racing grinds, and IVC from the 80-degree to low 100-degree range is all-out racing timing.

Camshaft Menu—Lifter Choices

The camshaft menu consists of two groups. The upper category provides a list of three common lifter types used to model camshaft acceleration rates. The lower part of the menu offers an application-specific group of individual cam grinds, and the final two "Other" choices allow the direct entry of cam timing events to simulate virtually any camshaft. Making a selection from each of these two groups "programs" the simulation to develop a valve motion curve for the selected camshaft.

The Filling-And-Emptying program uses a sophisticated model to accomplish this simulation, but the user must keep in mind that valve motion curves for both the intake and exhaust valves are being simulated from only

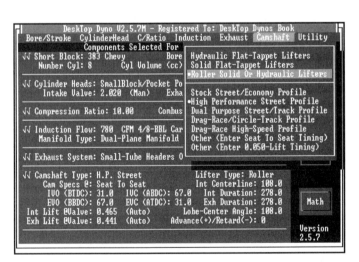

The upper category of the camshaft menu provides a list of three common lifter types used to model camshaft acceleration rates. The lower part of the menu offers an application-specific group of individual cam grinds, and the final two "Other" choices allow the direct entry of cam timing events to simulate virtually any camshaft. Making a selection from each of these two groups "programs" the simulation to develop a valve motion curve for the selected camshaft.

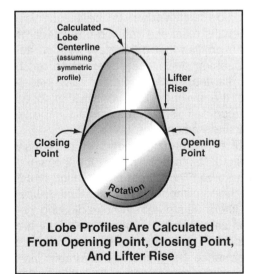

Lobe Profiles Are Calculated From Opening Point, Closing Point, And Lifter Rise

The Filling-And-Emptying program models valve motion curves from six data points, three for each lobe: 1) the opening point, 2) the closing point, and 3) the lobe lift. The simulation develops a symmetric valve motion curve. Although some cam grinds are asymmetric, performance differences between a symmetric model and actual asymmetric valve motion is quite small.

six data points, three for the intake valve and three for the exhaust valve. The starting point for each simulation is the opening and closing timing and the lobe lift. From these three points, and the lifters selection, the program creates a motion curve that pinpoints valve lift at each degree of crank position. The results are remarkably accurate, however, the simulation cannot model subtle differences between cam grinds that use the same event timing and valve lift specs. Furthermore, the model develops a symmetric valve motion curve, although some cam grinds are asymmetric (meaning that the "opening" side of the lobe differs in shape from the "closing" side). Asymmetric modeling is impossible with only three data input points, luckily, performance differences between symmetric models and actual asymmetric valve motions are often quite small.

The first part of the Camshaft menu offers three choices: 1) *Hydraulic Flat-Tappet Lifters*, 2) *Solid Flat-Tappet Lifters*, and 3) *Roller Solid Or Hydraulic Lifters*. Each of these choices instructs the simulation to apply a unique "ramp-rate" model to the valve motion curve. The first two choices are flat-tappet lifters. This lifter uses a flat surface to contact or "rub" on the cam lobes. Flat-tappets are simple and quite reliable in stock and many high-performance applications. However, their design limits the rate at which the valves can be opened and closed. Slower valve acceleration reduces the exposed curtain area and the flow capability of the cylinder heads at every point during the lift curve, except for the fraction of a second when the valve passes through maximum lift. (Interestingly, flat tappet lifters can be made to out accelerate roller lifters during the first several hundredths of an inch of the lift curve, but roller lifters easily surpass flat tappet lift rates by the time the valves reach 0.100- to 0.200-inch of lift.) The third choice in the lifter group is a roller lifter (either solid or hydraulic, more on these differences next). This design incorporates a cylindrical element that rolls over the cam lobe. While there are slight gains from reduced friction, the greatest benefit from a roller cam/lifter design lies "hidden" in the mechanical relationship between the roller and cam lobe. Roller cams can be ground with profiles that generate very high acceleration rates, opening and closing the valves much more quickly than flat-tappet cams. Faster valve acceleration increases the average curtain area exposed throughout the lift curve. This can substantially improve cylinder head flow and horsepower.

The three choices in the lifter menu, as previously indicated, establish a "ramp-rate" model for the simulated valve-motion curve. The lowest acceleration is assigned to the first menu choice: *Hydraulic Flat-Tappet Lifters*. Hydraulic lifters incorporate a self-adjusting design that maintains zero lash in the valvetrain. They are well-known for providing quiet, trouble-free operation in mild- to high-performance street engines. Hydraulic, flat-tappet cam profiles usually generate low acceleration rates to optimize valvetrain reliability and extend engine life. These are the characteristics of the model used by the simulation program when *Hydraulic Flat-Tappet Lifters* is

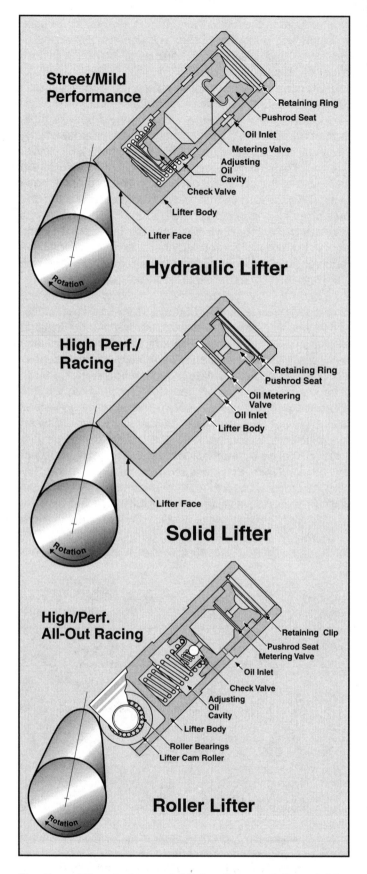

The three lifter choices establish a "ramp-rate" model for the simulated valve-motion curve. The lowest acceleration is assigned to *Hydraulic Flat-Tappet Lifters*. The next highest acceleration is applied to *Solid Flat-Tappet Lifters*. The highest acceleration is reserved for the last menu choice: *Roller Solid Or Hydraulic Lifters*.

chosen. The next highest acceleration rates are assigned to *Solid Flat-Tappet Lifters*. These lifters incorporate no lash adjusting mechanism and require an operating clearance (or lash) in the valvetrain, usually 0.020- to 0.030-inch. Clearance is typically adjusted at the rockerarm or with spacers in the case of overhead cams with cam followers. Solid lifter cams are often ground with faster acceleration rate ramps, generate more valvetrain noise and wear, and are designed for performance-oriented applications. These more aggressive characteristics are used by the simulation to derive a valve-motion curve when *Solid Flat-Tappet Lifters* is chosen from the menu. Finally, as described above, the highest acceleration rates are applied to the last menu choice: *Roller Solid Or Hydraulic Lifters*. This choice applies to very aggressive ramp acceleration rates and derives valve motion curves appropriate for most racing, roller-lifter camshafts.

The simulation uses increasing valvetrain acceleration to model hydraulic, solid, and finally roller-lifter camshafts. This is a good assumption, since cams typically use lifters that are suited for the intended application, and cam profiles for specific applications typically apply predictable valve acceleration rates. However, this is not always the case. For example, some camshafts currently available for mild street engines use roller lifters, not to achieve high valve acceleration rates, but to optimize reliability. In these cases, choosing roller lifters from the Camshaft menu will produce optimistic power curves from the simulation. So, to improve program accuracy, ask yourself if the camshaft you are modeling fits the follow-

ing application-specific description before you make a lifter selection:

Menu Choice	Intended Application
Hydraulic Flat-Tappet	Street/Mild Performance
Solid Flat-Tappet	High-Performance/Racing
Roller Solid Or Hydraulic	HP/All-Out Racing

If the cam you're modeling is a roller-lifter grind but a very mild-street profile, select Hydraulic or Solid Flat-Tappets from the menu since this choice will produce a lift curve that best matches a mild street camshaft. On the other hand, if the cam is a high-performance grind, select Solid Lifters since this will model the faster acceleration rates of aggressive performance grinds. If you are modeling a large-diameter, solid-lifter racing cam, like some "mushroom" lifter grinds, the Solid Lifter choice may underestimate the acceleration rate of these competition camshafts. In this case you may find more accurate predictions from the Roller Lifter selection.

Camshaft Menu—Application-Specific Camshafts

The second group within the Camshaft menu contains five camshaft "grinds" that are listed by application: 1) *Stock Street/Economy Profile*, 2) *High Performance Street Profile*, 3) *Dual Purpose Street/Track Profile*, 4) *Drag-Race/Circle-Track Profile*, and 5) *Drag-Race High-Speed Profile*. Any of the three lifter types can be applied to these cam profiles, adjusting the acceleration rates from mild to very aggressive. When any of these cam profiles are selected, the seat-to-seat IVO, IVC, EVO, and EVC are loaded into the Component Selection Box along with the camshaft description (valve lift specs are calculated and displayed as described next). Simulation versions 2.5 and later also display the Intake Centerline, Intake Lobe Center Angle, Intake Duration, and Exhaust Duration for all simulated camshafts.

*IMPORTANT NOTE: The **intake and exhaust valve lifts** for all application-specific cams are automatically calculated by the simulation and displayed on screen followed by the term "(Auto)". Valve lifts are based on the valve-head diameters chosen by the user and displayed in the Cylinder Head category of the Component Selection Box. Note: If **valve diameters** are also being automatically calculated—by selecting "Auto Calculate Valve Size" from the CylinderHead menu—a cylinder-bore diameter and a cylinder head selection must be made before the program can calculate the valve diameters and, consequently, the valve lifts. The simulation adjusts the intake and exhaust valve lifts to maintain appropriate lift-to-diameter ratios for a wide variety of applications, from single-cylinder small bore engines to large displacement racing engines with large valve diameters. The "auto calculation" feature for valve lift will be suspended and, instead, permanent values used for any camshaft by choosing one of the two "Other" selections at the bottom of the Camshaft menu AFTER choosing*

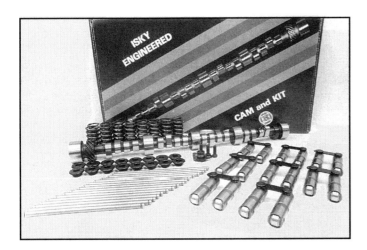

To improve program accuracy, ask yourself if the camshaft you are modeling fits the application-specific description listed in the above text. If your cam uses roller lifters but is a mild street profile, select *Hydraulic* or *Solid Flat-Tappets* from the menu since these choices will produce a lift curve that matches a mild camshaft. On the other hand, if the cam is a high-performance grind, select *Solid Lifters* or *Roller Lifters* since these will model the faster acceleration rates of an aggressive performance grind. If you are modeling a large-diameter, solid-lifter racing cam, like some "mushroom" lifter grinds, the Solid Lifter choice may underestimate the acceleration rate of these competition camshafts. In this case you may find more accurate predictions from the *Roller Lifter* selection.

This first menu profile simulates a typical factory-stock cam. This cam is generally used with hydraulic lifters.

```
Camshaft Type: Stock Street/Economy      Lifter Type: Hydraulic
   Cam Specs @: Seat To Seat             Int Centerline: 115.0
      IVO (BTDC): 12.0    IVC (ABDC): 62.0    Int Duration: 254.0
      EVO (BBDC): 66.0    EVC (ATDC): 10.0    Exh Duration: 256.0
Int Lift @Valve: 0.XXX   (Auto)          Lobe-Center Angle: 116.5
Exh Lift @Valve: 0.XXX   (Auto)          Advance(+)/Retard(-): 0
```

This profile simulates a high-performance cam. It is nearly identical to the *ISKY Hi-Rev Flat-Tappet* solid cam part 201025 for the SB Chevy.

```
Camshaft Type: High-Performance Street   Lifter Type: Hydraulic
   Cam Specs @: Seat To Seat             Int Centerline: 108.0
      IVO (BTDC): 31.0    IVC (ABDC): 67.0    Int Duration: 278.0
      EVO (BBDC): 67.0    EVC (ATDC): 31.0    Exh Duration: 278.0
Int Lift @Valve: 0.XXX   (Auto)          Lobe-Center Angle: 108.0
Exh Lift @Valve: 0.XXX   (Auto)          Advance(+)/Retard(-): 0
```

The third menu choice models a high-performance cam. The profile is close to *ISKY Hydraulic Series* part 201281 for the SB Chevy.

```
Camshaft Type: Dual-Purpose Street       Lifter Type: Solid
   Cam Specs @: Seat To Seat             Int Centerline: 109.0
      IVO (BTDC): 32.0    IVC (ABDC): 70.0    Int Duration: 282.0
      EVO (BBDC): 70.0    EVC (ATDC): 32.0    Exh Duration: 282.0
Int Lift @Valve: 0.XXX   (Auto)          Lobe-Center Angle: 109.0
Exh Lift @Valve: 0.XXX   (Auto)          Advance(+)/Retard(-): 0
```

the desired camshaft (more on this in the next section).

Stock Street/Economy Profile—This first profile is designed to simulate a typical factory-stock cam. All cam timing events displayed in the Component Selection Box are seat-to-seat measurements.

The EVO timing utilizes combustion pressure late into the power stroke and early IVC minimizes intake flow reversion. Late IVO and early EVC produce only 22 degrees of overlap, enough to harness some scavenging effects but restricted enough to prevent exhaust gas reversion into the induction system. The characteristics of this cam are smooth idle, good power from 1000 to 4500rpm, and good fuel economy. This cam works well in high-torque demand applications. The *Stock Street/ Economy Profile* cam is typically used with hydraulic lifters. As described earlier, the intake and exhaust valve lifts for all application-specific profiles are automatically calculated by the simulation and are based on the valve diameters.

High Performance Street Profile—This profile is designed to simulate a high-performance factory camshaft. All cam timing events displayed in the Component Selection Box are seat-to-seat measurements.

This camshaft uses relatively-late EVO to fully utilize combustion pressure and early IVC minimizes intake flow reversion. IVO and EVC produce 62 degrees of overlap, a profile that is clearly intended to harness exhaust scavenging effects. The modestly-aggressive overlaps allow some exhaust gas reversion into the induction system at lower engine speeds, affecting idle quality and low-speed torque. The characteristics of this cam are fair idle, good power from 1500 to 6000rpm, and good fuel economy. This cam develops considerable power at higher engine speeds and is especially effective in lightweight vehicles.

This *High Performance Street Profile* choice can be used with either hydraulic or solid lifters, and the simulation will accurately model this cam with either lifter selection (choose hydraulic lifters for more street-oriented applications and solid lifters for more high-performance oriented applications). This cam is nearly identical to the *ISKY Hi-Rev Flat-Tappet* cam part 201025 for the smallblock Chevy. As described earlier, the intake and exhaust valve lifts for all application-specific profiles are automatically calculated by the simulation and are based on the valve diameters.

Dual Purpose Street/Track Profile—This profile is designed to simulate a high-performance aftermarket camshaft. All cam timing events displayed in the Component Selection Box are seat-to-seat measurements.

EVO timing on this camshaft is beginning to move away from specs that would be expected for simply utilizing combustion pressure with more of an emphasis toward early blowdown and minimizing exhaust pumping losses. The later IVC attempts to strike a balance between harnessing the ram effects of the induction system while minimizing intake flow reversion. IVO and EVC produce 64 degrees of overlap, a profile that is clearly designed to harness exhaust scavenging effects. The modestly aggressive overlap can allow some exhaust gas reversion into the induction system at lower engine speeds, affecting idle quality and low-speed torque. The characteristics of this cam are lopey idle, good power from 2500 to 6500rpm, and modest fuel economy. This cam develops considerable power at higher engine speeds and is especially effective in lightweight vehicles. This *Dual Purpose Street/Track Profile* choice can be used with either hydraulic or solid lifters, and the simulation will accurately model this cam design with either lifter selection (choose hydraulic lifters for more street-

```
    Camshaft Type: Drag-Race Circle-Track      Lifter Type: Solid
      Cam Specs @: Seat To Seat                Int Centerline: 106.0
         IVO (BTDC): 42.0    IVC (ABDC): 74.0    Int Duration: 296.0
         EVO (BBDC): 77.0    EVC (ATDC): 45.0    Exh Duration: 302.0
  Int Lift @Valve: 0.XXX    (Auto)         Lobe-Center Angle: 106.0
  Exh Lift @Valve: 0.XXX    (Auto)         Advance(+)/Retard(-): 0

    Camshaft Type: Drag-Race High-Speed       Lifter Type: Roller
      Cam Specs @: Seat To Seat                Int Centerline: 108.0
         IVO (BTDC): 52.0    IVC (ABDC): 88.0    Int Duration: 320.0
         EVO (BBDC): 88.0    EVC (ATDC): 52.0    Exh Duration: 320.0
  Int Lift @Valve: 0.XXX    (Auto)         Lobe-Center Angle: 108.0
  Exh Lift @Valve: 0.XXX    (Auto)         Advance(+)/Retard(-): 0
```

This profile simulates a competition camshaft. The profile is similar to *ISKY Oval Track Flat Tappet Series* part 201555 for the SB Chevy.

This profile models an all-out competition cam. The profile of this cam is similar to *ISKY Roller Series* part 201600 for the SB Chevy.

oriented applications and solid lifters for more competition-oriented applications). The profile of this cam is close to the *ISKY Hydraulic Series* cam part 201281 for the smallblock Chevy. As described earlier, the intake and exhaust valve lifts for all application-specific profiles are automatically calculated by the simulation and are based on the valve diameters.

Drag-Race/Circle-Track Profile—This profile is designed to simulate a competition aftermarket camshaft. All cam timing events displayed in the Component Selection Box are seat-to-seat measurements.

EVO timing on this racing camshaft places less emphasis on utilizing combustion pressure and more emphasis on beginning early blowdown to minimize exhaust pumping losses. The later IVC attempts to strike a balance between harnessing the ram effects of the induction system while minimizing intake flow reversion. IVO and EVC produce 90 degrees of overlap, a profile that is clearly intended to optimize exhaust scavenging effects. This aggressive overlap is designed for open headers and allows exhaust gas reversion into the induction system at lower engine speeds, affecting idle quality and torque below 3500rpm. The characteristics of this cam

are very lopey idle, good power from 3600 to 7600rpm, with no consideration for fuel economy. This cam develops considerable power at higher engine speeds and is especially effective in lightweight vehicles. This *Drag-Race/Circle-Track Profile* choice can be used with either solid or roller lifters, and the simulation will accurately model this cam design with either lifter selection. The profile of this cam is similar to the *ISKY Oval Track Flat Tappet Series* cam part 201555 for the smallblock Chevy. As described earlier, the intake and exhaust valve lifts for all application-specific profiles are automatically calculated by the simulation and are based on the valve diameters.

Drag-Race High-Speed Profile—This profile is designed to simulate an all-out competition aftermarket camshaft. All cam timing events displayed in the Component Selection Box are seat-to-seat measurements.

All timing events on this camshaft are designed to optimize power on large displacement engines at very high engine speeds with large-tube, open headers, and high compression ratios. This camshaft may not be effective in small displacement engines. EVO timing on this racing profile places the utilization of combustion pressure on the "back burner" and focuses emphasis on beginning early blowdown to minimize pumping losses during the exhaust stroke. This technique will help power at very high engine speeds, especially on large-displacement engines that do not easily discharge the high volume of exhaust gasses they produce. The late IVC attempts to harness the full ram effects of the induction system while relying on intake pressure wave tuning to minimize intake flow reversion. IVO and EVC produce 104 degrees of overlap, a profile that is clearly intended to utilize exhaust scavenging effects. This very aggressive overlap seriously affects idle quality and torque below 4000rpm. The characteristics of this cam are extremely lopey idle, good power from 4500 to 8500+rpm, with no consideration made for fuel consumption. This *Drag-Race High-Speed Profile* is designed to be used with roller lifters. The profile of this cam is similar to the *ISKY Roller Series* cam part 201600 for the smallblock Chevy. As described earlier, the intake and exhaust valve

Several of the "generic" grinds that are included in the menu selection of the Filling-And-Emptying simulation were selected from the ISKY CAMS catalog. ISKY's catalog is "simulation-friendly," listing seat-to-seat valve event timing for nearly every cam in their line.

lifts for all application-specific profiles are automatically calculated by the simulation and are based on the valve diameters.

Each of the above application-specific cams can be modified in any way by directly entering valve-event or other cam-timing specs by choosing one of the two "Other" selections at the bottom of the Camshaft menu (more on this next).

Entering 0.050-Inch and Seat-To-Seat Timing

The last two selections in the Camshaft menu are "Other" choices that allow the direct entry of cam timing events to simulate virtually any camshaft. The first choice forces all specifications displayed and entered in the Camshaft category of the on-screen Component Selection Box to be treated as *Seat-To-Seat timing specs*. The second choice instructs the simulation to assume that all cam timing values are *0.050-inch timing specs*. Whenever an "Other" selection is made that requires the program to switch from one timing method to another, any currently displayed timing values are NOT changed; however, a warning message clearly indicates the timing method has changed. In addition, the new selected timing method is displayed next to "Cam Specs @:" in the Camshaft category. Furthermore, after an "Other" selection, the intake and exhaust valve-lift fields are switched to "(Man)," making entered or displayed valve-lift data permanent (turns off any auto-calculation techniques that may have been used to previously calculate valve lift).

Only the four basic timing events are affected by changes in seat-to-seat vs. 0.050-inch measurement methods. As you'll notice on the valve-motion curve drawing, changes in timing methods can only affect IVO, IVC, EVO, EVC, and the calculated intake and exhaust duration. The remaining timing events, including Intake Centerline (ICA), Exhaust Centerline (ECA), Lobe Center Angle (LCA), and Intake and Exhaust Valve Lift are <u>not altered</u> by either measurement method because none of these specs are derived relative to any of the basic four valve events.

The seat-to-seat timing method measures the valve timing—relative to piston position—when the valve or lifter has only just begun to rise or has *almost* completely returned to the base circle on the closing ramp. Unfortunately, there are no universal seat-to-seat measuring standards. These are some of the more common:

0.004-inch valve rise for both intake and exhaust
0.006-inch valve rise for both intake and exhaust
0.007-inch open/0.010-close valve rise for both valves
0.010-inch valve rise for both intake and exhaust
0.020-inch LIFTER rise for both intake and exhaust

The timing specs measured using these methods are meant to approximate the actual valve opening and closing points that occur within the running engine. Because of this, seat-to-seat valve events are often called the *advertised* or *running* timing. As we mentioned previ-

Seat-to-seat timing measures the valve timing—relative to piston position—when the valve or (more rarely the lifter) has just begun to rise. In the setup pictured here, the dial indicators are positioned on the valvespring retainers and are measuring <u>valve rise</u>, which is the most common technique used with seat-to-seat timing (0.020-inch LIFTER rise is a notable exception). Timing specs measured using these methods are meant to approximate the actual valve opening and closing points that occur within the running engine. Because of this, seat-to-seat valve events are often called the *advertised* or *running* timing and will always produce the most accurate simulations.

ously in this book, an engine simulation program needs just this type of information to calculate the beginning and end of mass flow in the ports and cylinders, a crucial step in the process of determining cylinder pressures and power output. *Because of this, seat-to-seat timing specifications produce the most accurate simulation results.* The 0.050-inch timing figures, while accepted by Motion's simulation, must be internally converted to seat-to-seat figures, unfortunately a less-than-perfect process, before they can be used in the simulation.

In the early days of the "cam wars," primarily during the 50's and 60's, the seat-to-seat timing method became popular with cam manufacturers as a way to "advertise" the duration of their popular grinds. Remember the bigger-is-better axiom? It probably reached its peak during this period. At that time, the way to be declared a winner in the marketplace was to offer the "biggest" and "baddest" camshaft, and that meant a cam with the longest duration. Manufacturers got so caught up in this foolishness that they used "trick" grinding methods to extend the clearance ramps and artificially increase seat-to-seat duration without appreciably affecting the valve-open du-

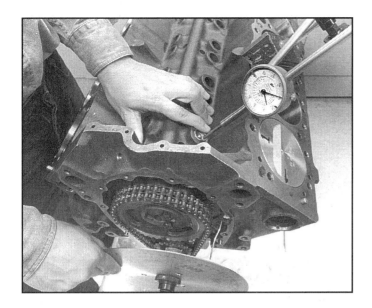

The 0.050-inch lifter rise cam timing method has become one of the few standards in the performance marketplace. It measures the valve timing—relative to piston position—when the lifter has risen 0.050-inch off of the base circle of the cam. In the setup pictured here, the dial indicator is positioned on an intake lifter and is reading 0.050-inch; the 0.050-inch valve timing point can now be read directly off of the degree wheel attached to the crankshaft. Timing specs measured using this method <u>are not meant</u> to approximate the actual valve opening and closing points, instead their purpose is to permit accurate cam installation. All 0.050-inch timing specs entered into the Filling-And-Emptying program are <u>internally converted</u> to seat-to-seat timing. Because there is no way to precisely perform this conversion, always try to obtain and use seat-to-seat event timing to optimize simulation accuracy.

ration (it was already too big). By this time, enthusiasts were confused by the myriad of seat-to-seat timing specs, and many were installing camshafts incorrectly. Even worse, the very nature of seat-to-seat timing makes it difficult to "nail down" the precise (rotational) position of the cam during engine assembly. To solve this problem, cam manufacturers united (picture water and oil!) to introduce a universal cam spec primarily aimed at making cam installation easier and more accurate. The new technique, called 0.050-inch timing, was based on the movement of the cam follower (lifter) rather than the valve. Since the lifter is moving quite quickly at 0.050-inch it was easy to accurately index the cam to the crank position. Today, regardless of who manufactures the cam, you will always find 0.050-inch lifter rise timing points published on the cam card, simplifying cam installation.

The 0.050-inch lifter rise timing method has become one of the few standards in the performance marketplace. In fact, some cam manufacturers have come to embrace this method so completely that they won't publish the old "advertised" or seat-to-seat timing events. This may go a long way toward establishing a standard, but it's a real step backwards from the standpoint of testing cams in engine simulation programs. As we have said, an engine simulation program MUST know when

the valves lift off the seats and when they return to their seats in order to calculate mass flow into and out of the engine.

Let's examine how much VALVE lift typically occurs at 0.050-inch of LIFTER rise:

Valve Lift @ 0.050-inch Lifter Rise =
$$= (0.050 \times \text{Rocker Ratio}) - \text{Valve Lash}$$
For example (for 1.5 rockers and 30 thousandths lash):
$$\textbf{Valve Lift @ 0.050} = 0.050 \times 1.5 - 0.030$$
$$= 0.045\text{-inch}$$

This example shows that the net valve lift is nearly equal to lifter rise. At this point in this book, your knowledge of IC valve events should tell you that substantial flow occurs during this seemingly insignificant period. Consider the EVO point for example. By 0.050-inch, the exhaust valve is well on its way to depressurizing the cylinder and having dramatic effects on the power balance between induced torque and pumping losses on the exhaust stroke. Furthermore, the EVO point blasts a pressure wave through the exhaust system that returns as a scavenging wave during the overlap period. Similar critical functions occur at the other valve timing points. Valve motion during the first 0.050-inch of lift cannot be disregarded as insignificant when performing engine simulations. But what do you do when you just can't find seat-to-seat timing specs?

The first answer to that question is provided in the second "Other" choice of the Camshaft pull-down menu (additional tips for finding "missing" valve event specs is provided later in this chapter). This selection declares that all specifications displayed and entered in the program are assumed to have been obtained using the *0.050-inch Lifter-Rise timing method*. (Whenever an "Other" selection is made that requires the program to switch from one timing method to another, a warning messages is displayed indicating a change has been made in cam timing methods.) All 0.050-inch timing specs entered into the program are <u>internally converted</u> to seat-to-seat timing points before the simulation is performed—remember, engine simulation is simply not possible without seat-to-seat valve timing specs. Unfortunately, there is no precise way to make this conversion, so an estimation is performed of where the seat-to-seat points might lie based on the known 0.050-inch timing points. Sometimes the program is able to guess very closely, and the power curves will match dyno results with that camshaft. At other times, the shape of the lobe is considerably different than the program's best guess, and accuracy will suffer.

We realize that this situation can be frustrating for some users, particularly when you consider that a few tech support people at cam manufacturers become belligerent when asked for seat-to-seat valve events or tell customers that the information is "proprietary." Until these behind-the-times individuals "wake up" and realize that enthusiasts have tools like engine simulations and want to "test" cams before they buy, our best suggestion is to take your business elsewhere. But before you give up completely on your favorite cam grinder, take a look at the upcoming section on calculating valve events. It may show you how to calculate the needed timing from the jumble of specs printed in their cam catalog.

Camshaft Advance and Retard

In our earlier discussions on overlap, we found that this important cam timing event can be adjusted in two ways: 1) the wrong way by changing the Lobe Center Angle, or 2) the right way by changing the appropriate valve events to complement overlap timing. Changing LCA alone effectively moves two valve events to improve high-speed performance and the other two events decrease high-speed power. This "schizophrenic" tuning approach also occurs when the cam is advanced or retarded.

Selecting an "Other" choice from the Camshaft menu moves the cursor to the Component Selection Box and allows the direct entry of cam timing specifications. After you have entered all four valve events and both valve lift specs, the cursor moves to the "Advance(+)/Retard(-)" field. Changing this spec from zero (the default) to a positive value advances the cam (in crank degrees) while negative values retard the cam. The *Advance/Retard* function "shifts" all the intake and exhaust lobes the same advanced or retarded amount relative to the crankshaft. Why would you want to do this? The answer is simple: It is just about the only "tuning" change available to the engine builder without regrinding or replacing the cam. While it's possible to "tune" the cam using offset keys, special bushings, or multi-indexed sprockets, let's investigate what happens when all the valve events are advanced or retarded from the cam manufacturer's recommended timing.

It is generally accepted that advancing the cam improves low-speed power while retarding the cam improves high-speed power. When the cam is advanced, IVC and EVC occur earlier and that tends to improve low-speed performance; however, EVO and IVO also occur earlier, and these changes tend to improve power at higher engine speeds. The net result of these conflicting changes is a slight boost in low-speed power. The same goes for retarding the cam. Two events (later IVC and EVC) boost high-speed power and two (later EVO and IVO) boost low-speed performance. The net result is a slight boost in high-speed power.

Advancing or retarding a camshaft has the overall affect of reducing valve-timing efficiency in exchange for slight gains in low- or high-speed power. Consequently, most cam grinders recommend avoiding this tuning technique. If advancing or retarding allows the engine to perform better in a specific rpm range, the cam profile was probably not optimum in the first place. More power can be found at both ends of the rpm range by installing the right cam rather than advancing or retarding the wrong cam. However, if you already own a specific camshaft, slightly advanced or retarded timing may "fine tune" engine output to better suit your needs.

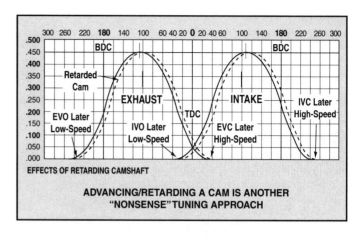

EFFECTS OF RETARDING CAMSHAFT

ADVANCING/RETARDING A CAM IS ANOTHER "NONSENSE" TUNING APPROACH

The "schizophrenic" tuning approach we discussed earlier involving LCA also occurs when the cam is advanced or retarded. If advancing or retarding the cam is actually "poor practice," why is it so popular? The answer is simple: It is just about the only "tuning" change available to the engine builder without regrinding or replacing the cam. Advancing the cam slightly improves low-speed power, while retarding the cam gives a small boost in high-speed power. If advancing or retarding allows the engine to perform better, the cam profile was not optimum in the first place.

Calculating Valve Events And Using The Cam Math Calculator

Valve-motion curve drawings clearly indicate that cam timing events are related. No specific event is entirely isolated from the others. With sufficient information about the derivative cam timing specs, it is possible to calculate the basic four valve events needed to run a simulation. What is the minimum amount of information needed to figure out valve-event timing? There is no one answer to this question, but the answer that applies to the specs found in many cam manufacturers' catalogs is: *Intake Duration, Exhaust Duration, Lobe Center Angle (LCA), and the Intake Centerline (ICA).* With these four cam specs, it is possible to calculate the IVO, IVC, EVO, and EVC. The calculated valve opening and closing events will be based on either seat-to-seat or 0.050-inch timing methods, depending on how the duration figures were measured. Remember, whenever you have a choice, always use seat-to-seat timing figures; the simulation results will have the highest accuracy. Also remember, the LCA and ICA do not change with timing methods, so the same LCA and ICA values can be used with either seat-to-seat or 0.050-inch duration figures.

Let's use the following example and work through the process of calculating the valve events hidden within this cam timing. A particular cam catalog lists a small-block Ford cam as:

Cam Type:	**Street Hydraulic**
Net Valve Lift (Int):	**0.448-inch**
Net Valve Lift (Exh):	**0.472-inch**
Duration @ 0.050 (Int):	**204-degrees**
Duration @ 0.050 (Exh):	**214-degrees**
Duration @ 0.006 (Int):	**280-degrees**

Duration @ 0.006 (Exh): 290-degrees
Overlap @ 0.006: 61-degrees
Intake Centerline: 107-degrees
Lobe Center Angle: 112-degrees

This is a lot of information, but none of the basic valve events are listed. Refer to the valve-motion drawings. See if you can discover the relationships described by the following equations (they assume all cam lobes are symmetric; while asymmetric profiles are quite common, the amount of asymmetry typically is very small, so the following calculations should be accurate to within two or three degrees regardless of the cam profile).

The first step is to calculate how many degrees before TDC the intake valve opens (when IVO occurs). This can be done with the following formula (we'll use seat-to-seat duration figures):

Intake Valve Opening (IVO) =
= (Intake Duration / 2) - Intake Centerline
= 280/2 - 107
= 140 - 107
= 33 degrees BTDC

Knowing the IVO, it is possible to calculate the intake valve closing point (IVC) by simply subtracting the IVO from the intake duration and then subtracting an additional 180-degrees to account for the full intake stroke:

Intake Valve Closing (IVC) =
= Intake Duration - IVO - 180
= 280 - 33 - 180
= 67 degrees ABDC

We're halfway there. The next step relates the known intake lobe timing to the exhaust lobe and then calculates the exhaust timing events. We must first locate the center of the exhaust lobe from the known intake centerline using the lobe center angle. The lobe center angle (LCA) is the distance (in cam degrees) between the exact center of both lobes. Since we know that the intake centerline (ICA) is the distance from TDC to the center of the intake lobe, it is possible to calculate where the center of the exhaust lobe lies relative to TDC:

Exhaust Centerline (ECA) =
= (2 x Lobe Center Angle) - Intake Centerline
= (2 x 112) - 107
= 224 - 107
= 117 degrees

Now that the exhaust centerline is known, we can repeat the same process to find exhaust event timing:

Exhaust Valve Closing (EVC) =
= (Exhaust Duration / 2) - Exhaust Centerline
= (290/2) - 117
= 145 - 117
= 28 degrees ATDC

Finally, knowing the EVC, we can calculate the Exhaust Valve Opening (EVO) point by subtracting the EVC from the exhaust duration and then subtracting another 180 degrees to account for the full exhaust stroke:

Exhaust Valve Opening (EVO) =
= Exhaust Duration - EVC - 180
= 290 - 28 - 180
= 82 deg. BBDC

So the valve events for this cam are:
IVO = 33 degrees BTDC
IVC = 67 degrees ABDC
EVO = 82 degrees BBDC
EVC = 28 degrees ATDC

If any of these valve events had turned out to be negative, which is possible for some stock-type cams measured using 0.050-inch timing, enter the calculated timing figures into the simulation with the minus sign. For example, if EVC was determined to be -10 degrees, this would mean that the valve closes 10 degrees BEFORE TDC rather than after it. To tell the simulation that this is the case, enter a -10 for EVC.

This series of calculations is performed automatically by the *Cam Math Calculator* included in Motion's Filling And Emptying simulation version 2.5 (under development as this book went to press). By clicking on the MATH button in the lower right of the screen, the *Cam Math Calculator* will open a window and pre-load it with the cam timing currently displayed on screen. If any single event is changed, the remaining events are instantly recalculated and may be saved to the main screen or discarded.

This handy addition to the program makes short work of not only entering cam data from manufacturer's catalogs, but also you can test the results of changes to Lobe Center Angle, Intake Centerline, Intake Duration and Exhaust Duration. Combined with the ability to change IVO, IVC, EVO, EVC, and overall advance and retard from the main screen, the new version 2.5 with the *Cam Math Calculator* allows changing virtually EVERY cam timing event and measuring its result.

The series of calculations performed on these pages can be done instantly by the *Cam Math Calculator* included in Motion's Filling And Emptying simulation version 2.5 (under development as this book went to press). By clicking on the MATH button in the lower right of the screen, the *Cam Math Calculator* will "pop up" a window pre-loaded with the current cam timing. Any single event can be altered and the remaining events will be recalculated. This handy addition to the program makes short work of entering cam data from some manufacturer's catalogs.

DeskTop Dynos
Using Computers To Build Horsepower
6—Gas Dynamics & Dynomation

Note: This chapter discusses wave interactions in the IC engine and utilizes the Dynomation engine simulation program to illustrate the concepts of gas dynamics. The Dynomation software was developed by V.P. Engineering (see pages 37-39 for more information about the development of this unique product). V.P Engineering is located at: 5261 N.W. 114th Street, Unit J, Grimes, IA 50111, voice: 515-986-9197, fax: 515-986-9130.

If you read the previous chapters, you've discovered some of the basics of gas dynamics as they apply to the IC engine. This chapter picks up where the others leave off and takes you considerably deeper into the theory of finite-amplitude waves. As part of this exploration, you'll get an inside look at one of the most advanced engine simulation programs available to engine builders and racing teams: *Dynomation*. While this program is quite expensive (about $600) and aimed at the professional, it provides a unique insight into many of the concepts discussed throughout this book. While the Filling-And-Emptying simulation incorporates a "mini-version" of the wave-action simulation used in Dynomation, all pressure analysis happens "behind the scenes," invisible to the user. The Dynomation program, on the other hand, is primarily a tool used *to investigate the interactions of pressure waves and particle flow within intake and exhaust sys-*

tem passages. Using the Dynomation program as a "test probe," we will examine how exhaust and intake runner lengths "tune," you'll see the effects of blowdown, you'll discover pressure waves as they "bounce" off of the open and closed ends of passages, you'll uncover how stepped headers affect cylinder pressures, and much more.

Before we proceed into the strange world of finite-amplitude waves and their actions inside the IC engine, it is essential to have a solid understanding of the fundamentals. As you read through the first part of this chapter you will find a fast review of familiar concepts. However, the basics are soon set aside as we delve into greater depths than in previous chapters. If, at first, you find this material difficult to grasp, a quick reexamination of chapters 3, 4, and 5 should be helpful.

THE IC ENGINE:
AND UNSTEADY FLOW MACHINE

The air-and-fuel and exhaust gasses that move within the passages of the internal-combustion (IC) engine behave in an *unsteady* manner. In other words, the gases are constantly changing pressure, temperature, and velocity throughout the four-cycle process of induction, compression, expansion, and exhaust. For example, when the intake valve is closed, the gas velocity at the valve is zero. When the valve begins to open, a difference in pressure between the cylinder and the port begins to accelerate gas particles into the cylinder. This gas motion—and all other gas particle motion within the engine—starts and stops, squeezes and decompresses, and heats up and cools down. To analyze and simulate these actions, designers and programmers must rely on the discipline of *Unsteady Gas Dynamics*. A basic knowledge of this subject and the ability to visualize (and calculate using simulations) wave interactions inside the IC engine is probably the single most important "tool" available to the modern engine builder.

The application of Unsteady Gas Dynamics does not require that we cover the development of gas-flow equations (thank goodness!!), but a general description of the mechanisms that apply to the IC engine are essential. After reading the following material, you should have sufficient understanding to comprehend what is possible and what is not possible with high-level simulation programs. In addition, if the writers and editors of this book have been at all successful in their tasks, this chapter—as a culmination of the subject—may help you gain a deeper insight into IC engine function!

Acoustic Waves Vs. Finite-Amplitude Waves

The sounds we hear around us are actually small pressure disturbances in the air. We call these pressure "pulses" *acoustic waves*. The pressure amplitude (volume) of these waves is very small. As an example, the volume at which you will begin to experience pain from sound occurs around 120 decibels and creates a peak pressure of only 0.00435psi above the ambient, undisturbed air. Since sea-level air pressure (barometric pressure) is about 14.7psi, then the *pressure ratio* at which sound become painful is:

$$Pr = P / Pa$$
$$\text{where}$$
$$P = 14.7 + 0.00435$$
$$= 14.70435 \text{ PSI}$$
$$\text{so:}$$
$$Pr = P/Pa$$
$$= 14.70435 / 14.7$$
$$= 1.0003$$

or three one-hundredths of one percent increase over atmospheric pressure!

Very loud acoustic waves create very small pressure disturbances. There are waves that produce substantially higher pressure ratios than even loud sound waves. These powerful energy-charged waves are called *finite-amplitude waves*. Pressure disturbances of these higher intensities can be found in the induction and exhaust passages of the IC engine. Remarkably, pressure ratios of 2.5 can be readily measured (that's a pressure ratio almost 10,000 times greater than painfully loud sound waves—certainly something you would never want to "hear"). This enormous difference in intensity between acoustic waves and finite amplitude waves gives some insight into why acoustic theory (still commonly used) for calculating the optimum "tuned lengths" of intake and exhaust passages is misleading (more on this later).

Compression And Expansion Waves

Finite-amplitude waves take two forms within IC engine ducting: Compression and Expansion. The compression wave is a positive pressure disturbance that will always have a pressure ratio greater than one. The expansion wave is a strong drop in ambient pressure, and therefore will always have a negative pressure ratio (less than one). Expansion waves are known by other names, such as "rarefaction waves" or "suction waves," however, they all refer to the identical phenomenon.

Compression and expansion waves act in similar—but uniquely different—ways as they move through IC engine passages. Understanding how these waves move and how they interact with their surroundings is an essential part of understanding how gasses move inside the IC engine. The first piece of the puzzle is shown in **figure 1**. This drawing illustrates a positive compression wave traveling from left to right through a pipe. As the pressure waves travel rightward, they drive gas particles in the same rightward direction. However, the velocity of the gas is considerably slower than the speed of the pressure waves. There are many analogs to this situation in everyday life. As we mentioned in Chapter 5, this same phenomenon can be visualized in the way logs are pushed ashore by waves on the surface of a lake. The waves wash through floating logs driving them forwards but at a much slower rate than the speed of the waves. An expansion wave is illustrated in **figure 2**. This low-pressure wave is also traveling from left to right, how-

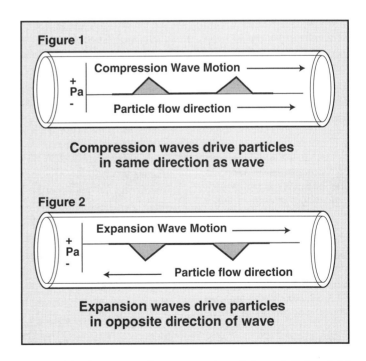

Figure 1

Compression Wave Motion →

+ Pa -

Particle flow direction →

Compression waves drive particles in same direction as wave

Figure 2

Expansion Wave Motion →

+ Pa -

← Particle flow direction

Expansion waves drive particles in opposite direction of wave

As positive compression waves travel from left to right through a pipe (top), they drive gas particles in the same rightward direction. When expansion waves (lower) travel from left to right, they pass through gas particles in the pipe and propel them in the *opposite* direction, in this case, leftward.

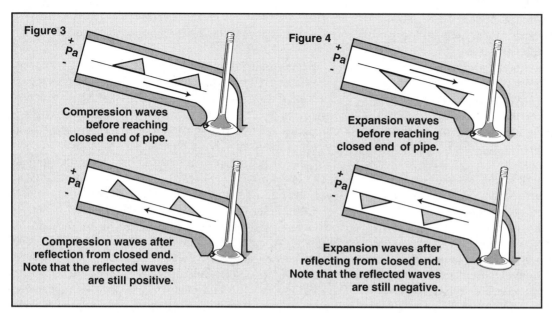

Figure 3

+Pa-

Compression waves
before reaching
closed end of pipe.

+Pa-

Compression waves after
reflection from closed end.
Note that the reflected waves
are still positive.

Figure 4

+Pa-

Expansion waves
before reaching
closed end of pipe.

+Pa-

Expansion waves after
reflecting from closed end.
Note that the reflected waves
are still negative.

Positive pressure compression waves striking the closed end of a passage return with their original profile intact. Expansion waves behave similar to compression waves. Net particle motion is zero.

ever, as it passes through gas particles in the pipe it propels them in the *opposite* direction, in this case, leftward. This phenomenon is similar to what you observe when you draw in a long, deep breath. As you inhale, gas particles flow into your mouth, yet the sound of in-rushing air (the low-pressure sound waves) travel in the opposite direction, out of your mouth.

Both compression and expansion waves change their character when they encounter sudden transitions in area. Area changes within engine ducting occur at an open end, a closed end, or at transition to smaller or larger diameter passages. Perhaps the most familiar area change occurs at the end of an exhaust header pipe. The primary tube either abruptly ends or it empties into a larger-diameter collector that opens to the atmosphere several inches downstream. Beyond this very visible (and easily heard) pipe transition, there are many other changes in area within engine ducting. For example, when the intake runner transitions into the manifold plenum or

directly into the atmosphere (in the case of injector stacks), a substantial area change is produced. Furthermore, the intake and exhaust valves create a pipe that is either closed or partially open, again creating significant changes in areas. What happens when a finite-amplitude wave reaches one of these areas?

First, let's examine the situation when pressure waves reach the closed end of a pipe. **Figure 3** illustrates a positive-pressure compression wave striking the closed end of a passage and returning with its original profile still intact. The only difference is that the pressure wave is now moving in the opposite direction. Consider how this affects gas particle motion. When the compression wave travels rightward, it nudges the gas particles toward the right. After reflection, the compression wave nudges the particles leftward. The gas particles are returned to their original position; there is no net flow in the pipe. This is exactly what you would expect to find in a pipe that is closed at one end! **Figure 4** depicts an ex-

A leftward-moving compression wave is reflected as a *rightward-moving expansion wave* when it reaches the open end of a pipe (figure 5). Particle movement is leftward in both cases. A leftward moving expansion wave is reflected as a *rightward-moving compression wave* (figure 6). Particle movement is rightward in both cases.

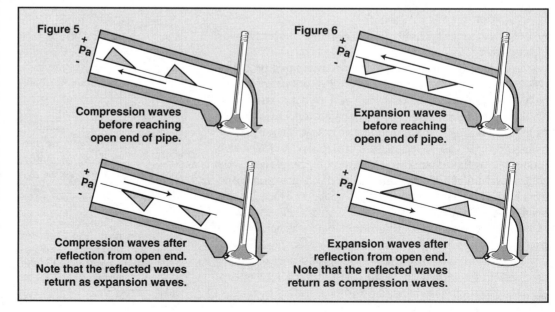

Figure 5

+Pa-

Compression waves
before reaching
open end of pipe.

+Pa-

Compression waves after
reflection from open end.
Note that the reflected waves
return as expansion waves.

Figure 6

+Pa-

Expansion waves
before reaching
open end of pipe.

+Pa-

Expansion waves after
reflection from open end.
Note that the reflected waves
return as compression waves.

pansion wave as it travels within the same closed-end pipe. Behaving similar to a compression wave, the reflected wave remains an expansion wave with the same profile. Net particle motion is again zero.

Now let's explore the interesting actions of finite-amplitude waves as they move within an open-end pipe. **Figure 5** shows the arrival of a compression wave at a transition to a much larger area. Notice that leftward-moving compression wave is reflected as a *rightward-moving expansion wave*. This has fascinating implications for particle movement. Initially, while the compression wave travels leftward, it helps propel gas particles in the same direction, toward the pipe end. When the expansion wave is created and it begins rightward movement, it continues to drive particles in the leftward direction (because expansion waves move particles in the opposite direction of wave travel). *Finite-amplitude compression waves moving <u>toward</u> the open end of a pipe provide a "double assist" to particle movement in the same direction.* Now consider the same open-end pipe, but this time picture a leftward moving expansion wave as illustrated in **figure 6**. As the expansion wave approaches the open end, it moves particles in the opposite direction, away from the end of the pipe. When the expansion wave reaches the pipe end, it is reflected as a compression wave and moves rightward, driving particles in the same direction. *So expansion waves "double-assist" particle movement <u>away</u> from the open end of the pipe.*

These pressure wave phenomena, particularly as they apply to the exhaust system, were not understood until the 1940s. Until that time, it was assumed that a high-pressure gas particle "slug" moved through the header pipe and created a vacuum behind it that helped to draw out residual gases. This "Kadenacy" theory—named after its inventor—is analogous to the compression waves traveling through a "Slinky™" coil-spring toy; a tight group of coils (representing high pressure waves) moves along the spring followed by a more open group of coils (representing low-pressure waves). Despite the fact that this theory was conclusively proven to be incorrect nearly 60 years ago, it is still believed by some engine "experts" to this day!

Pressure Waves And Engine Tuning

The goal of the high performance engine builder is to tune the lengths of IC engine passages so that the reflected waves reach the cylinder at the most effective times, either assisting exhaust-gas outflow or induction-charge inflow. If there ever was a statement that qualified for the adage "easier said than done," then this is it! There are many factors that affect the arrival of these waves. A short list would include valve timing, cam profiles, piston speed, pipe lengths, valve discharge coefficients, and cylinder blowdown pressures. To make matters worse, the peaks of finite amplitude waves travel faster than the base of the waves, causing wave profiles to distort as they travel through engine passages (see

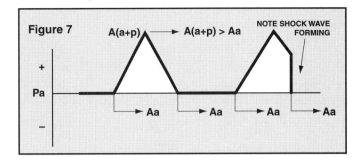

The peaks of finite amplitude waves travel faster than the bases of the waves, causing wave profiles to distort as they travel through engine passages. This can ultimately cause the waves to "tumble" over themselves forming shock waves and converting their energy into heat.

figure 7). This can ultimately cause the wave to "tumble" over itself forming shock waves and converting their energy into heat. All of these complex interactions occurring simultaneously make it easy to understand why the simple acoustic formulas that engine builders have traditionally used to determine "tuned lengths and pipe diameters" are simply misleading.

There are only two methods to determine effective pipe lengths and diameters. One is to build the engine, install it on a dyno, connect pressure-reading transducers to the intake and exhaust passages and in the cylinders and record pressure data. By analyzing these pressure signatures and running a series of tests with various component combinations, the engine builder can develop an effective engine for the desired purpose. The problem with this method is the associated high costs in time and money. Another method of finding effective pipe lengths and "zeroing in" on optimum component combinations is to *simulate* the pressure waves that occur within the IC engine. The problem with this method was that, until recently, an affordable four-cycle, pressure-wave simulation program for personal computers simply did not exist.

In 1993, V.P Engineering introduced *Dynomation*, the world's first PC computer program that applied the Method Of Characteristics mathematical solutions to the analysis of finite-amplitude waves within the 4-stroke racing engine (see Chapter 4 for more information about the development of Dynomation). Dynomation allows the engine builder to accurately analyze pressure-wave and particle-flow motions. It displays intake, exhaust, and cylinder pressure curves along with intake and exhaust flow velocities and directions. The experienced engine builder will find this information of great value when developing component combinations.

PRESSURE-TIME HISTORIES

The direct measurement of engine pressures can reveal a great deal about engine function. As discussed in Chapter 3, an analysis of engine pressures—throughout the complete four-cycle process—reveals the combined effects of all mechanical components, plus the ther-

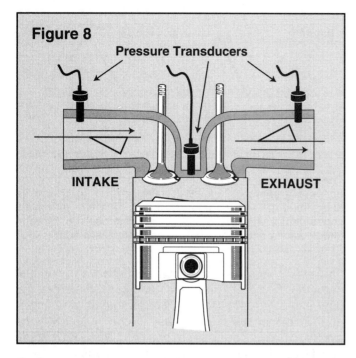

Figure 8

Pressure Transducers

INTAKE EXHAUST

Engine pressures can be directly measured with special transducers precisely positioned in the intake and exhaust passages and directly in the cylinders. The intake and the exhaust transducers are often located a few inches from the valves. The cylinder pressure transducer is located in the cylinderhead, protruding into the combustion chamber like a second sparkplug.

modynamic effects of heat transfer, the results of all the finite-wave interactions, and mass flow of induction and exhaust gasses within the engine. The measurement of these pressures requires the precise placement of pressure transducers in the intake and exhaust passages, and directly in the cylinders of the engine. **Figure 8** shows the typical locations. The intake and the exhaust transducers are often positioned a few inches from the valves. The cylinder pressure transducer is located in the cylinderhead, protruding into the combustion chamber like a second sparkplug. The typical pressures recorded by

these transducers is illustrated in **figure 9**.

This plot is referred to as a pressure crank-angle or pressure time-history diagram. (The reader will note the differences between this illustration and the more simplified versions on pages 21 and 23; also note that the starting points have been changed to coincide with the pressure plots produced by the Dynomation program). The horizontal axis displays the crank position throughout the 4-cycles from 0-720 degrees. The zero point on the left of the graph starts at TDC just before the power stroke. Moving rightward, the first vertical line indicates the exhaust valve opening point (EVO), typically occurring around 110 degrees. Continuing rightward, the next vertical line pinpoints intake valve opening (IVO) around 330 degrees. The exhaust valve closing point (EVC) occurs about 400 degrees. The distance between the IVO and EVC graphically indicates the valve overlap period. Around 600 degrees the intake valve closes (IVC). Finally, the diagram ends at 720 degrees with the piston back at TDC, marking the end of the compression stroke. The vertical axis of the diagram indicates the pressure in terms of the pressure ratio (Pr). A value of 1.0 represents standard atmospheric pressure (Pa). A value below this indicates subatmospheric pressure or expansion waves. Values above 1.0 are positive pressures above atmospheric or compression waves. The vertical axis can also be indexed in units of **bar** instead of pressure ratios (1.0 bar represents standard atmospheric pressure).

Referring to the same pressure crank-angle diagram (figure 9), let's trace out the pressures measured throughout all four engine cycles as recorded by the three transducers. Keep in mind that the pressures illustrated in this diagram reflect an engine that is "in-tune." (We'll explore out-of-tune pressures later.) When the exhaust valve opens (EVO), the formation of the primary exhaust pulse occurs. This high-pressure compression wave is created when the exhaust valve initially releases cylinder pressures (produced by the combustion of fuel and air) into the exhaust port and header pipe system. Cylinder pressure quickly falls and begins to approach exhaust port

This graph is called a pressure crank-angle diagram, and it traces out the pressures measured throughout all four engine cycles as recorded by three transducers. When the exhaust valve opens (EVO), the formation of the primary exhaust pulse occurs. Cylinder pressure quickly falls and begins to approach exhaust port pressure. The pressure wave created at EVO returns to the cylinder during overlap. It creates subatmospheric pressures that stop reversion and help draw in fresh charge. If the exhaust system was designed correctly, the expansion wave will continue to assist induction flow until the exhaust valve closes (EVC).

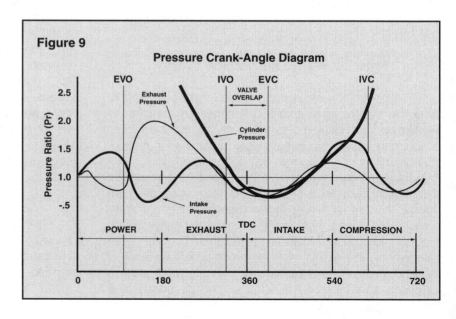

Figure 9

Pressure Crank-Angle Diagram

pressure. Until IVO, an intake pressure wave—created during the previous intake cycle—bounces between the closed inlet valve and the open end of the runner, as indicated by the oscillating wave on the diagram. When the intake valve opens, cylinder pressure is almost always higher than the pressure in the induction system. For the short period of time that this pressure differential exists, a reverse flow of exhaust gasses begins to move into the induction tract. Very little reverse flow generally occurs since piston speed is quite slow near TDC. During this time, the pressure wave that was generated when the exhaust valve opened reached the end of the header pipe and has now returned to the cylinder during the valve overlap period (between IVO and EVC) as an expansion wave. This wave creates subatmospheric pressures that stop reversion and help draw in fresh charge from the induction system <u>before</u> the piston begins to move down from TDC on the intake stroke. If the exhaust system (and several other engine parameters) was designed correctly, the expansion wave will continue to assist induction flow until the exhaust valve closes (EVC).

With the ending of the overlap period, the intake stroke begins in earnest. Throughout most of this period, inlet pressure closely follows cylinder pressure. Just before IVC a pressure surge or "hump" sends the cylinder pressure curve upwards. This surge is caused by a strong compression wave arriving from the induction system (created during the previous intake stroke), helping to "ram" fresh charge into the cylinder and minimize back flow. The arrival of this critically important compression wave is determined by runner length, engine speed, and other factors. After IVC, the cylinder pressure continues to rise as the piston heads for TDC on the compression stroke.

Gas Flow Vs. Engine Pressures

Up to this point, you may have assumed that there exists a direct relationship between the pressures measured in the ports and the flow of gasses. Furthermore, you may have assumed that when a pressure transducer registers a compression wave within a passage that opens on the right, gas flow would move in a rightward direction. In some instances pressures don't coincide with gas flow. **Figure 10** will help shed some light on this confusing issue. As compression **Wave 1** moves rightward it propels gas particles toward the right. A second compression wave, **Wave 2,** moves leftward in the same passage and propels gas particle toward the left. When **Waves 1** and **2** pass through each other they form the superposition **Wave 1 + 2**. Gas particles that were being propelled towards each other by the separate waves will collide and come to rest within **Wave 1 + 2**. A pressure transducer measuring this "new" wave will register a large pressure increase. It would be easy to assume that the higher pressure represented an increase in particle velocity.

This phenomenon makes the interpretation of pressure data difficult and easily misleading. Fortunately, the Dynomation simulation also calculates and displays *par-*

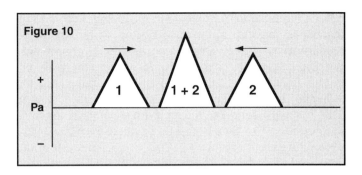

Figure 10

A direct relationship between the pressures measured and the flow of gasses within the ports does not always exist. Consider compression Wave-1 moving rightward and propelling gas particles toward the right. Wave-2 moves leftward in the same passage and propels gas particles toward the left. When Wave-1 and Wave-2 pass through each other they form the superposition Wave 1 + 2. Gas particles come to rest, but a pressure transducer measuring this "new" wave would register a large pressure increase.

ticle flow velocity and direction along with pressures for each degree of crank rotation. With displayed flow data, the engine builder is provided a comprehensive picture of port and cylinder pressures, intake and exhaust particle flow velocities, and the direction of flow. This is one of Dynomation's most powerful features, since not even the most precision pressure transducers can "reach into" the ports and measure instantaneous port velocity and direction.

INTAKE TUNING

The first part of effective intake tuning begins with good exhaust system tuning. As we mentioned previously, when the exhaust valve opens it generates a powerful positive pressure wave that travels to the end of the header pipe and returns to the cylinder as a strong expansion wave. When the timing is right, this suction wave will arrive during valve overlap and draw out burnt gases while starting the inflow of fresh charge. This scavenging effect lowers cylinder pressures just before the exhaust valve closes, early in the intake stroke. After EVC, the piston begins to move rapidly down the bore and when it reaches maximum speed, between 73- and 82-degrees after TDC, the rapid increase in cylinder volume will "yank" down the already low pressure in the cylinder. On the pressure-crank angle diagram this will occur between 433- and 442-degrees and is usually the lowest point on the cylinder pressure trace. This sudden drop in pressure generates a strong suction wave that travels toward the open end of the intake runner where it is reflected as a positive compression wave. Depending on the length of the runner and the speed of the engine, this compression wave will return to the cylinder just before the intake valve closes. The arriving compression wave provides two benefits: 1) As the wave moves through the port it pushes particles in the same direction, helping to fill the cylinder. When the compression wave reaches the intake valve just before IVC, the positive pressure 2) overcomes the buildup of pressure in the cylinder created by the piston moving up the bore on the early part of the compression stroke. This forces additional charge into the cylinder while delaying charge reversion until just before intake valve closes (an effect produced by the induction system sometimes described as ram tuning). This complex series of tuning events can add the winning edge to Pro Stock engines or other max-power applications, but the exhaust system, induction system design, and all cam timing events must all be synchronized to produce these effects.

When this synchronization is lost, intake charge will be driven back into the induction system before IVC. And reversion is a power killer. The Dynomation program can accurately predict when this will occur by examining the port flow velocity diagram (we'll provide examples of this later in the chapter).

After IVC the strong expansion wave created by the now completed intake stroke oscillates between the pipe end and the closed intake valve. It changes its sign from expansion to compression each time it encounters the open end of the runner. **Figure 11** shows the typical intake pressure trace throughout the full 720 degrees of crankshaft rotation. Each successive reflection returns with slightly lower peak pressures. To gain the greatest benefit from the reflected wave at peak engine speed, it is often best to tune the induction system to utilize the *second or third* returned pulse, since these retain the highest energy levels (engine timing and the physical length of the passages make it impossible to utilize the first pulse).

At lower engine speeds there will be more time for pressure reflections to return from the induction system, so additional waves will appear in the pressure crank-angle diagram. It is also possible to increase the number of pulsations at any given rpm by decreasing the length of the inlet runner. Similarly, a longer runner will decrease the number of pulsations since it takes more time for each pulse to return to the intake valve. Optimum runner length to return a second pulse at IVC can be "ballparked" with the following equation:

Second Pulse Length (inches) = 108,000 / RPM

This formula works best for engines that operate at relatively high rpm. However, at lower engine speeds this equation predicts a tuned length that is too long to be practical. Under these conditions, tuning to the third, fourth, or possibly even the fifth returned pulse requires a much shorter and more-practical length runner. The famous "Long Ram" of the early 1960s was designed by Chrysler to boost lower-speed torque on some of its big-block engines. It was based on second and third pulse tuning, requiring runners so long the carburetors wound up over the exhaust manifolds of the adjacent bank of cylinders. The runner lengths would have been much shorter if Chrysler engineers would have tuned to the third and fourth induction pulses. Here are good approximations for runner lengths tuned for the third, fourth, and

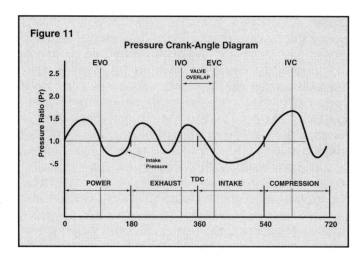

Figure 11

Pressure Crank-Angle Diagram

Here is a graph of typical intake pressures throughout the full 720 degrees of crankshaft rotation. Each successive wave reflection returns with slightly lower peak pressures. To gain the greatest benefit from the reflected wave at peak engine speed, it is often best to tune the induction system to utilize the *second or third* returned pulse since these retain the highest energy levels.

fifth returned induction pulse:

Third Pulse Length (inches)	**= 97,000 / RPM**
Fourth Pulse Length (inches)	**= 74,000 / RPM**
Fifth Pulse Length (inches)	**= 54,000 / RPM**

Engine designers and builders can use these equations to obtain good initial estimates for "fine tuning" using the Dynomation program.

Because of the "pulse-tuning" phenomenon, an intake manifold goes in and out of tune as the engine accelerates through its rpm range. The manifold transitions from fifth, to fourth, to third, and then, possibly, to second pulse tuning at maximum engine speed. As the engine passes through each of these tuning points, the runner phases in and out of sync with the expansion wave created when the piston reaches maximum speed on the intake stroke. As we mentioned, after the intake valve closes, a pressure wave bounces back and forth between the valve head and runner opening. At each successive return, the pulse loses energy. At lower speeds, when the engine tunes on the fifth or higher pulse, little benefit is derived from the weak returning pulse. However, by the time the engine speed reaches a level so that the third or second pulse arrives just before IVC, a substantial pressure differential strongly assists cylinder filling and prevents charge reversion. Since the second pulse delivers the strongest returning wave, the question arises: Why not use second-pulse tuning for all manifold designs? The answer is that the un-tuned gap between the second and third pulse is much greater than the gap between the third and fourth pulse. This means that engines using manifolds based on second-pulse tuning will have narrow, peaky, power bands, while third-pulse manifolds will tend to produce wider, although lower, power curves.

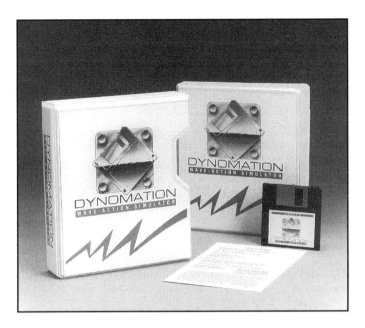

The Dynomation program is a powerful tool that simulates *the interactions of pressure waves and particle flow within intake and exhaust systems.* Dynomation acts as a "test probe," exploring subtle changes in camshaft timing and exhaust and intake system configuration.

Induction Runner Taper Angles

The taper angle of the inlet runner has a significant effect on the optimum tuned length. As the runner taper angle increases, the returning wave speeds up, so a higher engine speed is needed to regain the same level

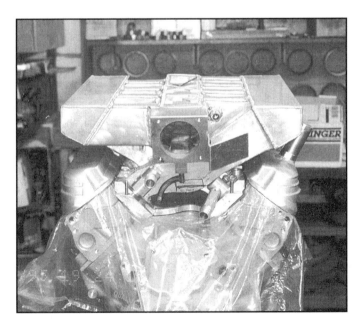

This custom intake manifold was designed with the help of Dynomation software. The manifold boosts low- and mid-range power on smallblock Ford engines. Initial dyno tests have confirmed the expected performance. Without simulation software, intake manifold design is strictly a trial-and-error process involving considerable time and money without any guarantee of success.

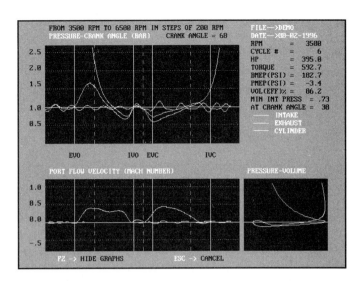

The Dynomation program reveals the entire spectrum of pressures and flow velocities within the simulated engine. This screen shows the pressure crank-angle diagram (top) displaying intake, exhaust, and cylinder pressures. Gas velocities are illustrated in the Port Flow graph (bottom left). A pressure-volume (PV) diagram (bottom right) illustrates cylinder pressure throughout the pumping loop. Studying the pressure curves can help professional racers locate inefficiencies and diagnose problems faster and cheaper than ever before.

of "tune." To put it another way, a 13-inch runner with a 4-degree taper angle will tune at approximately the same engine speed as a 10-inch straight runner.

Straight runners provide more power at lower engine speeds and work quite well for stock engines. However, to obtain peak performance from a high-speed racing engine, intake runners must incorporate a taper of 2 to 4 degrees (included). There are several complex reasons why taper angles are needed, but the easiest to explain are: 1) A tapered port has a greater volume to "store" air/fuel charge and feed the cylinder during the main portion of intake stroke, and 2) a taper angle acts somewhat like a stepped-header for the induction system, generating a series of positive pressure waves that return to the valve and assist cylinder filling.

Inlet runner taper angles can be adjusted in the Dynomation program to not only develop better-functioning induction systems, but also to gain a better understanding of how this important tuning element affects engine power. A particularly revealing test can be done by overlaying port velocities and cylinder pressures for various inlet taper angles.

Port Flow Velocities

Another very important element of intake and exhaust tuning is port flow velocity. The speed at which gasses move through the ports is essentially controlled by the port area and piston speed. For example, if intake port velocity is too low, gas particles flowing into the cylinder near IVC will not have sufficient momentum to overcome the rise in cylinder pressure, and fresh charge

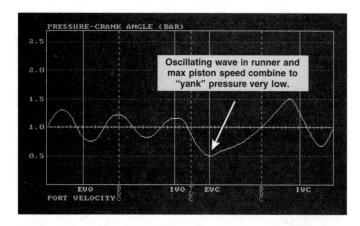

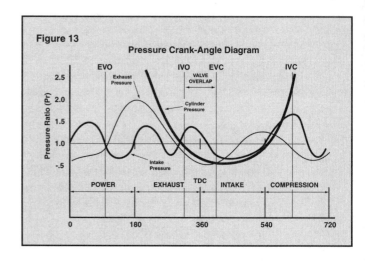

Figure 13

Pressure Crank-Angle Diagram

This is a good example of "in tune" induction pressures. The intake pressure wave is oscillating inside the runner and arrives at the intake valve during maximum piston speed (highest volume change) approximately 73- to 82-degrees after TDC. The "trough" of this wave combines with the suction created by the piston moving down the bore to "yank" the pressure wave to a very low amplitude. This low pressure generates a strong expansion wave that reflects back from the open-end runner as an equally strong compression wave that arrives at IVC. This not only drives additional charge into the cylinder, but reduces or eliminates reversion.

will flow back out of the cylinder into the inlet tract. Furthermore, when the ports are too large, all pressure waves generated by piston motion and exhaust gas outflow will be diminished. This will decrease the effectiveness of returning pressure waves during scavenging and cylinder filling. In fact, port size is so important that we can make this statement: Port sizing has a greater affect on engine performance than tuned runner lengths!

Research has shown that maximum port velocity through the minimum cross-sectional area of the runner should fall between 0.5 to 0.6 Mach, or about 600- to 720-feet-per-second. Port velocities higher than 0.6 Mach produce no further increases in volumetric efficiency. Since it is impossible for any port to provide optimum flow velocities at all engine speeds, it is essential that the engine builder accurately determine the required operating range for the engine and develop ports that flow appropriately during these selected speeds. If a broad power range is required, port areas should be sized so that maximum engine speeds produce port velocities of about 0.75 Mach. This will place optimum velocities (between 0.5 and 0.6 Mach) at lower engine speeds, optimizing volumetric efficiency where desired. If high-speed, maximum power is the goal, then port velocity at peak engine speed should be no higher than 0.6 Mach.

During your design sessions, here's an important concept to keep in mind. It is often possible to make port areas small enough—and velocities high enough—to completely eliminate intake reversion at IVC. When this is accomplished, it often produces insufficient port volume and constricted flow. A better approach, producing higher peak power, is to allow some reversion to occur. It is also possible to design ports that flow between 0.5 or 0.6

These engine pressures depict an engine with an exhaust system and cam timing that are "in-tune." The scavenging wave is wide enough to cover the overlap period, assisting exhaust gas outflow and preventing charge reversion.

Mach and do not show an increase in power. This situation can occur when valve restriction becomes too great. In these cases, the engine designer will simply have to experiment with several different port sizes, valve diameters, and valve lifts to find the optimum combination. The following formula will help you ballpark the required minimum port cross-sectional areas:

Minimum Area (Square Inches) =
$$= (RPM \times STROKE \times BORE^2) / 190{,}000$$
Note: This is an approximation and tends to be conservative; all variables are in inches.

One reason the above formula can only be an approximation is that port velocity is also dependent on the valve discharge coefficient. This value is the measured volume of flow across the valve divided by the perfect, theoretical (isentropic) flow. This value will always be less than one and is essentially a rating for the efficiency of the valve. The discharge coefficient is unique to each valve and cylinderhead design. The Dynomation simulation allows the direct input of flow-bench data and will calculate the discharge coefficients for specific cylinder head combinations. Since about 30 percent of flow loss through the port occurs at the valve, an improvement of the discharge coefficient can result in substantial performance gains.

EXHAUST TUNING

Incomplete removal of exhaust gases from the cylinder of an IC engine reduces performance in two ways. First, the volumetric efficiency is decreased when residual gases take up space within the cylinder that could have been occupied by fresh charge. Second, higher cylinder pressures from incomplete exhaust blowdown force residual burnt gasses into the inlet tract upon IVO. This "spoils" the fresh charge pulled back into the cylinder during the intake stroke.

When the compression wave generated at exhaust valve opening reaches the end of the header pipe a lower strength expansion wave is reflected back up the pipe. The positive compression wave, now of lower intensity, continues into the collector. When it reaches the atmosphere boundary, a second expansion wave is generated that moves back up the collector and the primary header pipe. If the header system and cam timing are properly coordinated, the first expansion wave will return to the cylinder at or slightly before IVO and begin to scavenge exhaust gasses from the cylinder and aid the flow of fresh charge from the induction system. Then, slightly later, the second expansion wave will arrive and continue the scavenging process until EVC. If the collector effectively broadens the scavenging wave to "cover" the entire overlap period, the engine and exhaust system are said to be "in tune". If any part of the overlap period is not accompanied by a scavenging wave, the engine and exhaust system fall "out of tune."

Engine pressures illustrating an in-tune condition are pictured in **figure 13**. As rpm increases, the pressure-

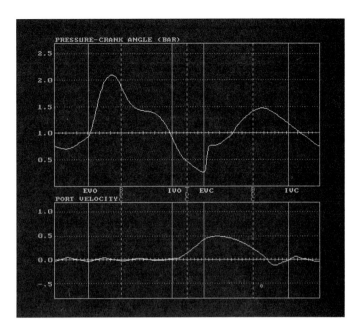

Exhaust tuning works by using the proper header pipe length to "time" the arrival of the suction wave to occur during the overlap, between IVO and EVC. When this happens, as shown on this Dynomation screen, it produces a negative pressure inside the cylinder that begins to draw fresh charge into the cylinder. The lower port-velocity diagram indicates *fresh charge is moving into the cylinder even though the piston is moving* *up* *the bore.*

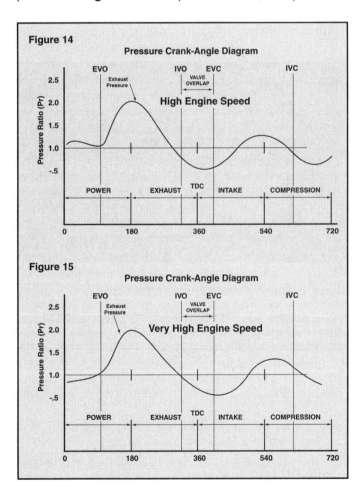

As rpm increases, the pressure-crank angle diagram curves "stretch" out to the right, as shown by these exhaust traces. If the scavenging wave is wide enough and the overlap is short enough, the exhaust system will remain in tune throughout a wide rpm range. Good scavenging is still taking place at higher rpm in figure 14 and to a lessor degree at even higher rpm in figure 15.

crank angle diagram traces "stretch" out to the right. If the scavenging wave is wide enough and the overlap is short enough, the exhaust system will remain in tune throughout a wide rpm range. Good scavenging is still taking place at higher rpm in **figures 14** and to a lessor degree at even higher rpm in **figure 15**. A wide scavenging wave is particularly desirable in engines with long overlap periods. A wide scavenging wave that maintains a low pressure differential at the exhaust valve throughout the entire overlap period will assist exhaust scavenging and prevent reversion, ensuring higher power levels over a wider range of engine speeds.

This fact brings to light an important point about exhaust header tuning. Optimum primary pipe and collector lengths are not very critical for low- to medium-performance engines. In these applications, overlap periods are short and cylinder pressures are often lower at the end of the exhaust stroke (lower performance engines produce a smaller volume of exhaust gasses and allow more time for cylinder blowdown). However, high-output, high-speed engines with long overlap periods require much more precise tubing lengths to optimize power. As power levels increase, the margin for error decreases.

Here's a final tuning note about collectors. When exhaust pulses from multiple cylinders enter a collector, primary and reflected waves interfere and interact with one another. The influence of this interaction is often overstated. The "interference" waves are considerably lower in magnitude and have much less effect than the primary and first reflection waves from cylinder blowdown. Dr. Jon C. Morrison of the *Institute of Mechanical*

Engineers conducted experiments on interference effects in collectors and concluded that multicylinder wave interference had an essentially insignificant affect on performance.

Exhaust Flow Velocities

Another important aspect of exhaust tuning is optimizing gas particle velocity throughout the exhaust system. When the exhaust valve opens (EVO), the piston is still moving downward on the power stroke. However, a large percentage of combusted gasses "blowdown" during this period between EVO and BDC. This occurs despite the fact that exhaust valve lift is relatively low. This phenomenon stresses the importance of the low-lift flow characteristics of the exhaust valve and port for optimum overall performance. If the header system is too restrictive—often from insufficient pipe diameter—to allow unrestricted blowdown, the piston will have to physically "pump" out the remaining gasses during the exhaust stroke. This will substantially increase the required pumping work and significantly increase cylinder pressures at IVO (in turn, reducing effective scavenging and creating reversion into the induction system). On the other hand, when primary pipe diameters are too large, the returning scavenging wave is so weak that it cannot effectively assist exhaust gas outflow and initiate induction flow during overlap. Optimum exhaust pipe diameters, like intake runners, will generate specific flow velocities that reach a balance between minimizing restriction and optimizing finite-amplitude wave actions.

Peak exhaust velocity typically occurs twice during the exhaust cycle. The first peak-flow event, at approximately 60 degrees after EVO, is produced by maximum flow during blowdown. The second event occurs at maximum piston speed on the exhaust stroke, about 73- to 82-degrees before TDC, and is the maximum flow during exhaust pumping. The first peak often will be the greater of the two. When the exhaust system is designed properly, the level of the first peak should fall between 0.45 to 0.5 Mach. If flow rates over 0.5 Mach are recorded, the exhaust system is too restrictive. If flow values fall below 0.45 Mach, blowdown will not generate expansion waves strong enough to effectively scavenge the cylinder during overlap. As is the case with intake tuning, it is possible to establish optimum flow velocities yet not measure a performance gain. When this occurs, the problem may be caused by excessive exhaust-valve restriction. Fortunately, this can be easily detected by reviewing the pressure-crank angle diagram or the pressure-volume diagram. More information on this phenomenon will be provided later in this chapter.

While it is impossible to predict exact primary lengths and diameters without using extremely complex formulas, it is helpful to have reasonable starting points. The book *Performance Tuning In Theory and Practice* by A. Graham Bell has excellent empirical formulas for header pipe length and diameters that can give you ballpark figures for most applications. These formulas work well

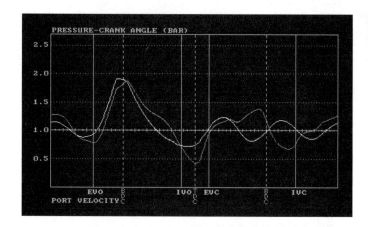

In this test, we changed the collector from 12-inch long, 4.5-inch diameter to 36-inch long, 3.75-inch diameter. Generally, increasing the collector length will broaden the scavenging wave. Smaller collector diameters place more tuning emphasis on the expansion wave generated at the open end as opposed to the header/collector boundary. The short-length, large-diameter collector (darker line) produced the lowest and narrowest scavenging pulse. This design tends to develop more low- to mid-range power. The longer collector produces a wider scavenging wave of lower amplitude, better for high engine speeds.

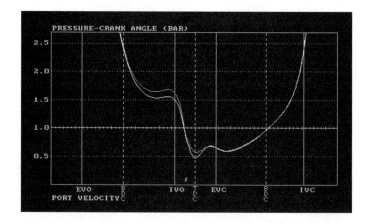

These cylinder pressure curves illustrate how stepped headers work. Stepped headers return small expansion waves at each step. These scavenging waves help exhaust gases flow out of the cylinder, particularly helpful on large-displacement, high-speed engines. Notice the lower cylinder pressures produced with stepped headers (darker line). The lower pressures reduce pumping work.

because they incorporate EVO timing as part of their solution. Here are Bell's exhaust formulas:

HPL (Header Pipe Length in inches) =
= ((850 * (360 - EVO)) / RPM) - 3
HPD (Header Pipe Diameter in inches) =
= ((SCID * 16.38) / ((HPL + 3) * 25))) * 2.1
Where
SCID is the displacement of a single cylinder in cubic inches.

These equations will only give good length and diameter estimations when the appropriate values for rpm are used. If the engine has been designed for street-driving, the selected rpm should correspond with peak torque speed. Racing engines should use either the engine speed at peak horsepower or some value in between.

While Bell's formulas come up with reasonably accurate estimations of primary tubing lengths and diameters, unfortunately, there are no reliable empirical formulas for collector length and diameter. However, there are rules-of-thumb to keep in mind when choosing starting values for these dimensions. Longer collectors force the peak torque to occur at lower engine speeds. This happens because, at higher engine speeds, expansion waves generated at the end of the collector take too long to travel back to the cylinder and don't assist exhaust scavenging. Longer collectors should be used to widen powerbands at lower engine speeds, whereas, shorter collectors optimize peak power at higher engine speeds.

Choosing collector *diameters* requires further development of a previous theory. We established that when a compression or expansion wave reached the open end of a pipe, a reflected wave was generated by this sudden change in area. What was not discussed, however, was that the <u>amplitude</u> of the reflected wave is dependent on the extent of the area change. If a wave reaches an open-end pipe that discharges into the atmosphere (effectively, has an infinite change in area), then the reflected wave will be of maximum possible amplitude, nearly equal to the originating wave but of the opposite sign. If the area change is small, for instance, a 1.00-inch pipe meeting a 1.05-inch pipe, a reflection wave will still be generated, but it will have a very small amplitude. The lesson to be learned from this for collector design is that *smaller collector diameters decrease the area change and reduce the amplitude of the first reflected wave.* As collector diameter is decreased, higher amplitude waves are generated at the open-end of the collector and smaller reflected waves are generated at the primary/collector pipe boundary. Since the open end is farther away from the cylinder, smaller collectors will boost low- to mid-rpm power. Larger diameter collectors generate stronger waves at the primary/collector boundary, and since this is closer to the cylinder, larger collectors generally boost high-rpm power.

While there are no reliable formulas to calculate these variables, the following simple formula can provide "large ballpark" figures for a high-speed, drag-racing engine:

Collector Diameter (inches) = 1.9 * HPD
Collector Length = .5 * HPL

VALVE EVENTS AND STRATEGIES

The four basic valve-event timing points (EVO, EVC, IVO, IVC) can be grouped into three categories based on their influence on engine performance: 1) EVC and IVO are the least important individually, but together comprise the overlap period that has a significant effect on power, 2) the EVO is the next most important timing point since is determines the beginning of the exhaust cycle and cylinder blowdown, and 3) IVC is the most critical since it fixes the balance between cylinder filling and intake reversion, each having a potent effect on engine output. Combining your knowledge of finite-amplitude waves with this information on valve timing will allow you to use the Dynomation program to design or select camshafts (and choose related intake and exhaust components) for virtually any application.

(IVO) Intake Valve Opening—This valve event marks the beginning of the intake process and valve overlap. IVO is probably the least sensitive timing point of all four valve events. However, when the exhaust system returns a broad, strong expansion wave, earlier IVO timing can boost performance. If a strong scavenging wave is not present, the same early IVO timing will cause exhaust gasses to flow into the induction system (reversion). This will substantially reduce power from not only "spoiling" the fresh charge but also charge heating.

There are several additional conditions that, along with IVO, influence intake reversion. Low engine speeds usually produce low port velocities. Since induction gasses have less momentum when they are moving at slower speeds, it is easier for the piston—moving upward at IVO—to force residual exhaust gasses into the inlet tract. Furthermore, low intake manifold pressures that occur during part-throttle operation or with restricted carburetion create large pressure differentials between the intake port and the cylinder, again contributing to reversion. A similar condition can occur at wide-open throttle when IVO is too early, as cylinder pressures are still quite high. Engines with these conditions might benefit from later IVO timing.

(EVC) Exhaust Valve Closing—This event marks not only the end of the exhaust process, but also the ending of the overlap period. At low rpm EVC strongly influences to what degree exhaust gasses will back flow into the cylinder from the exhaust system. This low-speed back flow happens for two reasons. First, at EVC, the piston is beginning to move down the bore on the intake stroke, and exhaust gas outflow velocity is low making it easy for the piston to draw exhaust into the cylinder. The second reason is more interesting. The negative scavenging wave created at the end of the header is always followed by another, <u>positive</u> compression wave. At low engine speeds both the scavenging and compression waves arrive prematurely. If the compression wave arrives during overlap, it forces exhaust gasses *back into the cylinder.* One solution to this problem is the reverse-megaphone "collector" often used on motorcycle exhaust systems. This device dampens the follow-up compression wave and reduces exhaust reversion at mid to low rpm. This discovery was made by accident (true for most discoveries!) when motorcycle racers tried using a reverse-megaphone in an effort to strengthen their flimsy megaphone style exhaust systems.

At higher engine speeds, later EVC will shift the power curve towards higher rpm at the expense of low-speed torque. At peak power the exhaust valve should close just slightly before exhaust back flow occurs. Don't forget that exhaust system tuning also has a significant influence on reversion. So, final EVC timing should only be determined after the exhaust system has been optimized.

(EVO) Exhaust Valve Opening—This timing point always occurs during the latter part of the power stroke and signals the start of the blowdown process. Optimum EVO timing allows a reduction in cylinder pressure that would otherwise cause exhaust reversion into the induction system at IVO and during overlap. However, at higher engine speeds it is almost impossible for some reversion not to take place. If there is no reversion flow at high speed, it is likely (but not certain) that EVO is too early, and pressure that could have been used to push the piston is being prematurely expelled from the engine. This will reduce thermal efficiency and horsepower. If EVO occurs too late, insufficient blowdown will increase pumping work during the exhaust stroke and, in turn, reduce horsepower. Late EVO will also increase cylinder pressures at IVO contributing to reversion and additional losses in power.

Thermal efficiency research has shown that within the normal range of EVO timing, this event has less affect on low-speed power than either IVC or EVC. Therefore, EVO timing should be early enough to satisfy high speed performance requirements, but no earlier than necessary to optimize thermal efficiency. EVO timing earlier than necessary for optimum power reduces thermal efficiency, albeit, only to a small degree.

(IVC) Intake Valve Closing—This is the most important valve event in the 4-cycle, IC engine. IVC occurs well into the compression stroke and intake flow is easily susceptible to reversion if induction velocity and/or pressure wave tuning do not provide sufficient energy to hold back increasing cylinder pressures. This is especially true at low to mid-range engine speeds where port velocity is still sluggish. Late IVC reduces volumetric efficiency at lower rpm and potentially increases volumetric efficiency at higher rpm. Optimum IVC at maximum engine speeds depends on port velocity, pressure wave tuning, and piston speed.

Using Dynomation To Optimize Valve Events

The Dynomation program includes a third plot of engine operating conditions. Called a pressure-volume diagram (or PV diagram), it graphically illustrates how cylinder pressures vary as a function of cylinder volume throughout the 4-cycle process. For an in-depth review of the basic characteristics of this pressure plot, refer to pages 22, 23, and 24 in Chapter 3, and the illustrations provided on these pages. Note: The lower "pumping" loop illustrated in the accompanying PV diagrams depict

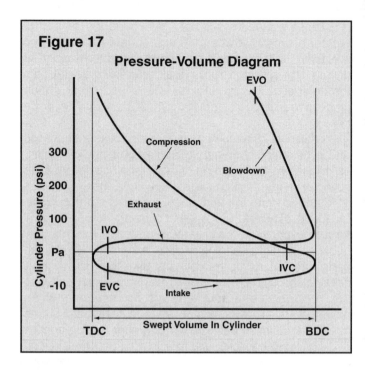

The Dynomation program displays pressure-volume (PV) diagrams that illustrate how cylinder pressures vary as a function of cylinder volume. The PV diagram can be a useful tool for optimizing valve-event timing, with the pumping loop providing the most helpful information.

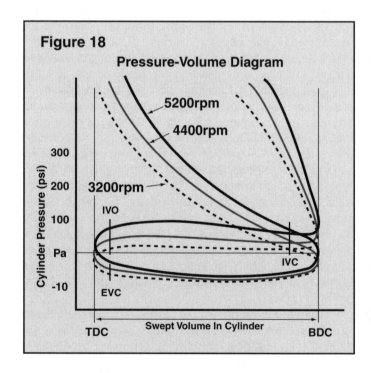

This PV diagram illustrates how the pumping loop changes as engine speed increases from 3200rpm to 5200rpm. Notice how the lower portion of the loop (the intake cycle) remains relatively constant, while the upper portion of the loop (the exhaust cycle) dramatically rises as rpm increases. The changes in exhaust pressure are caused by the decreasing <u>time</u> available to blowdown the cylinder as engine speed increases. Higher pumping pressures increase pumping work (increasing Pmep) and that consumes horsepower.

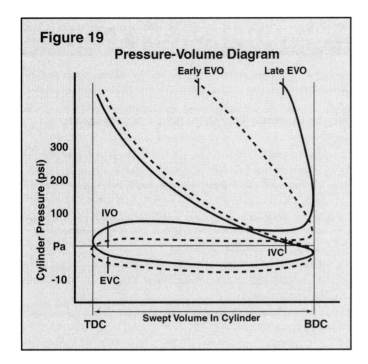

Figure 19

Pressure-Volume Diagram

Here are the effects of too early and too late exhaust valve openings. Early EVO (dotted line) causes the pressure curve to slope strongly from left to right as cylinder pressure decreases during blowdown. If EVO is too late the pressure curve takes much more of a vertical "dive" and tends to level out considerably above Pa.

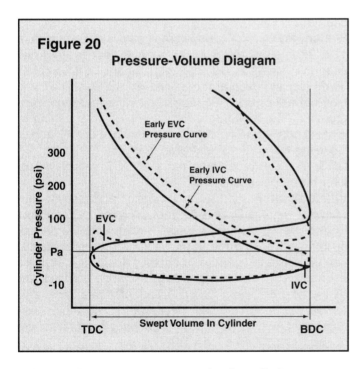

Figure 20

Pressure-Volume Diagram

This PV plot shows the sharp rise in cylinder pressure from too early EVC timing (dotted line). The "spike" at the left end of the loop is caused by the upward moving piston beginning to re-compress exhaust gasses. Also illustrated is too early IVC timing (solid line). Notice the "pointed tail" at the lower right. This is produced when the intake valve closes near BDC and prevents the inflow of fresh charge normally caused by the ram tuning effects of the induction system.

naturally-aspirated engines (it's called a "pumping" loop because the engine is either pumping in fresh charge or pumping out exhaust gasses; the average pressure of this loop is the pumping mean effective pressure—Pmep). *This pressure loop will look completely different for a supercharged engine because positive (forced induction) pressures will act on the piston during the intake stroke.*

The pressure-volume diagram can be a useful tool for locating optimum valve event timing, with the pumping loop providing the most helpful information. **Figure 17** shows a close-up view of the complete pumping loop. This period is also called the "valve-open cycle," since at least one of the valves is open throughout the entire loop. **Figure 18** illustrates how the pumping loop changes as engine speed increases from 3200rpm to 5200rpm. The loop obviously "balloons." Notice how the lower portion of the loop (the intake cycle) remains relatively constant, while the upper portion of the loop (the exhaust cycle) dramatically rises as rpm increases. The changes in exhaust pressure are caused by the decreasing time available to blowdown the cylinder as engine speed increases. Higher pumping pressures increase pumping work (increasing Pmep) and that consumes horsepower.

The 5200rpm curve in **figure 18** also illustrates a distinct bulge is forming around maximum piston speed on the exhaust stroke. This is a sign of exhaust flow restriction, sometimes caused by insufficient exhaust valve size and/or valve lift. This "restriction" bulge would be also visible on the pressure-crank angle diagram where cylinder pressure drops to parallel inlet pressure, at about 80 degrees before TDC.

Figures 19 show how too early and too late exhaust valve openings affect cylinder pressure. Notice the slope of the blowdown pressure at the upper right hand corner of the diagrams. If EVO is too early (dotted line), the pressure curve slopes strongly from left to right as cylinder pressure decreases during blowdown. If EVO is too late, the pressure curve takes much more of a vertical "dive" and tends to level out considerably higher above Pa. Ideal EVO timing will produce a pressure plot that will slope from left to right at a relatively steep angle (refer to figure 17).

Figure 20 shows the sharp rise in cylinder pressure from too early EVC timing (dotted line). The "spike" at the left end of the loop is caused by the upward moving piston beginning to re-compress exhaust gasses trapped in the cylinder when the exhaust valve closed too early. The intake valve opens at TDC and rapidly decompresses the cylinder. This figure also illustrates how too early IVC timing can change the lower part of the pumping loop (solid line). Notice the "pointed tail" at the lower right. This is produced when the intake valve closes near BDC and prevents the inflow of fresh charge normally caused by the ram tuning effects of the induction system.

One final note: IVO is the least sensitive valve event, and its opening point (within the range of typical valve event timing) is not distinguishable on the PV diagram.

Appendix-A Installation & QuickStart Guide

INTRODUCTION

(Note: If you can't wait to start your DeskTop Dyno™, feel free to jump ahead to **Beginning The Installation** *on the next page, but don't forget to read the rest of this Appendix when you have time. Also make sure you review Chapter 5; it contains extensive information about using this engine simulation.)*

Thank you for purchasing this book and Motion Software's DeskTop Dyno™ for IBM®-compatible computers. This software is the result of several years of development and testing. It is just one of several quality software products developed by Motion Software, Inc., that furthers your understanding and enjoyment of automobiles, performance, and racing technology. *Please take a moment and fill out the registration card included in this package and drop it in the mail. Stay in touch and get the most from this sophisticated engine simulation program (including discount upgrade pricing); mail in your registration card today!*

How It Works

The DeskTop Dyno program is based on a *Filling-And-Emptying* method of engine power simulation (see Chapters 3 and 4). We chose this mathematical model because of its excellent power prediction accuracy and reasonable processing times. To improve the accuracy even further, we made the DeskTop Dyno a *full-cycle* simulation. This means that it calculates the complete fluid-dynamic, thermodynamic, and frictional conditions that exist inside the cylinder throughout the entire 720 degrees of the four-cycle process.

You will find that many other simulation programs on the market (even a few that sell for several times the price of the DeskTop Dyno) are not true simulations. Rather, they calculate the volumetric efficiency (VE) and then derive an estimate of horsepower. There are many shortcomings to this technique. The two greatest drawbacks are: 1) since cylinder pressure is not determined, it is impossible to predict the pressure on the exhaust valve and the subsequent mass flow through the port when the exhaust valve opens, and 2) the inability to subtract the pumping horsepower (energy needed to move gasses into and out of the engine) from the predicted horsepower.

Since the DeskTop Dyno incorporates both filling-and-emptying modeling *and* full-cycle simulation that includes frictional and pumping-loss calculations, the program requires slightly more processing time than simpler programs (over a million calculations are performed for each point on the power curves), but if you're interested in accuracy and not just "playing games," we believe you'll be pleased with the overall performance of this software.

What You Need To Run Your DeskTop Dyno

Here is an overview of the basic hardware and software required to run the DeskTop Dyno:

- an IBM-PC compatible computer with a 3-1/2-inch floppy disk drive (a 5-1/4-inch floppy disk is available at no charge—see the "**Computer**" section, below) and at least 512K of RAM (random access memory)
- DOS, version 3.1 or later
- a gray-scale monochrome or color monitor (of EGA or better graphics capability if you wish to display power-curves)
- a math coprocessor is not required but is recommended
- a mouse is not required but simplifies program operation
- a printer (optional, needed to obtain printouts of test data).

Computer: An IBM-PC compatible computer with a 3-1/2-inch disk drive is required. (Note: If your system accepts only 5-1/4-inch floppy disks, return the enclosed disk with your registration card to Motion Software, Inc., and we will send you a 5-1/4-inch replacement disk at no charge.)

System Memory: Your system should have a <u>minimum</u> of 512Kbytes of installed memory. If your system has near the minimum memory requirement or if so-called "RAM resident" programs are installed, the DeskTop Dyno may not run properly—it may display the message "Program Too Big...". If you experience problems starting or running the DeskTop Dyno, try adding memory and/or disabling memory-resident programs.

DOS: The DeskTop Dyno requires DOS version 3.1 or later for proper operation.

Video Monitor: Virtually any monitor and display card will work with the DeskTop Dyno, however, systems with EGA or better graphics capability will permit the display of horsepower and torque curve graphics on screen. *If you do not have an EGA or better graphics system (you are using a CGA or another low-resolution graphics display), an on-screen "chart" listing of horsepower and torque will be substituted for power curves.* Note: Hercules graphics cards and non-gray-scale monitors <u>are not supported</u> by the DeskTop Dyno.

Math Coprocessor: You don't need a system with a math coprocessor to run the DeskTop Dyno, but since millions of calculations are performed for each power point (13 points for a full curve), a coprocessor will greatly speed program output and usability. The following PC systems have math coprocessors and allow the DeskTop Dyno to operate quickly (also refer to following table):
- All Pentium Pro, Pentium, and 486DX systems
- Any system with a separate math coprocessor chip

installed (very few systems are factory equipped with an external math coprocessors because of the added cost). The following systems <u>do not</u> have built-in math coprocessors: All 486SX, 386DX or SX, 286, or 8088 systems that are not equipped with a separate math coprocessor chip installed (by you or your computer dealer).

The following table gives an approximation of the time required to calculate a complete simulation on various PC systems:

Computer	Coprocessor	Calc. Time
Pentium at 133Mhz	Yes	1 Second
Pentium at 60Mhz	Yes	3.5 Seconds
80486DX at 33Mhz	Yes	11 Seconds
80386DX at 25Mhz	Yes (added)	40 Seconds
80486SX at 25Mhz	No	5 Min. 15 Sec.
80386DX at 33Mhz	No	7 Min. 55 Sec.
80286 at 10Mhz	No	21 Minutes
8088 at 8Mhz	Yes (added)	2 Min. 50 Sec.

Mouse: A mouse is not required to use the DeskTop Dyno, however a standard mouse is supported and makes program operation even easier. Note: A mouse driver must be loaded during bootup for the mouse to be functional when running the DeskTop Dyno under DOS.

Printer: You can print out a "dyno-test sheet" of any simulated run with any PC printer. You can also print power and torque curves to most graphic-capable printers using GRAPHICS.COM, a utility supplied with DOS (for instructions, see page 115). The DeskTop Dyno assumes that your printer is attached to LPT:1, the first parallel printer port. If your printer is connected to another port (i.e., a serial port) make sure your system is properly configured to support serial printing (by using the MODE command or other DOS printing-redirection software). Refer to your DOS manual for more information on configuring ports and system printers.

Important Note On Laser Printers: Some laser printers require special software drivers to allow them to communicate with specific programs (like *Windows®*, *WordPerfect®*, etc.). The DeskTop Dyno does not support laser printers that require software drivers to enable basic printer functions.

Windows: The DeskTop Dyno is not a Windows program, however, it will run in a DOS-program window under Windows 3.0 or later (no PIF file is required). Refer to your Windows documentation for instructions on running DOS programs in the Windows environment (also see page 115 for additional Windows operational notes).

BEGINNING THE INSTALLATION

IMPORTANT NOTE: If you encounter any problems during installation, refer to *Error Messages* on page 111. If you have problems after installation, see *Common Questions* on page 116.

Before You Begin

Installing the DeskTop Dyno is a quick and simple process on virtually all computers. To minimize the likelihood of problems, review the following sections that apply to your system:

ALL SYSTEMS
1) *Do Not Write-Protect (Lock) The Distribution Disk.* Make sure the lock tab (located on the upper right corner of the diskette) covers the small window. If the window is open, the disk is write protected and you cannot install the DeskTop Dyno.
2) If at all possible, install the software onto the (default) drive and directory suggested by the SETUP program included with the DeskTop Dyno.
3) In these and the upcoming installation steps we are assuming that your 3-1/2-inch floppy drive is labeled as drive "**A**", but if it is the "**B**" drive in your system, substitute "**B**" for "**A**" during the installation procedure.
DOS SYSTEMS—You must be running DOS version 3.1 or later, and you should have at least 512K of RAM memory.
WINDOWS® 3.0, 3.1, or 3.11—Exit Windows and install the DeskTop Dyno at the DOS prompt. The DeskTop Dyno will run under Windows (in a DOS-program window).
WINDOWS 95®—We recommend that you install the DeskTop Dyno after restarting your system in the MS-DOS Mode (choose "**Restart the computer in MS-DOS mode?**" from the Windows Shut-Down menu).
Additional Windows Installation Notes—If you encounter installation problems, there may be incompatible drivers or commands in your AUTOEXEC.BAT or CONFIG.SYS files. If you are a knowledgeable user, try commenting out any nonessential statements (even those that you may not suspect, like SETVER.EXE, HIMEM.SYS, etc.), then restart your system and try installing the program again.
OTHER OPERATING SYSTEMS—Begin the installation process from the lowest level DOS-compatibility box provided by your operating system.
INSTALLING ON A HARD DRIVE—If you will be installing the DeskTop Dyno program onto a hard drive, proceed to *Installing The DeskTop Dyno*.

Running The DeskTop Dyno
From A Floppy Disk

If you do not have a hard drive on your system, you can setup the DeskTop Dyno to run from a 3-1/2-inch floppy drive, however, we recommend that you first make a working copy of your distribution disk (not required for hard-disk installations). The standard DeskTop Dyno disk is supplied on 3-1/2-inch media, formatted double density (720K bytes), not HD (high density). You will need one additional blank, double-side, double-density, 720K disk to build a working copy.

Perform the following steps after your system has started (the following steps assume that your computer is equipped with a single floppy drive):

1) Place the DeskTop Dyno distribution disk in your "**A**" drive.

2) Type the following command:
   DISKCOPY A: A:
   (Be sure to enter one blank space between "**DISKCOPY**" and "**A:**" and another space between "**A:**" and the second "**A:**").
   Then press **Enter** and follow the instructions on your screen.

3) You will have to swap disks between the DeskTop Dyno (SOURCE) disk and a blank (TARGET) disk in order to complete the copy process. Make sure you carefully select the TARGET and SOURCE disks, because your computer will erase any files on the TARGET disk while transferring the DeskTop Dyno.

4) When the copy process is complete, store the original distribution disk in a safe place.

5) Now copy the DOS file "COMMAND.COM" to your working copy of the DeskTop Dyno disk by performing the following steps:
   a) Place your DOS start-up disk in your floppy drive and type:
   CTRL C
   That is, press and hold the "CTRL" key then press the "C" key, finally release both keys
   b) Now type:
   COPY COMMAND.COM B:
   Then press **Enter** and follow the on-screen instructions, using your working copy of the DeskTop Dyno disk as the Destination disk.

6) When COMMAND.COM has been copied to your DeskTop Dyno disk, you are ready to begin the installation process. With the working copy in your floppy drive, continue with the next section.

BEGINNING THE INSTALLATION

The files included on the DeskTop Dyno disk cannot be directly transferred to your hard dive. You must use the SETUP program included with your DeskTop Dyno.
Follow these steps to install your DeskTop Dyno:

1) Start your computer system. When DOS is loaded and you receive the "**C:\>**" prompt, place your DeskTop Dyno disk into the "**A**" floppy drive.
   Note: The following installation instructions assume that your floppy drive is named "**A**". If your floppy drive or hard drive have different system labels, substitute those labels in the following steps.

2) Log onto the drive containing the DeskTop Dyno disk by typing:
   A:
   followed by **Enter**.

3) Begin the installation process by typing:
   SETUP
   followed by **Enter**.

4) Read the pre-installation notes, then press **Enter** to begin the installation program.

5) After you have read the SETUP sign-on screen press **Enter** or click on **Continue**.

6) SETUP will now display the source drive for Dyno program files:
   Source: A:
   Accept the source by pressing **Enter** or clicking **Continue**.

7) SETUP now displays the default destination directory on your hard drive:
   Destination: C:\DYNO2
   Accept the destination directory by pressing **Enter** or clicking **Continue**. *NOTE: For a floppy-only installation using a working copy of the distribution disk, enter the same drive name as the source drive for the destination (**A:**) then press **Enter** or click **Continue**.*

8) When the program requests, enter your name (make sure you've typed it correctly) then press **Enter** or click **Continue**.

9) File transfer begins. When complete, SETUP will notify you of a successful installation. Press **Enter** or click **Continue** and you will see any post-installation notes included with the program. After you have read the messages, simply press **Enter** to begin the DeskTop Dyno for the first time (for subsequent Dyno startups, refer to the instructions in the next section *Starting The DeskTop Dyno*). Note: you may review the post-installation notes at any time by typing:
   READAFTR
   while in the DYNO2 subdirectory on your destination disk.

10) For a quick explanation of the Main Program Screen, the Simulator Screen, and various program functions, continue with *Program Overview* on the next page.

STARTING THE DESKTOP DYNO

The DeskTop Dyno is located in the DYNO2 subdirectory on the destination drive that you selected during the installation process. *For floppy-only installations, the program is located in the root directory of your working floppy.*

To start the DeskTop Dyno follow these simple steps:

1a) Hard Drive Installations
DOS: At the "C:\>" prompt enter the command:
CD \DYNO2
(That's **DYN** followed by an **O2**, not a zero two.) Then press **Enter**. Continue with step 2.
WINDOWS: Locate the DYNO2 subdirectory in the *File Manager* or the *Windows Explorer* and double click on the DYNO.EXE file located within that subdirectory.

1b) Floppy-Only Installations
After you boot your system with a DOS startup disk, insert the working copy of the DeskTop Dyno disk in your floppy drive and log to that drive:
A:
followed by **Enter**.

2) Start the program by typing:
DYNO
(That's **DYN** followed by an **O**, not a zero.) Then press **Enter**.

RUNNING THE DESKTOP DYNO UNDER WINDOWS

The DeskTop Dyno is a DOS-based program, however, it is also designed to run under Windows (you may notice some performance degradation under Windows 3.x vs. running at the DOS prompt).

To ensure stable operation, always run the DeskTop Dyno in full-screen mode under Windows versions 3.x. Here are some additional tips for Windows operation:

Read The Windows Documentation
There is no substitute for reading the documentation that is supplied with Windows (either printed or available from the on-screen help system). Refer to sections that cover running DOS programs in the Windows environment.

No PIF Files Required
The DeskTop Dyno will run under all versions of Windows without the need for a specific PIF (Program Information File). Because of the wide variety of hardware platforms available, this may not apply to all systems. Simply double click on the DYNO.EXE file or its icon to begin the program.

Create A DeskTop Dyno Icon
Windows 3.x: Copy any icon by clicking and holding the mouse button on the icon, then press the CTRL key and drag the icon to a new location. Use "Properties" under the file menu to change the attributes to run the DYNO.EXE file in the DYNO2 subdirectory.
Windows95: Simply click the right mouse button on the DYNO.EXE file and select "Create Shortcut." Drag the shortcut to your desktop.

INSTALLATION

ERROR MESSAGES

If the SETUP program encounters a problem, it can display the following error messages:
Distribution disk is write protected....
SETUP has determined that the installation disk is write protected. Slide the lock tab so that it <u>covers</u> the square hole in the upper right of the disk (with the label facing you) and restart the installation.
Dyno Execution Halted...
Program has not been properly installed. Reinstall the program; refer to pages 109 & 110 in this Appendix.
Cannot Read Sector... or **File Allocation Table Bad...**
SETUP cannot complete the installation due to a hardware problem with your system. Contact Motion Software for assistance.

PROGRAM OVERVIEW: THE MAIN PROGRAM SCREEN

The **Main Program Screen** allows you to select the components required to build virtually any four-, six-, or eight-cylinder engine for power testing. The screen is composed of the following main elements:

1) The **Title Bar** shows the name of the program.

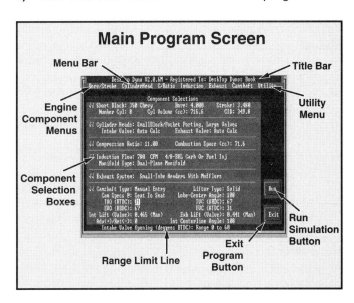

2) The **Menu Bar** contains the headings for all the pull-down menus. The six left-hand choices are the main engine component categories, and the final right-hand choice provides access to the utility menu.

3) The **Engine Component Menus** are the six left-hand choices in the Menu Bar. These easy-to-use, pull-down menus allow the selection of Bore/Stroke (Displacement), Cylinder Heads, Valve Size, Compression Ratio, Induction Flow, Manifold Type, Exhaust System, Camshaft, and Lifter Type.

4) The **Utility Menu** allows retrieving and deleting saved dyno tests and clearing previous choices from the Component Selection Boxes and pull-down menus.

5) The **Component Selection Boxes** list all the currently chosen engine components, plus calculated engine displacement, cylinder volume, and combustion volume (note: Combustion volume is not the same as *combustion-chamber* volume—refer to the question/answer on page 117 for more information).

6) Several menu choices have "OTHER" options that allow data to be entered directly into a Component Selection Box. During this procedure, the range of acceptable values will be displayed in the **Range Limit Line** at the bottom of the screen.

7) When all Component Selection Boxes have been filled in, the **Run Simulation Button** begins the engine simulation and switches to the *Simulation Screen* (described on page 114).

8) The **Exit Button** quits the DeskTop Dyno program and returns to DOS.

USING THE MOUSE OR KEYBOARD TO BUILD A TEST ENGINE

Begin using the DeskTop Dyno by "assembling" a test engine from component parts. For example, select a bore and stroke by using the **Bore/Stroke** pull-down menu. Activate the menu by:

Mouse
1) Move the mouse to the Bore/Stroke menu name in the Menu Bar.
2) Click and hold the left mouse button. This opens the menu.
3) Drag the mouse pointer down and over the selection of your choice.
4) If a submenu opens, move the mouse pointer over your selected choice in that menu.
5) Release the mouse button to complete the selection.
6) To close the menu without making any selection, drag the mouse pointer up into the Title Bar then release the mouse button.

Keyboard
1) Press and release the **Alt** key to highlight the Bore/Stroke menu name in the menu bar. Activate other menu choices—i.e., Cylinderheads, C/Ratio, etc.—by pressing the **Right-Arrow** or **Left-Arrow** keys. Note: If you do not see a highlight in the menu bar when you touch the Alt key, your computer probably has a monochrome (B&W) or Hercules graphics screen that is not supported by the DeskTop Dyno. You must obtain a gray-scale or color monitor to use this program.
2) Use the **Up-Arrow** or **Down-Arrow** keys to scroll through the menu choices. If the menu selections direct you to submenus (a small arrow points to the right at the end of the menu line), use the **Right-**

Arrow key to open the submenu. When you have highlighted your choice, press **Enter** to make the selection. To close the submenu <u>without</u> making a selection, press the **Left-Arrow** key.
3) To close <u>all menus</u> without making a selection, press the **Escape** key.
4) Use the **TAB** key to move the button highlight at the bottom of the screen between the Exit Simulation and Run Simulation buttons.

Both Mouse and Keyboard Users When an item in a menu has been selected and the same menu is opened again, a dot in the left hand column of the menu will indicate the previous choice.

USING THE "OTHER" MENU CHOICES

The Bore/Stroke, Valve Size, C/Ratio, Induction, and Camshaft menus have OTHER choices as the last selection in their menu lists. This allows direct data entry into one of the Component Selection Boxes for engine description, bore, stroke, number of cylinders, valve size, compression ratio, induction flow, camshaft name, and valve-event timing. When any of the OTHER choices are selected, a flashing cursor will be placed in the appropriate spot in a Component Selection Box. Entering a value replaces the currently displayed value. When you press **Enter** or **TAB**, the entered value will be tested for acceptability, and if it passes it will be used in the next simulation run. If you press **Enter** or **TAB** without entering a value, the currently displayed value is left unchanged.

Warning: Do not click the mouse on any of the menu choices, or on the RUN or EXIT buttons, until you have completed entering or TABing over all the required entry fields in any of the Component Selections Boxes. If you do not work your way through all data-entry fields, some of the entered values may not be properly incorporated into the next simulation run.

"OTHER" Choice Range Limits

Data entry into any Component Selection Box is limited to values over which the DeskTop Dyno can accurately predict power. The range limits are displayed in the **Range Limit Line**. If you enter an invalid number, the DeskTop Dyno will beep, erase the value, and wait for input.

For example, to use the OTHER choice in the Bore/Stroke menu, scroll down to the bottom of the menu using the **Down-Arrow** key, or click and hold the left mouse button then drag the highlight to the bottom of the menu. After selecting OTHER, a flashing cursor will be placed in the first field of the Bore/Stroke Component Selections Box, allowing you to directly enter an Engine

Description, then the Bore, Stroke, and the Number of Cylinders. Make an entry at each input point followed by **TAB** or **Enter**. The range limits for each value are displayed in the Range Limit Line (for example, acceptable bore diameters will be limited to 3.000- to 7.000-inches). After you've entered all values, the cylinder volume (in cc's) and the cubic-inch displacement (CID) will be calculated and displayed.

ABOUT THE COMPONENT MENUS

Chapter 5 in this book provides extensive information about using this software and the assumption behind each of the menu choices. However, you may find the following brief explanations helpful:

Head/Port Design: Under the Cylinderhead main menu, you'll find the Head/Port Design submenu. Choices range from: **Restrictive**, small-port heads (for low-performance engines, such as early 260cid Ford engines or, even worse, flatheads) where the ports are small and restrictive for the installed valve sizes; **Smallblock**, where the ports are sized with performance in mind; **Bigblock**, where the ports are large and the valves are canted for improved flow (the first three big-block choices model oval-port heads, the last two choices simulate rectangular-port heads); and **4-Valve Heads** for many import and some racing configurations. Combined with Valve Diameters (below), these choices provide the DeskTop Dyno sufficient information to accurately simulate a cylinder head flow curve for most engines.

Valve Diameters: Under the Cylinderhead main menu, you'll also find the Valve Diameter submenu. This menu includes: **1) Auto Calculation** of valve sizes, **2)** the selection of various valve sizes from the menu list, or **3)** by choosing OTHER, you can enter specific valve sizes directly in the CylinderHead Component Selection Box. If you do not know the exact valve sizes, use **Auto Calculate** and the DeskTop Dyno will determine the valve sizes automatically based on the cylinder bore diameter. In many cases, the DeskTop Dyno can predict power and torque with ±5% accuracy using auto-calculated valve sizes. If you enter the exact intake and exhaust valve sizes (particularly if they are larger or smaller than typical for a specific application), you will often further increase program accuracy.

Induction: The **Airflow** submenu is located under the Induction menu. Flow ratings range from 300cfm 2-bbl carburetors to 1100cfm 4bbl or 8bbl (single or multiple carburetor) configurations. By choosing OTHER, up to 3000cfm can be tested. The Induction menu also lists a series of intake manifolds. If you select **Individual Runner**, a message box will remind you that the chosen airflow will be divided by

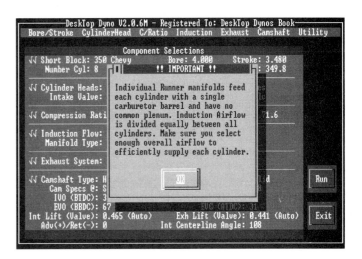

the number of cylinders. Make sure to select sufficient airflow for I.R. applications.

Camshaft: Selecting one of the OTHER choices at the bottom of the camshaft menu allows direct input of valve events measured at seat-to-seat or 0.050-inch lifter rise. These timing points can be found on the "cam card" supplied with your camshaft (they can also be found in some cam manufacturer's catalogs). Seat-to-seat timing is identified variously as "Cam Timing @ 0.004 or 0.006 <u>valve</u> rise," "0.007-open/ 0.010-close <u>valve</u> rise," or even "0.020-inch <u>lifter</u> rise." *These are all considered seat-to-seat timing specs.* If you select OTHER to change from seat-to-seat to **0.050-inch <u>lifter</u>** rise timing points, a popup message box warns that the timing values displayed in the Camshaft Component Selection Box are now based on the new, selected timing method.

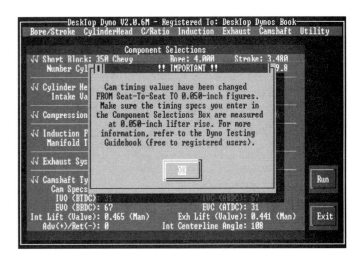

**Finding And/Or Calculating
Cam Timing Specs**

The DeskTop Dyno performs a complete gas-dynamic simulation as part of the power prediction process. This technique requires the input of valve event timing (intake and exhaust valve opening and closing points). Since valve events pinpoint the beginning and end of airflow into the cylinders, they are essential elements in accurately simulating the "physics" of the internal-combustion engine. But understanding valve-event timing, and calculating or obtaining this information from published cam data can be confusing. For information on entering and calculating valve-event timing, refer to pages 92 and 93.

THE UTILITY MENU

The Utility Menu at the right of the Menu Bar includes these selections:

Retrieve Previously Saved Dyno Tests loads previously saved test runs and all components into the Component Selections Box. Components displayed on-screen before this command is executed <u>will be replaced</u> with those from the saved run. The retrieved data will also be displayed as dotted lines on the Simulator graph (helpful for comparison testing).

Delete Previously Saved Dyno Tests selection <u>permanently</u> removes selected dyno test runs from the working DeskTop Dyno subdirectory on your disk. All component selections currently displayed on screen are unaffected by using this command.

*Warning: Once a dyno test file has been deleted (by clicking on **Delete** at the bottom of the file-selection box) it cannot be retrieved.*

Clear Current Choices removes all choices from the Component Selection Box, clears all "dots" from pull-down menus, and removes previous or "dotted-line" data from the Simulator Screen.

THE SIMULATOR SCREEN
AND RUNNING A POWER TEST

After all engine components have been selected, you can begin the power simulation. *Note: Selecting all components to complete an engine buildup requires opening some menus more than once. For example, Lifter Type is first selected from the **Camshaft** menu, then choosing a cam profile requires opening the **Camshaft** menu a second time.*

Begin the simulation by:

Mouse

Move the mouse pointer over the **Run Simulation** button on the bottom right corner of the Main Program Screen. Click the left mouse button to begin the simulation.

Keyboard

Use the **TAB** key to highlight the **Run** button located on the bottom-right corner of the Main Program Screen. Press **Enter** to begin the simulation.

The **Simulator Screen** shows the horsepower and

torque values calculated from the combination of components indicated in the Component Selection Box. If your computer does not have EGA or better graphics capability, the calculated figures will appear in a "chart" listing. Otherwise you will see a graph of horsepower and torque from 2000 to 8000rpm with the exact power values listed to the right of the graph.

The **Simulator Screen** is composed of the following main elements:

1) The **Horsepower/Torque Curves** provides a graphic representation of the results of the simulation. The

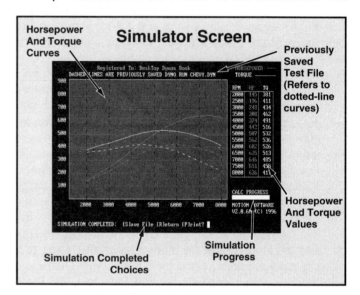

dotted-line curves (if displayed) indicate the results of the last saved or recalled test run (the file name used to display the dotted-line data is shown directly above the curves box—see *Previously Saved Test File* below).

2) The **Horsepower/Torque Values** are listed to the right of the curves and show the exact horsepower and torque values from 2000 to 8000rpm in 500rpm increments.

3) The **Simulation Progress** indicator shows the progress of each calculation in the power curve. Since a full simulation is calculated at each 500rpm increment in engine speed from 2000 to 8000rpm, the indicator will show the progress of 13 separate calculation cycles.

4) The **Previously Saved Test File** line at the top of the screen indicates the last saved or recalled test-file name—the source of the dotted lines in the curves box. If *Clear Current Component Selections* is chosen from the Utility menu on the Main Program Screen, the **Previously Saved Test File** line and any dotted-line test curves are cleared until a new test-run file is saved (saving tests is described next).

5) The **Simulation Completed Choices** line offers three options after a test run is completed: **1)** Press **S** to

save the current test to disk. The program will ask for a filename—use eight underlined numbers or underlined letters (avoid using any other keyboard characters in file names). A ".DYN" extension will automatically be added to the file name, and the file will be stored in the Desk-Top Dyno directory (a "File Saved" message will briefly appear to confirm that the file was saved). **2)** You can choose **R** to return to the Main Program Screen (NOTE: If you wish to save the current test run, you must choose the **S** option before you return to the Main Screen). And **3)** you can press **P** to send the results of the current test to your printer.

HALTING A SIMULATION TEST

You can halt a simulation by pressing the **ESCape** key. Pressing **Enter** will resume the calculation; however, a second press of the **ESCape** key will abort the simulation run and return to the Main Program Screen (helpful when you realize that you've selected an incorrect component).

PRINTING TESTS AND GRAPHICS

You can print a dyno test sheet by selecting "P" from the **Simulation Completed Choices** prompt after any simulation run. The DeskTop Dyno printout includes a listing (in chart form) of the exact horsepower and torque figures and a complete summary of the components selected for that test. Because of the limitations in DOS (the DeskTop Dyno operates under DOS even while running in Windows) graphics printing of the power curves is not directly supported. However DOS and Windows users can still obtain a printout of the Simulator Screen including the horsepower and torque curves. Here are some tips and hints that will help you obtain printed graphic output.

Printing under DOS or Windows 3.x
You can print the Simulator Screen, including power curves, on almost any IBM-compatible, graphics-capable printer using the DOS utility called GRAPHICS.COM. If you are using DOS version 5.0 or later, you will find this nifty program in your DOS subdirectory. Type GRAPHICS at the DOS prompt before you start the DeskTop Dyno to enhance the Print-Screen function to include graphics printing. Then, with the curves displayed on screen that you would like to print, simultaneously press the **Shift** and **PrintScreen** keys to send the current graphics screen to your printer.

GRAPHICS has several options that "fine tune" the command for various printers and output styles. Here are a few of the more useful methods of using GRAPHICS (refer to your DOS manual for a complete list of options):

Type at the DOS prompt:
GRAPHICS LASERJET
or
GRAPHICS LASERJETII
to tell the GRAPHICS command that the output will be printed on a HP or compatible laser printer.
Type at the DOS prompt:
GRAPHICS LASERJET /R
to print the image as it appears on screen rather than reversed. Reversed (black to white) printing is the default.

Printing under Windows 95
Windows 95 incorporates DOS version 7.0 and is not supplied (nor is compatible) with the GRAPHICS command. Instead, when a simulation is completed, press the **ALT** and **ENTER** keys together to switch the Simulator Screen from full-screen to a window. Then select and copy the screen, including the power curve graph, to the clipboard (see the Windows help system for instructions on how to accomplish this). Open the Windows *Paint* program and paste the clipboard into *Paint*. Then, simply print the image to your Windows printer.

General Simulation Assumptions

Motion's Filling-And-Emptying software closely simulates the conditions that exist during an actual engine dyno test. The goal is to reliably predict the torque and horsepower that a dynamometer will measure throughout the rpm range while the engine and dyno are running through a programmed test. However, engine power can vary considerably from one dyno test to another if environmental and other critical conditions are not carefully controlled. In fact, many of the discrepancies between dyno tests are due to variabilities in what should have been "fixed" conditions. Among the many interviews conducted during the research and development of the software and for this book, dyno operators and engine owners readily acknowledged the possibilities of errors in horsepower measurements; however, very few these individuals believe that underlined they had been lead astray by erroneous dyno readings. It seems that when test numbers "pop up" on a computer screen after a ground-pounding dyno test, the horsepower and torque values were accepted as "gospel." In other words, "dynos do lie, but they wouldn't do that to me"!

Unless the dyno operator and test personnel are extremely careful to monitor and control the surrounding conditions, including calibration of the instrumentation, dyno measurements are nearly worthless. Controlling these same variables in an engine simulation program is infinitely easier, but nevertheless just as essential. Initial conditions of temperature, pressure, energy, and methodology must be established and carefully followed. Here are some of the assumptions within the simulation software that establish a modeling baseline:

Fuel:

1) Gasoline rated at 19,000btu/lb as a standard fuel
2) The fuel is assumed to have sufficient octane to prevent detonation.
3) The air/fuel ratio is always maintained at 13:1 for optimum power.

Environment:

1) Air for induction is 68-degrees (F), dry (0% humidity), and of 29.86-in/Hg atmospheric pressure.
2) The engine, oil, and coolant have been warmed to operating temperature.

Methodology:

1) The engine is put through a series of "step" tests. That is the load is adjusted to "hold back" engine speed as the throttle is opened wide. Then the load is adjusted to allow the engine speed to rise to the first test point, 2000rpm in the case of the simulation. The engine is held at this speed for a few seconds and a power reading is taken. Then engine speed is allowed to increase to the next step, 2500rpm, and a second power reading is taken. This process is continued until the maximum testing speed is reached.
2) Since the testing procedure takes the engine up in 500rpm steps, and it is held steady during the measurement, the measured power does not reflect any losses from accelerating the rotating assembly (crank, rods, etc.) as would be found in a "real-world" application, such as drag racing.

COMMONLY ASKED QUESTIONS

The following information may be helpful in answering questions and solving problems that you encounter installing and using the DeskTop Dyno. If you don't find an answer to your problem here, send in the **Mail/Fax Tech Support Form** (*Motion Software provides Mail/Fax technical service to registered users only—mail in your registration form today*). We will review your problem and return an answer to you as soon as possible.

Question: Received an "Error Reading Drive A (or B)" message when attempting to run or install the DeskTop Dyno. What does this mean?

Answer: This means DOS cannot read the disk in your floppy drive. The disk may not be fully seated in your drive or the drive door (or lock arm) may not be fully latched. If you can properly read other disks in your drive, but the DeskTop Dyno distribution disk produces error messages, try requesting a directory of a known-good disk by entering **DIR A:** or **CHKDSK A:** and then perform those same operations with the DeskTop Dyno disk. If these operations produce an

error message only when using the DeskTop Dyno disk, the disk is almost certainly defective. Return the disk to Motion Software, Inc., for a free replacement (address at bottom of Tech Support Form).

Question: Encountered a "DeskTop Dyno Has Not Been Properly Installed..." error message when trying to run the DeskTop Dyno. Why?

Answer: This means that files required by the DeskTop Dyno were not found on your system. Reinstall the DeskTop Dyno using the SETUP program from the original distribution disk. Refer to pages 109 and 110 in this Appendix for installation help.

Question: The results of the simulation are listed in a simple chart on screen. Why are no power curves displayed?

Answer: Any monitor and display card will work with the DeskTop Dyno, however, systems with EGA or high-resolution graphics capability will allow the display of horsepower and torque curve graphics. If you do not have an EGA or better graphics system (you are using a CGA or another low-resolution display), an on-screen "chart" listing for horsepower and torque will be substituted for power curves.

Question: When I choose a carburetor that is too large for an engine (for example 1200cfm on a 283 Chevy), why does the power increase without the typically seen "bog" at low speeds?

Answer: The DeskTop Dyno, along with virtually any current computer simulation program, cannot model over-carburetion and show the usual reduction in low-end performance that this causes. In reality, carburetors that are too large for an engine develop fuel atomization and air/fuel ratio instabilities. Unfortunately, this phenomenon is extremely complicated to model. The DeskTop Dyno assumes an optimum air/fuel ratio regardless of the selected CFM rating. While you can get positive results from larger-and-larger induction flows (by the way, this is not far from reality when optimum air/fuel ratios can be maintained, as is the case in electronic fuel-injection systems), you can't go wrong if you use common sense when selecting induction/carburetor flow capacities.

Question: I built a relatively stock engine but installed a drag-race camshaft. The engine only produced 9 hp @ 2000 rpm. Is this correct?

Answer: Yes. Very low power outputs at low engine speeds occur when radical camshafts are used without complementary components, such as high-flow cylinder heads, high compression ratios, and exhaust system components that match the performance potential of the cam. In fact, some low performance engines with radical camshafts will show zero horsepower at low speeds. This means that if the engine was assembled and installed on a dynamometer, it would not produce enough power to offset any measurable load.

Question: The power predicted with the DeskTop Dyno seems too high for the Oldsmobile 455 engine that I am testing. Why?

Answer: You selected cylinder heads for your Olds engine from the **Big Block** choices in the CylinderHead menu. While this may seem like the logical choice, some big-block engines are equipped with heads that flow significantly less air than other large (big-block) engines. You will obtain more accurate power predictions by choosing one of the **Smallblock** head selections when building one of these large-displacement engines. In addition to Oldsmobile, versions of the 429-460 Ford engines also came with restrictive cylinderheads. When you make cylinderhead choices, keep these tips in mind: **Restrictive** applies to small-port heads (e.g., low-performance engines, such as early 260cid Ford engines or even flatheads) where the ports are small and restrictive for the installed valve sizes; consider **Smallblock** to describe heads with ports that are sized adequately or with performance in mind; **Bigblock** applies to heads where the ports are large or the valves are canted for improved flow (the first three big-block choices model oval-port heads, the last two choices simulate rectangular-port heads); and **4-Valve Heads** apply to many import and some racing configurations.

Question: The DeskTop Dyno produced an error message "THE SELECTED COMBINATION PRODUCED A CALCULATION ERROR..." What went wrong?

Answer: The combination of components you have selected produced a calculation error in the simulation process (this is usually caused by a mathematical instability as the program repeatedly performed calculations to "home in" on a variable—called iteration). This is often caused by using restrictive induction flow on large-displacement engines, or by using radical cam timing on otherwise mild engines. Try reducing the EVO timing specs, increasing the induction flow, selecting a cam with less duration, or reducing the compression ratio. A balanced group of components should not produce this error.

Question: The DeskTop Dyno takes 15 minutes to complete a simulation and draw horsepower and torque curves. Is there a problem with my computer or the software?

Answer: Your computer does not have a math coprocessor (speeds up the simulation from 50 to 300 times—see the information on page 108 and 109 in this Appendix). The DeskTop Dyno uses a powerful full-cycle simulation that performs millions of calculations for each point on the power curves, and this takes some time. But what you lose in speed with the DeskTop Dyno, you gain in accuracy over less sophisticated programs.

Question: The DeskTop Dyno calculated the total Combustion Volume at 92ccs. But I know my cylinder heads have only 75ccs. What's wrong with the DeskTop Dyno?

Answer: Nothing. The confusion comes from assuming that the calculated Total Combustion Volume is the same as your measured combustion-chamber volume. The Total Combustion Volume is the <u>entire volume</u> that remains when the piston reaches top dead center. This includes the combustion chamber, the remaining space above the piston top and below the deck surface, and the valve pockets; but it excludes any portion of the piston that protrudes into the combustion chamber. Compression ratio is calculated by this formula:

$$CR = \frac{Cyl/Volume + Comb/Vol}{Comb/Volume}$$

Both cylinder volume and combustion volume are calculated and displayed in the Component Selection Boxes.

Question: The horsepower produced when I enter the seat-to-seat timing on my cam card does not match the horsepower when I enter the 0.050-inch timing figures for the same camshaft. Why are there differences?

Answer: The DeskTop Dyno uses the timing specs found on your cam card, and in cam manufacturer's catalogs, to develop a valve-motion curve (and from this, develops the instantaneous airflow for each port). Neither the seat-to-seat nor 0.050-inch timing fig-

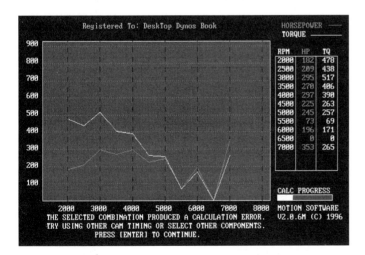

When severely unbalanced components are selected from the menus or entered manually, the iterative process of simulation can fall into mathematical instabilities, typically causing the curves to form a ragged "sawtooth" plot. Simply selecting a more balanced combination of parts and component specs will eliminate instabilities.

ures precisely describe actual valve motion; you would need to measure valve position at each degree of crank rotation to come close to developing an exact valve-motion diagram! Lacking this, the DeskTop Dyno "creates" its own valve-motion diagram for use in later calculations of power and torque. A lot can happen in induction airflow between the time the valve is on the seat and when is reaches 0.050-inch of <u>lifter rise</u>. It is impossible (without exact measurement) to precisely "guess" the shape of the cam or the motion of the valve. This is the reason for the calculated differences. When in doubt, use seat-to-seat timing figures. They provide the DeskTop Dyno more information about valve motion, and are more likely to produce accurate simulated power levels.

Question: When I build an engine, the menus close after each component selection. Why don't the menus open, one-after-the-other, until the entire engine is assembled?

Answer: This would make engine assembly *from scratch* easier. But it gets in the way when you want to change individual components to evaluate the changes in torque and horsepower. And since the true power of the DeskTop Dyno lies in its ability to make back-to-back tests—and it's these back-to-back tests that are essential steps in finding the best combination—we designed the menus to optimize changing individual components and quickly running back-to-back tests.

Question: How does the DeskTop Dyno allow for hydraulic, solid, and roller lifters?

Answer: The DeskTop Dyno calculates a valve-motion diagram that is used in the subsequent calculations to predict horsepower and torque. When the choice is made to move from hydraulic to solid, and then from solid to roller lifters, the DeskTop Dyno increases the valve acceleration rates to coincide with the lobe shapes that are commonly found on these cam grinds. It is impossible (without exact measurement of valve position at each degree of crank motion) to "guess" the precise shape of the cam or the motion of the valve, but the DeskTop Dyno has proven to be remarkably accurate in simulating real-world valve motion and horsepower.

Question: Why can't I just enter my port flow? Wouldn't that result in more accurate power predictions?

Answer: If you could input the flow of both the intake and exhaust ports at valve lifts from zero to maximum lift for each 0.010-inch of valve motion, yes. <u>Published flow figures</u> for ports are virtually meaningless when it comes to predicting power potential. This is because the peak port flow only occurs when the valve reaches some maximum lift figure specified by the head manufacturer (and maximum lift in

your engine may not be the same as the maximum lift that was used to rate port flow). Furthermore, the valve is only at maximum lift for a small fraction of its motion. To predict power you need to know the flow at each point of valve lift. This is calculated by the DeskTop Dyno from: 1) the valve head diameter, 2) knowing how the port shape (restrictive, smallblock, big-block, etc.) will affect flow across the valve, and 3) the valve motion diagram calculated from the valve-event timing.

Question: Can I change rockerarm ratios with the DeskTop Dyno?

Answer: Yes. Simply use this formula to alter valve lift (the DeskTop Dyno will calculate the new valve motion throughout the lift curve):

$$\text{New Lift} = \text{Old Lift} \times \frac{\text{New Ratio}}{\text{Old Ratio}}$$

When you have calculated the new maximum valve lifts for the intake and exhaust valves, enter these numbers directly into the Component Selections Box by choosing one of the OTHER choices in the Camshaft menu.

Question: I found the published factory seat-to-seat valve timing for Pontiac engine that I am building, but I can't enter the valve events into the DeskTop Dyno. The IVC occurs at 110 degrees (ABDC), and I can only enter up to 100 in the program.

Answer: There are so many ways that cam specs can be described for cataloging purposes that it's confusing to anyone trying to enter timing specs into an engine simulation program. Your Pontiac is a classic example of this lack of standards. The Pontiac cam listed in the factory manual is a hydraulic grind with seat-to-seat timing measured at 0.001-inch valve rise. Because the cam is designed for long life and quite operation, it has shallow opening ramps. This is the reason for the large number of crank degrees between the opening and closing points. In fact, during the first 35 degrees of crank rotation, the lifter rises less than 0.010-inch. If this wasn't the case and the valve opened and closed at the specified timing points listed in the factory manual, the cam would have over 350-degrees duration, and it's unlikely the engine would even start! The DeskTop Dyno can use 0.004- or 0.006-inch <u>valve</u> rise, 0.007-open/0.010-close <u>valve</u> rise, or even 0.020-inch <u>lifter</u> rise for seat-to-seat timing. But the 0.001-inch figures published in your factory manual are useless for engine simulation purposes.

Question: My cam manufacturer's catalog does not list seat-to-seat valve-event timing. But it does list seat-to-seat intake and exhaust duration, lobe-center angle, and intake centerline. Can I calculate the valve-event timing from these figures?

Answer: Yes. To calculate the intake and exhaust opening and closing points, you must have all of the following information:
1) **Intake Duration**
2) **Exhaust Duration**
3) **Lobe-Center Angle** (sometimes called lobe separation angle).
4) And the **Intake Centerline Angle**.

To perform the required calculations refer to the step-by-step procedure described on pages 92 and 93. Note: Version 2.5.7M of the DeskTop Dyno (under development when this book was published) incorporates a *Cam Math Calculator* that performs this calculation instantly. Send in your registration card to receive information about upgrades and new products (including the DeskTop DragStrip, and others).

Question: I have been attempting to test camshafts from a listing in a catalog. I can find the duration and lobe center angle. The cam manufacturer won't give me the seat-to-seat timing (they act like it's a trade secret). Can I use the available data to test their cams?

Answer: No. As stated in the previous answer, you also need the intake-center angle to relate cam lobe positions to TDC and, therefore, crank position. Freely providing seat-to-seat timing or any of the other cam specs discussed in this booklet poses no threat to any cam grinder. It takes a lot more than valve-event timing to manufacture a quality cam; full profiles of the lobes are needed to ensure mechanically and dynamically stable operation. Cam companies that refuse to provide potential customers with simple valve-event information for evaluation in programs like the DeskTop Dyno are simply living in the "dark ages." Our suggestion is to contact another cam manufacturer.

Question: Everyone talks about how longer rods make more power. Why isn't rod length one of the choices

in the pull-down menus?

Answer: Tests we have performed with the DeskTop Dyno show that rod length has virtually no affect on power. We realize that many actual dyno tests have shown power increases, but our simulation tests tell us that the power, when found, probably has little to do with piston dwell at TDC (and the associated thermodynamic effects) or changes in rod angularity on the crank pin. The measured power differences are most likely due to a reduction of friction on the cylinderwall from changes in side-loading on the piston. This can vary with bore finish, ring stability, piston shape, the frictional properties of the lubricant, etc. These variabilities are highly *unpredictable*. Some development, after all, can only be done in the real world on a engine dynamometer.

Question: I have an NEC Ready computer system. When I run a simulation, the curves are displayed properly, but the numbers and other words surrounding the power curves is garbled and completely unreadable. How can I fix this?

Answer: The NEC *Ready* series of computers was released for sale in the U.S. during the 1995 Christmas sale season. This system has a "bug" in firmware (unchangeable, internal code stored in ROM chips) that causes it to improperly display EGA graphics characters. It maps the lower 128 ASCII to their upper 128 counterparts. Motion Software has developed a fix for this problem (a VGA version of the power curves screen) that is available at no charge from Motion Software. Return your DeskTop Dyno disk, along with a note mentioning your NEC computer problem, to: Motion Software, Inc., NEC replacement, 535 West Lambert, Bldg. E, Brea, CA, 92821.

Question: I have tried many different engine combinations using the same engine displacements and have noticed that several of the power curves begin at nearly the same horsepower and torque values at 2000rpm. Why are they so similar at this engine speed?

Answer: Since the DeskTop Dyno uses a simulation technique that iterates toward an answer—performs a series of calculations that approach a more and more accurate result—the first power point must be developed based on educated "guesses" about mass flow and other variables. The next point, at 2500rpm, is calculated from the starting point, plus the data obtained from the completed simulation, so accuracy is higher. By 3000rpm, the power points are based on simulation calculations with virtually no remaining influence from the initial estimations.

0.050-Inch Cam Timing Method—See Cam Timing, @ 0.050-inch.

ABDC or **After Bottom Dead Center**—Any position of the piston in the cylinder bore after its lowest point in the stroke (BDC). ABDC is measured in degrees of crankshaft rotation after BDC. For example, the point at which the intake valve closes (IVC) may be indicated as 60-degrees ABDC. In other words, the intake valve would close 60 degrees after the beginning of the compression stroke (the compression stroke begins at BDC).

Air-Fuel Ratio—The proportion of air to fuel—by weight—that is produced by the carburetor or injector.

ATDC or **After Top Dead Center**—Any position of the piston in the cylinder bore after its highest point in the stroke (TDC). ATDC is measured in degrees of crankshaft rotation after TDC. For example, the point at which the exhaust valve closes (EVC) may be indicated as 30-degrees ATDC. In other words, the exhaust valve would close 30 degrees after the beginning of the intake stroke (the intake stroke begins at TDC).

Atmospheric Pressure—The pressure created by the weight of the gases in the atmosphere. Measured at sea level this pressure is about 14.69psi.

Back Pressure—A pressure developed when a moving liquid or gaseous mass passes through a restriction. "Backpressure" often refers to the pressure generated within the exhaust system from internal restrictions from tubing and tubing bends, mufflers, catalytic converters, tailpipes, or even turbochargers.

BBDC or **Before Bottom Dead Center**—Any position of the piston in the cylinder bore before its lowest point in the stroke (BDC). BBDC is measured in degrees of crankshaft rotation before BDC. For example, the point at which the exhaust valve opens (EVO) may be indicated as 60-degrees BBDC. In other words, the exhaust valve would open 60 degrees before the exhaust stroke begins (the exhaust stroke begins at BDC).

Big-Block—A generic term that usually refers to a V8 engine with a displacement that is large enough to require a physically "bigger" engine block. Typical big-block engines displace over 400 cubic inches.

Blowdown or **Cylinder Blowdown**—Blowdown occurs during the period between exhaust valve opening and BDC. It is the period (measured in crank degrees) during which residual exhaust gases are expelled from the engine before the exhaust stroke begins. Residual gasses not discharged during blowdown must be physically "pumped" out of the cylinder during the exhaust stroke, lowering power output from consumed "pumping work."

Bore or **Cylinder Bore**—The internal surface of a cylindrical volume used to retain and seal a moving piston and ring assembly. "Bore" is commonly used to refer to the cylinder bore diameter, unusually measured in inches or millimeters. Bore surfaces are machined or ground precisely to afford an optimum ring seal and minimum friction with the moving piston and rings.

Brake Horsepower (bhp)—Brake horsepower (sometimes referred to as *shaft* horsepower) is always measured at the flywheel or crankshaft by a "brake" or absorbing unit. *Gross brake horsepower* describes the power output of an engine in stripped-down, "race-ready" trim. *Net brake horsepower* measures the power at the flywheel when the engine is tested with all standard accessories attached and function-

ing. Also see Horsepower, Indicated Horsepower, Friction Horsepower, and Torque.

Brake Mean Effective Pressure (bmep)—A theoretical average pressure that would have to be present in each cylinder during the power stroke to reproduce the force on the crankshaft measured by the absorber (brake) on a dynamometer. The bmep present during the power stroke would produce the same power generated by the varying pressures in the cylinder throughout the entire four-cycle process.

BTDC or **Before Top Dead Center**—Any position of the piston in the cylinder bore before its highest point in the stroke (TDC). BTDC is measured in degrees of crankshaft rotation before TDC. For example, the point at which the intake valve opens (IVO) may be indicated as 30-degrees BTDC. In other words, the intake valve would open 30 degrees before the intake stroke begins (the intake stroke begins at TDC).

Cam Timing, @ 0.050-Lift—This method of determining camshaft valve timing is based on 0.050 inches of tappet rise to pinpoint timing events. The 0.050 inch method was developed to help engine builders accurately install camshafts. Lifter rise is quite rapid at 0.050-inch lift, allowing the cam to be precisely indexed to the crankshaft. Camshaft timing events are always measured in crankshaft degrees, relative to TDC or BDC.

Cam Timing, @ Seat-To-Seat—This method of determining camshaft timing uses a specific valve lift (determined by the cam manufacturer) to define the beginning or ending of valve events. There is no universally accepted valve lift used to define seat-to-seat cam timing, however, the Society of Automotive Engineers (S.A.E) has accepted 0.006-inch valve lift as its standard definition. Camshaft timing events are always measured in crankshaft degrees, relative to TDC.

Camshaft Advance/Retard— This refers to the amount of advance or retard that the cam is installed from the manufacturers recommended setting. Focusing on intake timing, an advanced cam closes the intake valve earlier. This setting typically increases low-end performance. The retarded cam closes the intake valve later which tends to help top end performance.

Camshaft Follower or **Lifter**—Usually a metal cylinder (closed at one end) that rubs against the cam lobe and converts the rotary motion of the cam to an up/down motion required to open and close valves, operate fuel pumps, etc. Cam followers (lifters) can incorporate rollers, a design that can improve reliability and performance in many applications. Roller lifters are used extensively in racing where valve lift and valve-lift rates are very high, since they can withstand higher dynamic loads. In overhead cam engines, the cam follower is usually incorporated into the rocker arm that directly actuates the valve; in this design push rods are eliminated.

Camshaft Grind—The shape of the cam lobe. Determines when the intake and exhaust valves open and close and how high they lift off of the seats. The shape also determines *how fast* the valves open and close, i.e., how much acceleration the valves and springs experience. High acceleration rate cams require large-diameter solid, mushroom, or roller lifters.

Camshaft Lift—The maximum height of the cam lobe above the base-circle diameter. A higher lobe opens the valves further, often improving engine performance. Lobe lift must be multiplied by the rocker ratio (for engines using rocker arms) to obtain total valve lift. Lifting the valve more than 1/3 the head diameter generally yields little additional performance. Faster valve opening rates add stress and increase valvetrain wear but can further improve performance. High lift rates usually require specially designed, high-strength components.

Camshaft Lobe—The eccentrically shaped portion of a camshaft on which the camshaft follower or lifter rides. The shape of intake and exhaust cam lobes are important engine design criterion. They directly affect engine efficiency, power output, the rate (how fast) the valves open and close, and control valvetrain life and maximum valvetrain/engine rpm.

Camshaft Timing—The rotational position of the camshaft, relative to the crankshaft, i.e., the point at which the cam lobes open and close the valves relative to piston position. Two common methods are used to indicate the location of valve events: the Seat-To-Seat and 0.050-inch timing methods. For simulation purposes, Seat-To-Seat timing values yield more accurate horsepower and torque predictions. Camshaft timing can be adjusted by using offset keys or offset bushings (or by redesigning the cam profile). Valve-to-piston clearance will vary as cam timing is altered; always ensure that adequate clearance exists after varying cam timing from manufacturer's specifications. See Cam Timing @ Seat-To-Seat, Cam Timing @ 0.050-Inch Method.

Carburetor—A device that combines fuel with air entering the engine; capable of precision control over the air volume and the ratio of the fuel-to-air mixture.

Centerline—An imaginary line running through the center of a part along its axis, e.g., the centerline of a crankshaft running from front-to-back directly through the center of the main-bearing journals.

Closed Headers or Closed Exhaust System—Refers to an exhaust system that includes mufflers; not open to the atmosphere.

Combustion Chamber or Combustion Chamber Volume—The volume contained within the cavity or space enclosed by the cylinder head, including the "top" surfaces of the intake and exhaust valves and the spark plug. Not the same volume as the *combustion space volume*.

Combustion Space or Combustion Space Volume—The volume contained within the cylinder head, plus (or minus) the piston dome (or dish) volume, plus any volume displaced by the compressed head gasket, plus (or minus) any additional volume created by the piston not fully rising to the top of the bore (or extending beyond the top of the bore) of the cylinder at TDC. This volume is used to calculate compression ratio.

Compression Pressure—The pressure created in the cylinder when the piston moves toward top dead center (TDC) after the intake valve closes, trapping the induced charge (normally a fuel/air mixture) within the cylinder. Compression pressure can be measured by installing a pressure gauge in the cylinder in place of the spark plug and "cranking" the engine with the starter motor. To improve measurement accuracy, the throttle is usually held wide open and the remaining spark plugs are removed to minimize cranking loads and optimize pressures in the cylinder under test.

Compression Ratio—The ratio of the total volume enclosed in a cylinder when the piston is located at BDC compared to the volume enclosed when the piston is at TDC (volume at TDC is called the *combustion space volume*). The formula to calculate compression ratio is: (Swept Cylinder Volume + Combustion Space Volume)/Combustion Space Volume = Compression Ratio.

Compression Stroke—One of the four 180-degree full "sweeps" of the piston moving in the cylinder of a four-stroke, internal-combustion engine (originally devised by Nikolaus Otto in 1876). During the compression stroke, the piston moves from BDC to TDC and compresses the air/fuel mixture. Note: The 180-degree duration of the compression stroke is commonly longer than the duration between the intake valve-closing point and top dead center or ignition, sometimes referred to as the true "Compression Cycle." The compression stroke is followed by the power stroke.

Cubic Inch Displacement or CID—The swept volume of all the pistons in the cylinders in an engine expressed in cubic inches. The cylinder displacement is calculated with this formula: (Bore x Bore x Pi x Stroke x No.Cyl.)/4. When the bore and stroke are measured in inches, the engine displacement calculated in cubic inches.

Cylinder and Cylinder Bore—The cylinder serves three important functions in an internal-combustion (IC) engine: 1) retains the piston and rings, and for this job must be precisely round and have a uniform diameter (for performance applications 0.0005-inch tolerance is considered the maximum allowable); 2) must have a surface finish that ensures both optimum ring seal (smooth and true) and yet provides adequate lubrication retention to ensure long life for both the piston and rings; and 3) the cylinder bore acts as a major structural element of the cylinder block, retaining the cylinder heads and the bottom end components. The cylinder bore design, finish, and its preparation techniques are extremely important aspects of performance engine design.

Cylinder Block—The casting that comprises the main structure of an IC engine. The cylinder block is the connecting unit for the cylinder heads, crankshaft, and external assemblies, plus it houses the pistons, camshaft and all other internal engine components. The stability, strength, and precision of the block casting and machining are extremely important in obtaining optimum power and engine life. Cylinder blocks are usually made from a high grade of cast iron.

Cylinderhead—A component (usually made of cast iron or cast aluminum) that forms the combustion chambers, intake and exhaust ports—including water cooling passages—and provides support for valvetrain components, spark plugs, intake and exhaust manifolds, etc. The cylinderhead attaches to the engine block with several large bolts that squeeze a head gasket between the block deck and head surfaces; and when attached, the head becomes a load-carrying member, adding strength and rigidity to the cylinder block assembly. Modern cylinderhead designs fall into three major categories: 1) overhead-valve with wedge, canted-valve, or hemispherical combustion chambers; 2) single-overhead cam with wedge or hemispherical cambers; 3) double-overhead cam with hemispherical chambers.

Degree—1) An angular measurement. A complete circle is divided into 360 degrees; equal to one crankshaft rotation; 180 degrees is one-half rotation. 2) A temperature measurement. The temperatures of boiling and freezing water are: in the Fahrenheit system 212 and 32 degrees; in the Celsius system 100 and 0 (zero) degrees.

Density—A measurement of the amount of matter within a known space or volume. Air density is the measurement of the amount of air per unit volume at a fixed temperature, barometric pressure, altitude, etc.

Detonation—The secondary ignition of the air/fuel mixture in the combustion space causing extreme pressures. Detonation is caused by low gasoline octane ratings, high combustion temperatures, improper combustion chamber shape, too-lean mixtures, etc. Detonation produces dangerously high loads on the engine, and if allowed to continue, will lead to engine failure. Detonation, unlike preignition, requires two simultaneous combustion fronts (fuel burning in two or more places in the combustion chamber at once); whereas preignition occurs when the fuel-air mix ignites (with single burning front) before the spark plug fires. Both preignition and detonation produce an audible "knock" or "ping," but detonation does not produce the rapid "wild pinging" noise that is typically associated with preignition. The extreme pressures of detonation can lead to preignition, but even worse the high temperatures of preignition can cause detonation.

Duration or **Valve Duration**—The number of crankshaft degrees (or much more rarely, camshaft degrees) of rotation that the valve lifter or cam follower is lifted above a specified height; either seat-to-seat valve duration measured at 0.006-, 0.010-inch or other valve rises (even 0.020-inch lifter rise), or duration measured at 0.050-inch lifter rise called 0.050-inch duration. Intake duration is a measure of all the intake lobes and exhaust duration indicates the exhaust timing for all exhaust lobes. Longer cam durations hold the valves open longer, often allowing increased cylinder filling or scavenging at higher engine speeds.

Dynamometer—A device used to measure the power output of rotating machinery. In it's simplest terms, a dynamometer is a power-absorbing brake, incorporating an accurate method of measuring how much torque (and horsepower) is being absorbed. Braking is accomplished through friction (usually a hydraulic absorber) or by an electric dynamo (converts energy to electricity). Modern computer-controlled dynamometers for high-performance automotive use have sophisticated speed controls that allow the operator to select the rpm point or range of speeds through which the torque is to be measured. Then the operator opens the throttle and the dynamometer applies the precise amount of load to maintain the chosen rpm points; horsepower is read out directly on a gauge and/or computer screen.

Dynomation—A engine simulation program developed by V.P. Engineering that uses full wave-action analysis, currently using the Method Of Characteristics to provide solutions to the complex equations of wave dynamics.

Empirical or **Empirical Testing**—Meaning "after the fact" or "experimental," empirical testing involves actual "real-world" experiments to determine the outcome of component changes.

Exhaust Center Angle/Centerline or **ECA**—The distance in crank degrees from the point of maximum exhaust valve lift (on symmetric cam profiles) to TDC during the valve overlap period.

Exhaust Manifold—An assembly (usually an iron casting) that connects the exhaust ports to the remainder of the exhaust system. The exhaust manifold may include a heat-riser valve or port that heats the intake manifold to improve fuel vaporization.

Exhaust Ports—Cavities within the cylinder head that form the initial flow paths for the spent gases of combustion. One end of the exhaust port forms the exhaust valve seat and the other end forms a connecting flange to the exhaust manifold or header.

Exhaust Stroke—One of the four 180-degree full "sweeps" of the piston moving in the cylinder of a four-stroke, internal-combustion engine (originally devised by Nikolaus Otto in 1876). During the exhaust stroke, the piston moves from BDC to TDC and forces exhaust gases from the cylinder into the exhaust system. Note: The 180-degree duration of the exhaust stroke is commonly shorter than the period during which the exhaust valve is open, sometimes referred to as the true "Exhaust Cycle." The exhaust stroke is followed by the intake stroke.

Exhaust Valve Closing or **EVC**—The point at which the exhaust valve returns to its seat, or closes. This valve timing point usually occurs early in the intake stroke. Although EVC does not have substantial effects on engine performance, it contributes to valve overlap (the termination point of overlap) that can have a significant effect on engine output.

Exhaust Valve Duration—See Duration

Exhaust Valve Lift—See Valve Lift

Exhaust Valve Opening or **EVO**—The point at which the exhaust valve lifts off of its seat, or opens. This valve timing point usually occurs late in the power stroke. EVO usually precedes BDC on the power stroke to assist exhaust-gas *blowdown*. This EVO timing point can be considered the second most important cam timing event.

Exhaust Valve—The valve located within the cylinder head that control the flow of spent gases from the cylinder. The exhaust valves are precisely actuated (opened and closed) by the camshaft, usually through lifters, pushrods, and rockerarms. Exhaust valves must withstand extremely high temperatures (1500 degrees-F or higher) and are made from special steels, e.g., SAE J775 that has excellent strength at high temperatures and good resistance to corrosion and wear.

Filling & Emptying Multidimensional Simulation—This engine simulation technique includes multiple models (e.g., thermodynamic, kinetic, etc.), and by dividing the intake and exhaust passages into a finite series of sections it describes mass flow into and out of each section at each degree of crank rotation. The Filling And Emptying method can accurately predict average pressures within sections of the intake and exhaust system and dynamically determine VE and engine power. However, the basic Filling And Emptying model can not account for variations in pressure *within* individual sections due to gas dynamic effects. See Gas-Dynamic Multidimensional Simulation.

Finite-Amplitude Waves—Pressure waves of higher energy levels higher than acoustic waves. Finite-amplitude waves exhibit complex motions and interactions when traveling through engine passages. These actions make their mathematical analysis very complex.

Flat-Tappet Lifter—A camshaft follower having a flat surface at the point of contact with the cam lobe. Flat-tappet lifters actually have a shallow convex curvature at their "face" to allow the lifter to rotate during operation, extending the working life.

Flow Bench and **Flow-Bench Testing**—A flow bench is a

testing fixture that develops a precise pressure differential to either "suck" our "blow" air through a cylinder head or other engine component. A flow bench determines the flow capacities (restrictions) of cylinder head ports and valves and assists in the analysis of alterations to port contours.

Four-Cycle Engine—Originally devised by Nikolaus Otto in 1876, the four-cycle engine consists of a piston moving in a closed cylinder with two valves (one for inlet and one for outlet) timed to produce four separate strokes, or functional cycles: Intake, Compression, Power, and Exhaust. Sometimes called the "suck, squeeze, bang, and blow" process, this technique—combined with a properly atomized air/fuel mixture and a precisely timed spark ignition—produced an engine with high efficiency and power potential. The software discussed in this book is designed to simulate the functional processes of a four-cycle engine.

Friction Horsepower (Fhp)—The power absorbed by the mechanical components of the engine during normal operation. Most frictional losses are due to piston ring pressure against the cylinder walls. Frictional power losses are not easily measured, however, they can be accurately *calculated* knowing the brake horsepower (from dyno testing) and the indicated horsepower (from pressure measurements). Also see Indicated Horsepower and Brake Horsepower.

Friction Mean Effective Pressure (Fmep)—A theoretical average pressure that would have to be present in each cylinder during the power stroke to overcome the power consumed by friction within the engine. Fmep is usually calculated by first determining the Indicated Mean Effective Pressure (Imep)—the maximum horsepower that can be produced from the recorded cylinder pressures. The Brake Mean Effective Pressure (Bmep) is then measured by performing a traditional "dyno" test. The Fmep is calculated by finding the difference between the Imep and the Bmep: Fmep = Imep - Bmep. Fmep can also be directly measured with a motoring (electric) dyno.

Friction—A force that opposes motion. Frictional forces convert mechanical motion into heat.

Full Three-Dimensional (CFD) Simulation—This highly advanced engine simulation technique incorporates multiple models (e.g., thermodynamic, kinetic, etc.), including full three-dimensional modeling that subdivides an area, such as the combustion chamber or port junction, into a series of volumes (or cells) through which the model solves the differential equations of thermodynamics and fluid flow (using Computational Fluid Dynamics—CFD). The interaction of these cells can reveal very subtle design features within the induction and exhaust systems. It can thoroughly evaluate their effect on horsepower, fuel efficiency, and emissions throughout the rpm range. This simulation is not available as a commercial program and it currently remains a "laboratory-only" tool.

Gas-Dynamic Multidimensional Simulation—This engine simulation technique includes multiple models (e.g., thermodynamic, kinetic, etc.), plus powerful finite-wave analysis techniques that account for variations in pressures within individual sections of the ports due to gas dynamic effects. This detailed, highly math-intensive technique can predict engine power with remarkably high accuracy. The Dynomation program from V.P. Engineering is an example of a program using this simulation method.

Helmholtz Resonator—A device that increases the ampli-

tude of pressure wave through a resonance phenomenon (an effect similar to the deep "whir" produced when air is blown over the neck of a jug). In some cases, the induction system in an IC engine can be modeled by employing Helmholtz resonance equations.

Horsepower—Torque measures how much work (an engine) *can* do, power is the rate-based measurement of *how fast* the work is being done. Starting with the static force applied at the end of a torque arm (torque), then multiplying this force by the swept distance through which the same force would rotate one full revolution finds the power per revolution: Power Per Revolution = Force or Weight x Swept Distance. James Watt (1736-1819) established the current value for one horsepower: 33,000 pound-feet per minute or 550 pound-feet per second. So horsepower is currently calculated as: Horsepower = Power Per Revolution/33,000, which is the same as Horsepower = (Torque x 2 x Pi x RPM)/33,000, or simply: Horsepower = (Torque x RPM)/5,252. The horsepower being calculated by these equations is just one of several ways to rate engine power output. Various additional methods for calculating or measuring engine horsepower are commonly used (to derive friction horsepower, indicated horsepower, etc.), and each technique provides additional information about the engine under test.

Hydraulic Lifter—See Lifters, Hydraulic

IC Engine—See Internal Combustion engine.

Inches of Mercury and **Inches of Water**—A standard method of pressure measurement, where pressures are compared to atmospheric or ambient pressure. Inches of displacement are recorded for a water or mercury column measured in a "U" shaped tube with one end open to the air and the other end connected to the test pressure. Commonly called a manometer, this pressure comparison device is quite sensitive and accurate. When mercury is used in the manometer tube, one psi differential from atmospheric pressure will displace 2.04-inches of mercury. However, when water is the liquid in the "U-tube," a substantial increase in pressure sensitivity is obtained: one psi will displace 27.72 inches of water. A water manometer is used to measure small vacuum and pressure signals.

Indicated Horsepower (Ihp)—is the maximum power that a particular engine can *theoretically* produce. It is calculated from an analysis of the gas pressures measured by installing pressure transducers in the cylinders throughout the entire four-cycle process (with no losses due to friction). Also see Brake Horsepower and Friction Horsepower.

Indicated Mean Effective Pressure (Imep)—A theoretical average pressure that would have to be present in each cylinder during the power stroke to generate the maximum horsepower possible from the pressures recorded within the cylinder of an engine during an actual dyno test. The Imep pressure assumes that the recorded pressures within the test engine will be entirely converted into motive force (with no losses due to friction).

Induction Airflow—The airflow rating (a measurement of restriction) of a carburetor or fuel injection system. Four-barrel carburetors are rated by the measured airflow when the device is subjected to a pressure drop equal to 1.5-inches of Mercury. Two-barrel carburetors are tested at 3.0-inches of Mercury.

Induction System—Consists of the carburetor or injection system and the intake manifold. The intake manifold can be of many designs such as dual plane, single plane, tunnel ram, etc.

Intake Centerline Angle—The distance in crank degrees from the point of maximum intake valve lift (on symmetric cam profiles) to TDC during the valve overlap period.

Intake Stroke—One of the four 180-degree full "sweeps" of the piston moving in the cylinder of a four-stroke, internal-combustion engine (originally devised by Nikolaus Otto in 1876). During the intake stroke, the piston moves from *TDC* to *BDC* and inducts (draws in by lowering the pressure in the cylinder) air/fuel mixture through the induction system. Note: The 180-degree duration of the intake stroke is commonly shorter than the period during which the intake valve is open, sometimes referred to as the true "Intake Cycle." The intake stroke is followed by the compression stroke.

Intake Valve Closing or **IVC**—Considered the most important cam timing event. The point at which the intake valve returns to its seat, or closes. This valve timing point usually occurs early in the compression stroke. Early IVC helps low-end power by retaining air/fuel mixture in the cylinder and reducing charge reversion at lower engine speeds. Late IVC increases high-speed performance (at the expense of low speed power) by allow additional charge to fill the cylinder from the ram-tuning effects of the induction system at higher engine speeds.

Intake Valve Duration—See Duration

Intake Valve Lift—See Valve Lift

Intake Valve Opening or **IVO**—The point at which the intake valve lifts off of its seat, or opens. This valve timing point usually occurs late in the exhaust stroke. Although IVO does not have a substantial effect on engine performance, it contributes to valve overlap (the beginning point of overlap) that can have a significant effect on engine output.

Internal Combustion Engine—An engine that produces power from the combustion and expansion of a fuel-and-air mixture within a closed cylinder. Internal-combustion engines are based on two methods of operation: two cycle and four cycle. In each method, a mixture of fuel and air enters the engine through the induction system. A piston compresses the mixture within a closed cylinder. A precisely timed spark ignites the charge after it is compressed. The explosive burning produces very high temperatures and pressures that push the piston down and rotate the crankshaft, generating a motive force. Also see combustion space, compression ratio, compression stroke, power stroke, exhaust stroke, and intake stroke.

Lifters, Hydraulic Flat-Tappet—A camshaft follower having a flat surface at the point of contact with the cam lobe. Flat-tappet lifters actually have a shallow convex curvature at their "face" to allow the lifter to rotate during operation, extending the working life. A hydraulic lifter incorporates a mechanism that automatically adjusts for small changes in component dimensions, and usually maintains zero lash in the valvetrain. Hydraulic lifters also offer a slight "cushioning" effect and reduce valvetrain noise.

Lifters, Roller Solid Or Hydraulic—A camshaft follower having a round, rolling element used at the contact point with the cam lobe. A hydraulic lifter incorporates a mechanism that automatically adjusts for small changes in component dimensions, and usually maintains zero lash in the valvetrain. Hydraulic lifters also offer a slight "cushioning" effect and reduce valvetrain noise. Solid lifters lack this hydraulic adjusting mechanism and require a running clear-

ance in the valvetrain, usually adjusted by a screw or nut on the rockerarm.

Lifters, Solid Flat-Tappet— A camshaft follower having a flat surface at the point of contact with the cam lobe. Flat-tappet lifters actually have a shallow convex curvature at their "face" to allow the lifter to rotate during operation, extending the working life. Solid lifters lack an automatic hydraulic adjusting mechanism and require a running clearance in the valvetrain, usually adjusted by a screw or nut on the rockerarm. Solid lifter cams usually generate more valvetrain noise than hydraulic-tappet cam.

Lobe-Center Angle or **LCA**—The angle in <u>cam degrees</u> from maximum intake lift to maximum exhaust lift. Typical LCAs range from 100 to 116 camshaft degrees (or 200 to 232 crank degrees).

Multi Dimensional—As it refers to engine simulation programs, multi dimensional indicates that the simulation is based on multiple models, such as thermodynamic and kinetic, plus the multidimensional geometric description of inlet and outlet passages and a dynamic model of induction and exhaust flow. Also see Quasi Dimensional and Zero Dimensional.

Negative Pressure—A pressure below atmospheric pressure; below 14.7psi absolute. Very low pressures are usually measured by a manometer. See Inches of Water.

Normally Aspirated—When the air-fuel mix is inducted into the engine solely by the lower pressure produced in the cylinder during the intake stroke; aspiration not aided by a supercharger.

Otto-Cycle Engine—See Four-Cycle Engine

Overlap or **Valve Overlap**—The period, measured in crank degrees, when both the exhaust valve and the intake valve are open. Valve overlap allows the negative pressure scavenge wave to return from the exhaust and begin the inflow of air/fuel mixture into the cylinder even before the intake stroke begins. The effectiveness of the overlap period is dependent on engine speed and exhaust "tuning."

Pocket Porting—Relatively minor porting work performed below the valve seat and in the "bowl" area under the valve head. These changes, while straightforward, can produce a significant improvement in airflow and performance. Proper contours must be maintained, particularly below the valve seat, to produce the desired results.

Porting or **All-Out Porting**—Aggressive porting work performed to the passages within the cylinderhead with intention of optimizing high-speed airflow. Often characterized by large cross-sectional port areas, these ports generate sufficient flow velocities only at higher engine speeds; low speeds produce weak ram-tuning effects and exhaust scavenging waves. This porting technique is a poor choice for low-speed power and street applications.

Pounds Per Square Inch—See PSI.

Power Stroke—One of the four 180-degree full "sweeps" of the piston moving in the cylinder of a four-stroke, internal-combustion engine (originally devised by Nikolaus Otto in 1876). During the power stroke, the piston moves from TDC to BDC as the burning air/fuel mixture forces the piston down the cylinder. Note: The 180-degree duration of the power stroke is commonly longer than the duration between top dead center and the exhaust-valve opening point, sometimes referred to as the true "Power Cycle." The power stroke is followed by the exhaust stroke.

Pressure Crank-Angle Diagram—Also called a *"Pie-Theta*

"diagram, the crank-angle diagram is a plot of the indicated cylinder pressures vs. the angular position of the crankshaft during the entire four-cycle process. This diagram provides an easily understood view of the widely varying pressures in the cylinder. Also see Pressure-Volume Diagram.

Pressure—A force applied to a specific amount of surface area. A common unit of pressure is psi, i.e., pounds per square inch. The force that develops the pressure is sum total of all the slight "nudges" on a surface generated by each molecule striking the surface; the greater number of impacts or the more violent each impact, the greater the pressure. Therefore, the pressure increases if the same number of molecules are contained in a smaller space (greater number of impacts per unit area) or if the molecules are heated (each impact is more violent). Also see psi.

Pressure-Volume Diagram—Also called a *PV* (pronounced *Pee-Vee),* or "*indicator*" *diagram,* the pressure-volume diagram plots indicated pressure against the displaced volume in the cylinder. A PV diagram has the remarkable feature of isolating the *work consumed* from the *work developed* by the engine. The area within the lower loop, drawn in a counterclockwise direction, represents the work consumed by the engine "pumping" the charge into the cylinder and forcing the exhaust gasses from the cylinder. The upper loop area, drawn in a clockwise direction, indicates the work produced by the engine from pressures generated by expanding gasses after combustion.

PSI or **Pounds Per Square Inch**—A measure of *force* applied on a surface, e.g., the force on the wall of a cylinder that contains a compressed gas. A gas compressed to 100 psi would generate a force of 100 pounds on each square inch of the cylinder wall surface. In other words, psi equals the force in pounds divided by the surface area in square inches. Also see *pressure*.

Restriction—A measure of the resistance to flow for (usually) a liquid or gas. Exhaust or intake flow restriction can occur within tubing bends, within ports, manifolds, etc. Liquid restriction can occur in needle-and-seat assemblies, fuel pumps, oil filters, etc. Some restriction is always present in a flowing medium.

Roller Lifter—See Lifters, Roller

Roller Tappet Lifter— See Lifters, Roller

RPM—Revolutions Per Minute. A unit of measure for angular speed. As applied to the IC engine, rpm indicates the instantaneous rotational speed of the crankshaft described as the number of crank revolutions that would occur every minute if that instantaneous speed was held constant throughout the measurement period. Typical idle speeds are 300 to 800rpm, while peak engine speeds can reach as high as 10,000rpm or higher in some racing engines.

Seat-To-Seat Cam Timing Method—See Cam Timing, @ Seat to Seat.

Simulation and **Engine Simulation**—A engine simulation process or program that attempts to predict real-world responses from specific component assemblies by applying fundamental physical laws to "duplicate" or simulate the processes taking place within the components.

Smallblock—A generic term that usually refers to a V8 engine with a displacement small enough to be contained within a "small" size engine block. Typical smallblock engines displace under 400 cubic inches.

Solid Lifter—See Lifter, Solid.

Stroke—The maximum distance the piston travels from the top of the cylinder (at TDC) to the bottom of the cylinder (at BDC), measured in inches or millimeters. The stroke is determined by the design of the crankshaft (the length of the stroke arm).

Top Dead Center or **TDC**—The position of the piston in the cylinder bore at its uppermost point in the stroke. Occurs twice within the full cycle of a four-stroke engine; at the start of the intake stroke and 360 degrees later at the end of the compression stroke.

Torque—The static twisting force produced by an engine. Torque varies with the length of the "arm" at which the twisting force is measured. Torque is a force *times* the length of the measurement arm: *Torque = Force x Torque Arm*, where *Force* is the applied or the generated force and *Torque Arm* is the length through which that force is applied. Typical torque values are ounce-inches, pound-feet, etc.

Valve Head and **Valve Diameter**—The large end of an intake or exhaust valve that determines the diameter. Valve head temperature can exceed 1200 degrees F during engine operation and a great deal of that heat is transferred to the cylinder head through the contact surface between the valve face and valve seat.

Valve Lift Rate—A measurement of how fast (in inches/degree) the camshaft raises the valve off of the valve seat to a specific height. If maximum valve lift is increased but the duration (crankshaft degrees) that the valve is held off of the valve seat is kept the same, then rate at which the valve opens must increase (same time to reach a higher lift). High lift rates can produce more horsepower, however, they also increase stress and valvetrain wear.

Valve Lift—The distance the valve head raises off of the valve seat as it is actuated through the valvetrain by the camshaft. Maximum valve lift is the greatest height the valve head moves off of the valve seat; it is the lift of the cam (lobe height minus base-circle diameter) multiplied by the rockerarm ratio.

Valve Motion Curve or **Valve Displacement Curve**—The movement (or lift) of the valve relative to the position of the crankshaft. Different cam styles (i.e., flat, mushroom, roller) typically have different displacement curve acceleration rates. Engine simulation programs calculate a valve motion curve from valve event timing, maximum valve lift, and other cam timing specifications.

Volumetric Efficiency—Is calculated by dividing the mass of air inducted into the cylinder between IVO and IVC divided by the mass of air that would fill the cylinder at atmospheric pressure (with the piston at BDC). Typical values range from 0.6 to 1.2, or 60% to 120%. Peak torque always occurs at the engine speed that produced the highest volumetric efficiency.

Work and **Net Work**—Work is the energy required to move an object over a set distance. Both motion and force must be present for work to occur. In an IC engine, work is developed from pressures within the cylinder acting on the face of the piston (producing a force) times the distance through which the piston travels. In the internal combustion engine some of the work produces power output (such as pressures producing piston movement during the power stroke) and some of the work is negative (like compressing the fresh charge on the compression stroke). The difference between the positive and negative work is the net work produced by the engine.

Appendix-C Bibliography

The following books are generally not available in auto stores or "speed shops." These references can be found in well-stocked engineering libraries (particularly at state universities) or at technical book stores. Many of these books are serious engineering works requiring substantial math and physics background for complete understanding, however, all of these books have least some "readable" material that might be of interest to performance enthusiasts.

Anderson, Edwin P., Facklam, Charles G, **Gas Engine Manual**, G.K. Hall & Co., 70 Lincoln Street, Boston, MA 02111, 800-343-2806. A very readable, non-engineering look at the four and two-cycle internal combustion engine. Includes a detailed look at individual components and their function. Published 1962. ISBN-0-8161-1707-1

Cummins Jr., C. Lyle, **Internal Fire**, Internal Fire, SAE. In-depth history of the internal-combustion engine, from the early attempts at gunpowder engines in the 1600's to "modern" designs of the early 1900's. Easy, interesting reading. Orig. Published 1976, revised 1989. ISBN 0-89883-765-0

Benson, Roland S., **The Thermodynamics and Gas Dynamics of Internal-Combustion Engines, Volume 1**, Oxford University Press, New York. Considered by many to be the original "bible" of gas dynamics as applied to the IC engine. This book has been the jumping off point for many engineers and scientists into the world of computer engine modeling. This book is mathematically rigorous and demands much of the reader. A knowledge of differential and integral calculus is required to get the most from this text. Published 1982 for the late Rowland Benson (1925-1978) by J.H. Horlock F.R.S and D.E. Winterbone, editors. ISBN 0-19-856210-1

Ferguson, Colin R., **Internal Combustion Engines, Applied Thermosciences**, John Wiley & Sons, New York, An interesting combination of "nuts and bolts" and thermodynamics. A much more rigorous look at thermal science (encompasses two thirds of the book) than the design of IC engines. Requires knowledge of differential and integral calculus. Includes some computer code listings, however, calls are made to subroutines that may not be available to many readers. Published 1986. ISBN 0-471-88129-5

Stone, Richard, **Introduction To Internal Combustion Engines**, Macmillan Publishing. A text for college-level students. Includes some high-level math, but much of the text is accessible to the advanced enthusiast. Covers thermodynamics (with a quick look at modeling theory), combustion, turbocharging, mechanical design, dynamometers. Published 1985; second edition published 1992. ISBN 0-333-37593-9

Heywood, John B., **Internal Combustion Engine Fundamentals**, McGraw-Hill, Inc. A very thorough text for researchers and professionals. Includes both in-depth technical treatments (with thorough mathematical analysis) and a considerable amount of material that should be accessible to many enthusiasts. Nearly 1000 pages with many fascinating photos and drawings of research work. Published 1988. ISBN 0-07-028637-X

Markatos, N.C., **Computer Simulation For Fluid Flow, Heat And Mass Transfer, And Combustion In Reciprocating Engines**, Hemisphere Publishing Corp., New York. A book that evolved from a course on computer simulation for fluid flow held in Dubrovnik, Yugoslavia in September 1987. Heavy mathematical treatment; very little light reading here. Published 1989. ISBN 0-89116-392-1

Ramos, J.I., **Internal Combustion Engine Modeling**, Hemisphere Publishing Corp., New York. A text intended for researchers in fluid mechanics, combustion, turbulence and heat transfer at the graduate level. Rigorous mathematical treatment includes rotary, diesel, two- and four-stroke spark ignition engines. Published 1989. ISBN 0-89116-157-0

Ganesan, V., **Internal Combustion Engines**, Tata McGraw-Hill Publishing Company Limited. A book written by V. Ganesan, a Professor of Mechanical Engineering at the Indian Institute of Technology in Madras, India. Readable text intended for the student beginning serious study of the I.C. engine. Good balance between textual explanations and mathematical/physics study. Contains many solved problems. First published 1994. ISBN 0-07-462122-X

Mail/Fax Tech Support Form For DeskTop Dyno

Please use this form (or a copy) to obtain technical support for the DeskTop Dyno (version 2.0.7M) from Motion Software, Inc. Fill out all applicable information about your system configuration and describe your problem as completely as possible. We will attempt to duplicate the problem and respond to your question. Mail or fax this form to the address below. *Note: We will only respond to problems from registered users—if you haven't already, please take a moment and fill out the registration card supplied with your DeskTop Dyno.* Registered users receive information about upgrades and new products that will help you get the most from your DeskTop Dyno software and book investment.

Your Phone ( ) _____-_____   Your Fax ( ) _____-_____

Your Name _____

Address _____ Apt. or Building _____

City _____ State _____ ZipCode _____

Brand of computer _____ CPU _____ Speed _____

Floppy ❑—5-1/4 ❑—3-1/2 Size of hard drive _____ Amt of RAM _____

Describe your monitor and graphics card _____

_____

Version of DOS (enter the command VER at the DOS prompt) _____

List the TSR (Terminate and Stay Resident) programs loaded by your Autoexec.bat or Config.sys files that are present when you are running the DeskTop Dyno.

_____

_____

_____

_____

_____

Please describe the problem, the point in the program at which the problem first occurred and, if necessary, the menu choices that caused the problem to occur.

_____

_____

_____

_____

_____

_____

Can you duplicate the problem? _____

Mail this form to: Motion Software, Inc., 535 West Lambert, Bldg. E, Brea, CA 92821
Or fax to: 714-255-7956 (24 hours)   Version 2.0.7M (DeskTop Dynos book)

Using Computers To Build Horsepower

Running Time Approx. 65 Min..
U.S. NTSC Format Only

A terrific companion to the *DeskTop Dynos* book, this fascinating video will show you how computers and computer-simulation programs have become essential tools in performance and racing. Renown simulation programmer, Curtis Leaverton, is your guide as you move from the basics through an in-depth investigation of this ground-breaking technology. Noted automotive and racing experts add insight from their unique perspectives and describe how they use this new technology on a daily basis. Packed with practical advice and tips, this quality video will help you with any project from a street performer to an all-out Pro Stock racer.

Featuring Expert Writers, Engineers, And Racers

John Baechtel
WesTech Dyno Testing

Jim McFarland
AutoCom, Inc.

Mike Sullivan
Wayne County Racing

Includes:

- **Building Horsepower**

- **Climbing The Learning Curve**

- **History Of Simulations**

- **Wave Theory: The Basics**

- **Exhaust System Tuning**

- **Induction System Tuning**

- **Program Assumptions**

- **Simulation Accuracy**

- **Practical Racing Applications**

- **Future Of Simulations**

Jeff Smith
Hot Rod Magazine

Paul "Scooter" Brothers
Competition Cams, Inc.

David Vizard
Advanced Perf. Tech.

This quality video is available from Motion Software, Inc., and CarTech Books for the special price of $19.95 plus $4.50 postage and handling per copy. Call either Motion Software, Inc., at 714-255-2931 or CarTech Books at 1-800-551-4754 to place your order.

Mail Your Registration Card Today!

Stay up to date on the latest products from Motion Software, Inc. Find out about new simulation software, like the DeskTop DragStrip, DeskTop Bonneville, and DeskTop Circle Track programs. PLUS: Sending in your registration card will entitle you to receive special discounts on new products and upgrades. In addition, tech support is only provided to registered users. So, don't miss out. Stay up to date and get the best prices on software. Mail in your registration card now!